ONE NATION UNDER GUNS

*How Gun Culture
Distorts Our History and
Threatens Our Democracy*

ONE NATION UNDER GUNS

DOMINIC ERDOZAIN

CROWN
NEW YORK

Published in the United States by Crown, an imprint of the
Crown Publishing Group, a division of Penguin Random House
LLC, New York.

CROWN and the Crown colophon are registered trademarks of
Penguin Random House LLC.

Library of Congress Cataloging-in-Publication Data
Names: Erdozain, Dominic, author.
Title: One nation under guns / by Dominic Erdozain.
Description: First edition. | New York : Crown, 2024 |
Includes bibliographical references and index.
Identifiers: LCCN 2023034012 (print) |
LCCN 2023034013 (ebook) | ISBN 9780593594315 (hardcover) |
ISBN 9780593594322 (ebook)
Subjects: LCSH: Firearms—Social aspects—United States. |
Firearms—Law and legislation—United States. |
Gun control—United States.
Classification: LCC HV7436 .E73 2024 (print) |
LCC HV7436 (ebook) | DDC 363.330973—dc23/eng/20231002
LC record available at https://lccn.loc.gov/2023034012
LC ebook record available at https://lccn.loc.gov/2023034013

PRINTED IN THE UNITED STATES OF AMERICA ON ACID-FREE PAPER

crownpublishing.com

9 8 7 6 5 4 3 2 1

First Edition

To my father

"But don't you see, this is just the point—what has for centuries raised man above the beast is not the cudgel but an inward music: the irresistible power of unarmed truth, the powerful attraction of its example. . . ."

"I haven't understood a word. You should write a book about it!"

—Boris Pasternak, *Doctor Zhivago*

Contents

"YOU'RE NEXT"

In the first five years that I lived in America, four of the five deadliest shootings in the nation's history took place—at a school, a nightclub, a concert, a church. Of the twenty deadliest shootings in the nation's history, seventeen have occurred since 1999. And throughout this period, like an athlete shedding clothes, America has been loosening her gun laws, scrapping training requirements, and protecting firearms manufacturers from liability. As an outsider, then as a citizen, my question was the same: Why do Americans tolerate it?

Then the matter became personal. I was sitting on a leather couch in a rented apartment when a series of mysterious, abusive, and finally threatening messages came flooding through from an angry acquaintance. First came a picture of a handgun, then bullets, then an image of a man with his head blown off—followed by the words "You're next."

The sender was someone I hadn't seen for months— a woman my wife and I had hired to look after our children for a few hours every week, before parting with her on friendly terms. She had been badgering my wife, who is a journalist, about a story she wanted her to cover, and the disagreement had escalated bizarrely. When I stuck my oar in, hoping to smooth things over, the fury turned on me. And there I was, swaying under the motion of death threats, as my reading matter faded into irrelevance. The words "You're next" were followed by a series of coded messages about my children being angels and the sender's "father" preparing to punish me for ten thousand years. Today I was going to find out "how clever" I really was: death for me, a better life for my children.

While I was absorbing the shock, I heard a rap on the door. I rolled onto the ground like a shot fox before establishing that it was the UPS man, announcing a delivery. Still, I thought, it would be a good idea to pick the children up early, to avoid any encounters, so I scuttled off to the school in a state of agitation. Housed, as we were, in temporary accommodation, it seemed the only weakness in my strategy of avoidance would be if she were to find out from the neighbors where we were staying. As I texted them, explaining what was going on, the gravity of the situation hit home. Credible or otherwise, a death threat was a crime. Within the flood of outrage and concern, one message stood out. "Hope everything is ok!" said my Tennessee-born, NRA-member friend, Michael. "And believe me, if she steps foot in OUR house it'll be a HUGE mistake!"

I did not reply. But I wasn't as offended by the sentiment as I should have been. I remember something Tim O'Brien wrote about how a crisis catches you cold. You think that by having the right views you will build up a reservoir of courage that will be ready when you need it. But thoughts are only thoughts. To say that you don't believe in violence means nothing until somebody is trying to hurt you.

When I chatted with Michael the following day, he asked me straight: "Do you think you will get a weapon?"—a careful choice of words, I thought. He knew my feelings on the subject, and he probably saw me flinch, a few months earlier, when I spotted his assault rifle hanging on the wall of his basement while he was digging around for a wrench. Would this be a turning point, a teachable moment for an incorrigible liberal? Michael was not what you would call a gun nut. He was an intense, ambitious, energetic guy who never wasted a moment of his life. We bonded over subwoofers, audio streaming, and every kind of technology. We spent many hours sipping Miller Lite on his driveway, plotting the next overhaul of something that was not quite as it should be. Years later, when I started writing articles about guns, Michael gallantly indulged my heresies. When I told him I had wimped out on attending the annual meeting of the NRA, having written a scathing article on the organization for CNN, Michael said that next time he would take me round himself. I loved that. It was not that our friendship transcended our comically divided opinions: it was built on them—a mutual curiosity that an intelligent person could be so very wrong. I was sorry when Michael moved to another city and our conversations about lawn seed and loudspeakers came to an end. But would I get a gun? No.

Instead of buying one, I started to think more seriously about guns and why people place their trust in them. Why did every conversation come back to "the law-abiding citizen" and the importance of not offending him? Who were these people whose rights eclipsed all considerations of public safety? Does the law-abiding citizen even exist?

The clinching argument, and the catalyst for this book, was a series of visits to the Fulton County Superior Court in the aftermath of the text messages. Contrary to my expectation of some sort of private hearing, the whole thing was open, like a town hall in which every member of the audience makes a public submission to the chair. Forced to make more than one visit, we were, by the end, quite conversant with the situations that drive people to seek the protection of the state. These were people living in fear of someone they knew. In one case, the judge adopted a compassionate, almost pastoral tone as she counseled a couple to stay apart, seek help, or face the consequences of the law. These were not "law-abiding citizens" tormented by a "criminal class." They were feuding spouses and estranged lovers—the kind of people who shoot one another every day in the United States. It was, I recall, impossible to determine from the appearance of the assembled parties who would take the stand as the plaintiff and who would be the defendant.

The idea that these disputes could have been resolved by a gun struck me as an absurdity. As I began to study the statistics, one thing became clear: anybody is capable of killing. Most gun fatalities are committed by law-abiding citizens, who become "criminals" only when they pull the trigger. A gun, said Edward Kennedy, is unlike other weapons. It is "an instrument of instant and distant death," capable of killing from afar, wounding without contact. Guns make killing as easy as buying groceries, yet America's gun laws seemed to exceptionalize it under the belief that most people are responsible and gun violence is rare.

Even liberals talked about keeping guns away from dangerous people, as though they are perfectly harmless in the right hands. I began to think of gun violence the way William James thought of war. People assume that wars are caused by acts of aggression and failures of diplomacy, he wrote. But "the real war" is the preparation. The "battles are only a sort of public verification" of a state of play established in the so-called interval of "peace." Self-defense and aggression are two sides of the same coin.

In the 1960s, this kind of thinking was widespread, and eloquently stated. Six out of ten Americans favored a total ban on handguns, and journalists dismantled the pieties of the National Rifle Association with panache. In a gun culture, argued a series of editorials in *The Washington Post,* there is no such thing as an "accident," and the word "tragedy" starts to become a misnomer. There are only choices. As Martin Luther King, Jr., wrote after the assassination of John F. Kennedy: all murders are "political" in a nation that worships "the one who masters the art of shooting" and allows "arms to be purchased at will and fired at whim." Violence was a "plague," not an event. And "the plague spread until it claimed the most eminent American."

Comparing these statements to the fatalism of the America I had arrived in, a simple question began to form in my mind: When did America make peace with the gun? A series of commissions in the 1960s found that there were 24 million handguns in circulation, recommending that the figure be reduced to 2.4 million within ten years, through rigorous and selective licensing. The policy was backed by more than three quarters of the population, and urged by President Lyndon Johnson as the only solution to the crisis. Instead, Congress refused the request, and the moment passed. Decrying the role of a militant gun lobby that had prevailed over the will of an "aroused nation," Johnson expressed his hope that Congress would confront the problem soon.

History has disappointed that hope. Instead of Congress catching up with the nation, the nation—to a degree that nobody could have imagined—has fallen in line with the gun lobby. In the fifty years since Johnson's National Commission on the Causes and Prevention of Violence delivered its findings, almost every recommendation on firearms has been ignored, and both parties have adopted interpretations of the Second Amendment that were unthinkable in the 1960s. A weapon described as "the curse of America" in the mid-twentieth century, and one that most of the population wanted to ban, has become an accepted reality of American life. The number of handguns in private possession is now around two hundred million. Not only are these weapons more deadly than the ones Americans wanted to regulate in the sixties, they are carried outside the home.

When states such as Texas began to issue permits for concealed weapons in the 1990s, the policy was deeply controversial. "On this day," declared Governor Ann Richards as she vetoed such a measure in 1994, "we say no to the amateur gunslingers who think they will be braver and smarter with gun in hand." She could not ask law enforcement officers to patrol streets in which they could expect citizens to be armed, and she thought the law would disgrace the great state of Texas "as a place where gun-toting vigilantes roam the streets." Since then, the American heritage has moved fast. Almost as soon as Americans began to accept the idea of concealed weapons, gun activists decided that the permits and training requirements were irksome, unnecessary, and a violation of their freedom. Liberties that were startling and offensive in the 1990s are small beer in our age of "constitutional carry" and "stand your ground." Where does it end? In 1934, the United States prohibited the ownership of machine guns, as "the paramount example of peace-time barbarism." Now they are back, and semiautomatic handguns of the kind used in the Virginia Tech massacre of 2007 exceed the firepower of the repeating rifles that horrified Americans when they first appeared in the nineteenth century. Native Americans called them "spirit guns"—because they put the power of God into the hands of men.

As friends schooled me on what they believed to be the American tradition, I began to see that both conservatives and liberals were trapped in an illusion: the belief that today's "freedoms" are the norms of American history and the mandates of the Constitution. They are not. As I delved into the constitutional history, I was stunned to discover that it was not in the eighteenth, nineteenth, or even twentieth century that the Supreme Court recognized an individual right in the hallowed terms of the Second Amendment. It was the twenty-first—in a decision that turned two hundred years of settled law on its head. When I read that decision, in *District of Columbia v. Heller* (2008), I knew at once that something was wrong. Here was a group of judges playing with words, turning phrases upside down. With a background in intellectual history, I thought it unlikely that the framers of the Constitution would have issued a blank check to the armed citizen. And they didn't. The court's decision in 2008 did not bring the law in line with the Constitution. It wrestled the Constitution into the dogmas of a gun culture.

There is no mystery to the Second Amendment. The mystery is how one part of America convinced itself that privately held guns are the foundation of democracy, and how everyone else was bullied into acquiescence. The term is not too strong. My intuition was that some powerful forces were at work in the conversion of a well-regulated militia into the licensed anarchy of today. This book is about those forces: the politics beneath the plague. It is the story of a counterrevolution, a false liberty triumphing over that original freedom to live.

"A government which cannot preserve the peace," wrote Thomas Paine in a pamphlet that helped to crystallize the American nation in 1776, "is no government at all." The allusion was to the Boston Massacre, in which British troops opened fire on unarmed civilians, killing five and causing many to lose faith in the Crown. In raw numbers, a Boston Massacre occurs every hour in modern America. If we cannot stop the bloodshed, we can tell the truth about the Constitution. In the pummeled idealism of James Baldwin: "Not everything that is faced can be changed; but nothing can be changed until it is faced."

ONE NATION UNDER GUNS

Chapter 1

THE MYTH OF THE LAW-ABIDING CITIZEN

> I never knew a man who had better motives
> for all the trouble he caused.
>
> —Graham Greene, *The Quiet American*

R ichard Venola was a pillar of the gun culture—a retired U.S. Marine who wrote a fiery column for *Guns & Ammo* magazine, having previously served as editor. Venola was a vivid and engaging writer, expert at drawing the reader into the zip and terror of a shoot. He loved to dispel stereotypes about the "bitter, clinging types" of the gun community, tirelessly asserting the claims of the gun owner as "a person of substance and responsibility."

Venola was not merely a defender of gun rights: he was an evangelist—a restless advocate of firearms-as-citizenship, and the importance of supporting organizations such as the NRA. In an absorbing piece on "Empowering the Euros," Venola described the pleasure of teaching European travelers how to shoot, and the confidence that the experience generated in the tourists. Coaching a Dutchman into the "John

Wayne position," Venola described the transformation "evident in the eyes" of the visitor as he began to master a semiautomatic rifle. "It was almost as if an aroma of personal independence was drifting over him instead of oil smoke coming off the barrel," he wrote.

"So much power," marveled the Dutchman. "And anyone can own one of these?"

"Yes," Venola responded, "and they *should* if they have not committed a felony and are not crazy. This," he added, "is what keeps our politicians from getting rid of the Bill of Rights."

Such was the theory. On a warm night in 2012, Venola shot and killed a neighbor after an evening of high spirits. James O'Neill was unarmed and facing away from Venola's house when Venola shot him in the shoulder, killing him as the bullet passed through the heart. The men were friends and had spent the evening drinking before the amity dissolved in a haze of liquor. Venola claimed that O'Neill had turned to grab a weapon from his house, and that his life was in danger. He had killed in self-defense.

State prosecutor Rod Albright disagreed. "An extremely drunk man shot a friend in the heart," said Albright. "That's murder." "He had so many possible options," Albright advised the jury when the case came to trial. "Did he need to use deadly force?"

Perhaps not. But the law was on Venola's side. The state of Arizona allows a resident to use deadly force if they believe their life is being threatened—"believe" being the operative word. Venola's state of intoxication did not impair his credentials under that heading. The prosecution needed to prove beyond reasonable doubt that he had *not* acted in self-defense, which was impossible when the only eyewitness was dead. When successive juries failed to reach a verdict, Venola walked. Exhausted and relieved, he said the process had restored his faith in American justice. How would the saga feed into the national debate on firearms? wondered a reporter. "That's a little over my head," demurred Venola. "People on both sides are going to infer what they want. All I know is that I'm alive."

The killing of James O'Neill was the classic American homicide: starting with an argument and ending with a bullet. O'Neill was just one of the hundred lives lost to firearms every day in America. The cost is more than the numbers. It is the fear, the anxiety, the dread of public spaces that an armed society has created under the tortured rubric of freedom.

It does not have to be this way.

The norms of today are not the norms of American history or the values of the founders. They are the product of a gun culture that has, for now, won its battle with the Constitution and imposed its vision on a sleeping nation. How did this new freedom, this godlike entitlement to deadly force, talk its way into American law? How did citizens become kings?

The first answer, and the foundation of all others, is a myth of innocence—what I call the myth of the law-abiding citizen. It is the belief that mass shootings and domestic violence are exceptions to the rule of responsible gun ownership, and that any attempt to go after "the criminal element" must be studiously mindful of this silent and saintly majority.

It is a theory that attaches guilt and risk to one portion of the community, and perfect innocence to another, so that any attempt to curb the flow of weapons meets the same protest: We are not the problem! You cannot make "peaceable and innocent gun owners" suffer for the crimes of "the guilty," as NRA chief Wayne LaPierre protested in the pages of *American Rifleman*. The law-abiding citizen is not only safe and responsible in the use of firearms: he is brave and courageous against the bad guy.

This is the belief that has stood in the way of gun control from the days of Franklin D. Roosevelt to the present, the difference being the degree to which liberals now accept a version of the glib dichotomy. Screen for troublemakers, and all will be well! Not only is the theory flawed on the practical level, but this doctrine of innocence is one of the engines of violence in America: an inducement to kill based on an illusion of purity. The good guy, it seems, is not the solution: he's the problem. The first truth of the gun culture is a raging myth.

I

"It's only in mediocre books that people are divided into two camps and have nothing to do with each other," wrote Boris Pasternak in his classic novel *Doctor Zhivago*. "In real life everything gets mixed up." The same is true in history and the mottled terrain in which most of us live.

Gun laws as they stand are a "heads, I win—tails, you lose" scenario in which the status of the law-abiding citizen is preserved by a trick of language. Law-abiding citizens, we are told, have a right to arm themselves against criminals and madmen. When one of them acquires a private arsenal and murders more than fifty people from a hotel room, his status is reassigned, and we are told that he should never have had a gun in the first place. One law-abiding citizen has become a "wolf," and the concept survives the trauma. Indeed, the scale of such atrocities bolsters the belief that murderers are a different kind of animal: monsters, for whom we need to be even more rigorously prepared.

It may not be a coincidence that two of the architects of our gun culture, Ronald Reagan and Charlton Heston, were actors who brought the charisma of Hollywood to the theater of politics. Theirs was a cinematic vision, subjecting the tensions of reality to an unsustainable clarity. "Any gun in the hands of a bad man is a bad thing," averred Heston in a radio interview. "Any gun in the hands of a decent person is no threat to anybody—except bad people." We are trapped in a cartoon.

Physician and professor Arthur Kellermann began his research on gun violence when he heard that Marvin Gaye had been murdered by his father, with a pistol that the Motown star had given him as a Christmas present. "This is nuts," he thought as the story broke in 1984. Every day, it seemed, there was a report about a husband shooting a wife, or a father shooting a son. Yet the narrative persisted: guns keep us safe from the bad people.

Kellermann conducted a series of studies that proved otherwise. Of 398 gun-related deaths in King County, Washington, only two were justifiable killings of intruders—what might be termed a "good guy with a gun" scenario. The remaining 396 consisted of suicides, accidents, and criminal homicides by hitherto law-abiding citizens. Of these, 84 percent were defined as "altercation homicides" involving spouses or friends. There was no romance, no mystery to these findings. Kellermann drew similar conclusions from data collected in Atlanta, where a third of households contained guns. As he summarized his contribution in 2008: "Citizens did not realize then, nor do we realize today, that the most likely person to do us harm already has a key to the house."

Kellermann's findings enraged firearms activists, who lobbied Congress to defund firearms-related research at the Centers for Disease Control, where he was based. But the truth did not go away. A wealth of privately funded studies reached similar conclusions, undermining the claim that gun violence is the province of a mythical group of bad guys, "so different from the rest of the population as to virtually constitute a distinct species." Even mass murderers, the monsters of the popular imagination, were shown to be ordinary citizens moved by common grievances. The typical mass murderer, wrote one scholar, is "a white male who has a history of frustration and failure, who is socially isolated and lacking support systems, who externalizes blame onto others, who suffers some loss or disappointment perceived to be catastrophic, and has access to a powerful enough weapon." The boundaries begin to blur.

Much of this was known in the 1920s, when coroners, police commissioners, and Progressive politicians began to expose the unglamorous realities of gun ownership. By the 1960s, when the government commissioned several reports on the subject, the overwhelmingly domestic nature of gun violence was well established. The bedroom, concluded the director of a task force on gun violence, was the most dangerous room in America, and murder the most prosaic and transparent of crimes. Every homicide detective knew that the circle of investigation around a murder was generally smaller than for other types of crime, because the offender was typically known to the victim. People liked to blame "hoodlums" and "delinquents," but Johnson's Violence Commission found that only 3 percent of gun deaths in Chicago could be attributed to "teen gang disputes." Four out of five were committed by ordinary citizens over such perennial enigmas as love, money, and sex. As a frazzled police chief reported on Chicago's six hundredth homicide of 1968: "There was a domestic fight. A gun was there. And then somebody was dead. If you have described one, you have described them all."

A study of fifty-one murderers in a New England prison found that only four had prior convictions for violent crime. Most came from respectable homes in which standards of decency had been rigorously observed—too rigorously, thought the author. But these were ordinary men, and few had planned their crimes.

"Society's greatest concern," wrote the psychologist Manfred S. Guttmacher in another important study, "must be with the non-psychotic murderer; with the individual who exhibits no marked psychopathology, since by far the greatest numbers of homicides are committed by them." Feelings of hostility and alienation were as natural as the circulation of blood, as poets and philosophers had always known. Guttmacher distilled his thesis with a quotation from the German writer Goethe: "There is no crime of which I do not deem myself capable."

II

The really subversive insight, however, was not the obvious point that good people have bad days. It was the unnerving hypothesis that good people might *be* the problem—their self-righteousness providing a permission structure for aggression. "Nobody is more dangerous than he who imagines himself pure in heart," wrote James Baldwin in 1961, "for his purity, by definition, is unassailable."

Social science began to prove the point. A number of psychologists had toyed with this concept before Hans Toch and Rollo May made it the centerpiece of landmark studies on the social origins of violence. Toch's 1969 study, *Violent Men: An Inquiry into the Psychology of Violence,* was inspired by the riots, assassinations, and police brutality of the 1960s, and it pioneered a method of peer-to-peer interviewing to get closer to the fundamental question: What authorizes people to kill? The answers included the usual suspects of pride, reputation, and masculine honor—and some less-familiar candidates, including virtue, justice, and respectability. The critical insight was that criminal violence, and violence committed in the name of law and order, were psychologically kindred. Toch showed that the so-called hoodlums on the streets and the men presuming to police them were strangely alike—prisoners of pride and social esteem.

Many of these killers lived in a world of "minor detail,"

where insults registered like mortal blows, and where standards had to be maintained. One of Toch's types was "the norm enforcer," whose aggression sprang from a passion for decorum. The norm enforcer was a one-man posse who "knew" when the rules had been broken. Self-driven and self-appointed, the norm enforcer regards himself as "the conscience of society and the insurer of its integrity"—although his primary concern is for his friends and family. "These men," writes Toch, "perceive themselves as arbiters of disputes, as slayers of dragons, as protectors of the weak, and as dispensers of justice; they define themselves as policemen, prosecutors, judges, and executioners. They patrol their beat alertly searching for black knights carrying off maidens. They attack any abuser of power or violator of decency they spot, often without much prior notification." Although the men perceived themselves as exercising whatever process was due, the truth was quite the contrary. These were America's vigilantes: moralists, whose morality did not shrink from murder.

Such was the paradox that Rollo May considered the master key to America's infatuation with force. In *Power and Innocence: A Search for the Sources of Violence,* published in 1972, May posed some awkward questions about the connection between Christian bourgeois morality and America's exceptional levels of violence. Americans were, at once, more moralistic and more violent than citizens of comparable nations—a tension that baffled the psychologist until he grasped the relationship: the morality providing the assurance that *we* are good and *they* are not. This morality is real and typically sincere, May concedes, but he ultimately defines it as "pseudoinnocence" for its capacity to obscure and encrypt the dynamics of power.

Americans are warm, tender, and idealistic, almost by default. They are serious about their values. But the intensity comes at a price. It fosters crude Manichaean judgments about good and evil, and it frowns at compromise. The result was a type of personality strong on justice but weak on "the element of mercy," which, May suggests, "may well turn out to be a *sine qua non* of living in this world with an attitude of humanity." The sooner we grasp the "fact that good and evil are present in all of us," he writes, the sooner we can develop "a sense of restraint," at home and abroad.

The resonance of these ideas for an armed society is unmistakable. In the year May published his book, the *Los Angeles Times* ran an editorial on "Law-Abiding Killers," disputing the very language of the gun culture. "Opponents of legislation to outlaw handguns argue incessantly that law-abiding American citizens have a right to possess firearms," observed the writer. But the statistics suggested that "the law-abiding citizen is a significant factor in the nation's rising murder rate," including the man who concealed a revolver in his briefcase before killing an attorney and wounding two others in a California courtroom.

Ralph McGill, a Pulitzer Prize–winning journalist based in Atlanta, went further. Not only were law-abiding citizens responsible for some of the deadliest shootings of the 1960s: the notion of two classes of Americans seemed to issue an invitation to violence. Phrases like "law and order" and "crime on the streets" were green lights to the vigilante. There was violence in the very grammar of the gun culture.

The same is true today. Gun owners often describe themselves as "sheepdogs" and "Samaritans," protecting the weak from the "wolves." They have lobbied for laws to enable "victims" to use deadly force against "criminals." The result has been a proliferation of violence in which Samaritans have played no small part. One study found that concealed-weapon carriers were more eager to confront criminals than to assist the victims of crime, often exacerbating situations in which they intervened. The withering conclusion was that "the Samaritans have a low boiling point." Another found that motorists who keep guns in their vehicles are more prone to road rage than those who do not. In Florida, road-rage shootings increased so sharply after the state relaxed its gun carry laws that legislators passed a law making it illegal to drive more than ten miles below the speed limit in the left lane of the interstate—as though driving slowly were the clear and present danger.

The data is clear: homicide rates rise with gun density and fall where guns are less common. There is a dreary consistency. Where guns have been promoted as peacemakers, they have consistently failed on their brief. "This is a bill to make Texas a safer place," declared Governor George W. Bush as he signed a concealed carry law in 1995. Within a month, the state witnessed its first deadly shooting by a license holder, over a brushing of mirrors at a traffic light. Within a year, 940 concealed weapon carriers had been arrested for gun-related offenses.

If an armed society is a polite society, writes Jim Atwood, "we should have already reached a level of politeness that would be the envy of the whole world." Instead, we kill over music at gas stations, or for talking during a movie. And this is called freedom.

Since emerging as a political force in the 1920s, the National Rifle Association has valorized this brand of citizen justice as an American birthright. In 1932, it launched a Guns vs. Bandits column in *The American Rifleman,* with bracing headlines like "Thug Medicine" and "No Freedom for Crooks." The criminal was learning that "his victims will not tamely submit to his depredations but will meet him with his own weapons and a skill a shade better than that possessed by the thug." The stories followed a David-and-Goliath formula, in which the good guy never misses, but questions of justice were assumed rather than explained. Guns vs. Bandits survives as the Armed Citizen® column, a registered trademark of Smith & Wesson. These "amazing stories" of "law-abiding gun owners . . . using their Second Amendment rights for self-defense" are clearly vetted and intended to inspire. Yet even here, in curated purity, the stories raise more questions than answers. Who is the good guy? What authorizes him to kill? A recent example suggests the problem:

> A good Samaritan came to the aid of a neighbor during a domestic dispute that ended in the death of the aggressor. In Gonzales, La., a man in his home heard people arguing outside. He went to investigate. The neighbor approached the two people—a man and a woman—who were arguing and was accosted by the male. The instigator pointed a handgun at the good Samaritan, who in turn drew his own firearm and shot. When police officers arrived, they deter-

mined that the man who had been arguing with the woman was dead. The police said that charges would not be filed against the armed citizen, saying that he ended a dispute that might have led to the death of the woman.

That is a big "might."

In *Good Guys with Guns,* a study of concealed-weapon carriers in Texas, the sociologist Angela Stroud got closer than anyone to the paradox of the law-abiding citizen: a self-defined elite who felt empowered to break the law. Describing themselves as "the good guys," and "the cream of the crop of our community," they held it as gospel that "our behavior patterns are different from the criminal class." Many of them were genuinely baffled that businesses would want to prevent them from bringing guns into their premises, and deeply offended by the policy. Such restrictions simply "punish the righteous," complained one of them. Because "bad guys don't read signs." Infuriated by the policy, many of them admitted to ignoring prohibitions against concealed weapons and taking their guns wherever they wanted.

There are, explained one of Stroud's respondents, three types of people: sheep, sheepdogs, and wolves. The sheep are the ordinary folks who take life as they find it and do little to stop crime. The sheepdogs are "the heroes," who "do what has to be done." "They're the ones who see the raccoon that's obviously got rabies . . . and get the gun and shoot it." The wolves were the bad guys, the predators, who never change. Some "are such a predator that all you can do is shoot them," said one respondent. Some people, explained another, were "just innately bad." They "just need killing."

When Stroud asked one of the gun owners whether she had pondered the magnitude of taking a human life, the response was swift: "I have. I have no problem with that," she said. "I have always said that I will shoot first and ask questions later." One man felt that his gun sent a message to anyone who might annoy him: "Don't piss off an old guy because he'll probably just kill ya'?" Another respondent admitted to pointing his .45-caliber semiautomatic handgun at a man who remonstrated with him for driving dangerously, which happened to be true. "Dude! I have a fuckin' gun!" he told the other motorist. "Get away from here." The story was told as a laughing mea culpa, the-one-time-I-crossed-the-line, but it said everything about the sense of power and entitlement that each of these armed citizens seemed to possess. Convinced of their superiority to a criminal class, the sheepdogs carried themselves like lords.

Michael Dunn's last words to Jordan Davis, before he killed the seventeen-year-old for playing "thug music" at a gas station in 2012, were: "No, you're not gonna talk to me that way." Dunn was a member of the NRA, and he seemed to regard himself as a keeper of the peace. So did George Zimmerman when he killed Trayvon Martin in the same year. Something is awry when one group of people feels empowered to control another at gunpoint. Where does it come from? Where does it sit with the cultured liberty of the Constitution?

III

Rollo May felt that innocence was as old as America— a "chosen nation" carried from the quagmire of Europe to the virgin soil of New England. Religion is certainly an influence. A more pressing and tangible source, however, is race and a racially infused patriotism. From its emergence as the "honest American" of the 1920s to its consolidation as the myth of the law-abiding citizen in the 1960s, the doctrine of the good guy with the gun has been suffused with racial anxiety.

The gun culture's narrative of equality and empowerment, writes the historian Caroline Light, has always embodied "deep-seated exclusionary principles," which decide in advance who is really entitled to kill. Over the course of American history, guns have been enforcers, not equalizers. When nonwhites claim the privileges of the dominant caste, they typically discover that they are not the law-abiding citizens that the laws were intended to serve. Sold as democracy, gun rights have functioned more like a gentlemen's club, "reserved only for the select few."

Stroud found the same chemistry at work. "It is remarkable," she writes, "how often respondents simultaneously employed race in their descriptions of threat while at the same time trying to distance themselves from sounding racist." The association was so instinctive, it was difficult to know whether the dangers were real or imagined. The good guys seemed to interpret every unsettling encounter as a crime in the making, the presence of "gangster guys" enough to put the watchdogs on high alert. "In none of my interviews," reported Stroud, "did a respondent identify a potentially threatening person as white." The hushed sagacity, the vaunted insight into the criminal mind, boiled down to racial fear. Crime was black. Innocence was white and moderately prosperous.

Scott Melzer, who spent several months interviewing an inner circle of NRA members, came to regard the very term "law-abiding citizens" as "a code word for whites." He found the same childlike certainty that "you don't have any problems with law-abiding citizens and firearms," and the same visceral connections between color and crime. "If three big ol' Black dudes come at you," said one of the NRA men, "you gotta be able to protect your family." The case was not argued: it was simply assumed that criminals were Black or Hispanic, and one had to be ready. Discussions about the Founding Fathers would drift into monologues about race and national decline. "If you don't like the damn country, get out," said one of Melzer's respondents. "But don't tell me I have to say I'm Hispanic-American or Black-American or Arabian-American or something like that. Because I was born here and I choose to live here. I'm American."

Once again, it is the sense of superiority that justifies an arms race—even though, as Melzer notes, white Americans are more likely to be victimized by other whites than by other racial groups. But in explaining why people buy guns, and resist all efforts to regulate them, it is the belief that matters. Melzer defined it as a militant and nostalgic patriotism—a "frontier masculinity," in which roles are assigned and enemies known. And this is what I mean by a "gun culture"—a body of assumption about innocence and guilt, power and entitlement: an affinity for violence flowing from convictions of preeminence.

How did Americans come to think in such terms? No other country, mourned the journalist Tom Teepen in 2009, puts up with such a reckless level of domestic armament, or suffers the violence that flows from it. Our "answer to a plague of locusts," he wrote, "is more locusts." Yet to speak against the plague was to be covered in opprobrium. Advocates of gun control have been called communist, un-American, and traitors to the Constitution. They have been bullied into silence. But where is the real betrayal? Does the Constitution authorize citizens to wield the arbitrary power that was feared and despised in kings?

This visceral entitlement, the dancing glee of the Armed Citizen column, cannot be traced to republican philosophy. It is, I will argue, rooted in some of the least democratic of American traditions—better understood as a counterrevolution than as an authentic expression of democracy. American gun culture is not the story of a Second Amendment unleashing its terrible logic. It is the story of a Constitution captured and travestied by a culture of violence.

The first of these traditions is slavery, "the tyranny beneath the stripes and stars," in Sojourner Truth's phrase: the original monarchy within a democracy. The second is militarism and a crusading nationalism that always felt that the end justified the means. It is here, not in the Constitution, that a militant gun culture cut its teeth. The difference between regulated and unregulated power was critical to the founders, and it is no less important now. It is time to rescue the Second Amendment.

Chapter 2

LIBERTY AS LIFE: THE SECOND AMENDMENT YOU NEVER KNEW

Remember, all men would be tyrants if they could.
—Abigail Adams

In May 1983, Ronald Reagan addressed the annual meeting of the National Rifle Association in Phoenix, Arizona, the first sitting president to do so. The speech signaled a new era of gun rights in America.

"It does my spirit good to be with people who never lose faith in America," he began. People "who never back down one inch from defending the constitutional freedoms that are every American's birthright. . . . You live by Lincoln's words: 'Important principles may and must be inflexible.' Your philosophy put its trust in people."

"And, by the way," he added with a masterful change of pace, "the Constitution does not say that government shall decree the right to keep and bear arms. The Constitution says, 'The right of the people to keep and bear arms, shall not be infringed.'" The crowd roared.

Liberals whined that guns create "a violent, shoot-em-up

society." But "just a minute," protested Reagan. Couldn't they see that most violent crimes were committed by criminals, not decent, law-abiding citizens? "And locking them up . . . and throwing away the key is the best gun-control law we could ever have." Deafening applause.

It was "a nasty truth," he coolly advised, but those who seek to inflict harm are not fazed by gun control laws. So the emphasis had to change. He was working with the NRA leadership to draft a bill that would truly protect the rights of "legitimate gun owners like yourselves." He was also looking to extend the sale of M1 rifles to participants in civilian marksmanship programs. This, he said, was a tradition that went back to the Revolutionary War, when courageous patriots, who learned by "plinking as young boys," outgunned a professional army. Thus began the age of the assault rifle, the high-capacity magazine, and that strangest of misnomers: "constitutional carry."

Leaving aside the thought of "plinking" with a weapon that could bring a small aircraft out of the sky, this was not a speech that Lincoln, Jefferson, or Madison could have delivered. Reagan's "trust in people" was really a doctrine of division, which held the difference between good guys and bad guys to be so profound that violence was the only remedy. Was this the meaning of the right to keep and bear arms?

While Reagan was sending the crowd into raptures over the Second Amendment, he was of course misquoting it— omitting the part about a "well regulated militia, being necessary to the security of a free State." Whatever one might suppose the words to mean, their inclusion in a constitutional amendment would suggest their importance—perhaps a controlling stake. But for nearly fifty years, the gun rights movement has invoked the Second Amendment while cutting it in two: marshaling its authority while shrinking from its terms. In 2008, the strategy reached the Supreme Court in *District of Columbia v. Heller,* where a 5–4 majority established the meaning of the Second Amendment by reading it backwards: declaring the second half the substance, and the part about the militia a species of eighteenth-century waffle, best avoided.

But if trust is the commodity and truth the aim, why not take it in full? Why not read the words in the order in which they were written? It is striking that those who talk loudest of Second Amendment rights—from the National Rifle Association to the Supreme Court—are so resistant to an unabridged reading, so cool on the notion of a "well-regulated militia." There is a reason for the reticence: a properly understood Second Amendment would spell disaster for the gun rights agenda.

I

Before we can establish what the founders meant by "the right to bear arms," we need to understand what they meant by "liberty." This was something very different from the modern sense of unfettered freedom. The great irony of American gun culture is that when individuals insist on unlimited access to weapons, they are closer to the values of the monarchy that the founders wanted to escape than the republic they actually established.

When the founders placed their trust in "the people," they did not mean the imperious individual. They meant the community. The whole thrust of their philosophy was to move the sword away from the storms of private judgment to the calmer waters of collective wisdom. Although the term "individualism" had not been invented at the time of revolution, noted Alexis de Tocqueville in his classic study *Democracy in America,* the closest thing to it was "egoism" or self-love—and this was the "menace" that the political process aspired to contain. As Abigail Adams advised her husband in a legendary exchange of 1776: "Remember, all men would be tyrants if they could."

Modern democracy differed from its classical forebears in two critical respects. The first was the principle of equality—the belief that every life is sacred, and none are born to rule. The second was the belief that all men are equally flawed: creatures of passion and slaves to self-love. Modern philosophers placed a higher value on the sanctity of ordinary life than any of the ancient philosophers, yet they were more skeptical about the possibilities of virtue. If men are born free, wrote Milton, Locke, and Rousseau, they are free to flounder as well as prosper; free to fall as well as rise. The political process had to acknowledge both sides of the human enigma. Understanding this tension is the key to grasping the shrewd and cultured freedom at the heart of the Constitution—and why it could never have conferred its blessing on the armed individual.

The American system was based on a theory of social contract, crafted by the philosopher John Locke, drawing on deep wells of political thought. It was the attempt to reconcile two burning convictions: the principle of equality and the problem of passion. It was one thing to say, with the radicals of Locke's time, that all humans are born "equal and alike in power, dignity, authority, and majesty." But what did that look like in practice? What happens when one man's dignity runs into another man's power? No sooner had political theory rejected the divine right of kings than it ran into a more profound and subtle conundrum: the yearning of all men to be kings.

Thomas Hobbes proposed the surrender of natural liberty to a strong and wise ruler. Locke's alternative, which supplied the architecture of the U.S. Constitution, was the suspension of hostilities under a social contract, where power is shared and subject to mutual consent. The political process is not going to turn sinners into saints, agrees Locke, but it can help them get along. When laws are reasonable and deftly weighted, self-interest can serve the greater good. Men will vote, not fight. And nature's "war of all against all" gives way to such benign institutions as a well-regulated militia. In a political society, sovereignty lies with the people, not the person, and the welfare of the people is the supreme law.

When libertarians quote Locke's *Second Treatise of Government,* they often cite passages in which he sets out the awesome freedoms of the state of nature. This, however, is not his destination. It is the nightmare from which he wants to deliver us. Locke is as worried about the tyranny of the individual as the tyranny of kings. Both spring from pride—the passion that makes monsters of men.

Humans, Locke agrees with the rosier philosophers, are endowed with some sort of conscience, but few live up to its demands. Students of history would have to admit that the greater part of humankind are "no strict observers of equity and justice." Why? Because men are "partial to themselves" and biased toward their friends. Their natural sense of justice is warped into vengeance, making men soft on themselves and cruel to those who injure them. A state of nature is one clenched fist from a state of war.

In a state of nature, everyone is lord and nobody is free. Men act on their own authority, and the earth is drenched in blood. Civilization arises when individuals agree to surrender some of their natural liberty to the sober judgment of the community. That is the price of survival. The faculty of reason that is so unreliable while it is governed by passion is perfectly competent when it doesn't have a dog in the fight: when it is balanced by other minds. And the physical energies that were at once necessary and devastating in a state of nature are cooled and pacified in the waters of consensus.

In this new political society, the natural power of punishing is "resigned" into "the hands of the community," which "comes to be umpire, by settled standing rules, indifferent, and the same to all parties." That is where freedom begins.

Freedom, Locke insists, is not "a liberty for everyone to do what he lists, to live as he pleases." It is to live in peace, under laws common to all. And "where there is no law, there is no freedom, for liberty is, to be free from restraint and violence from others; which cannot be, where there is no law." For "who could be free," he wonders, "when every other man's humour might domineer over him?" French philosopher Montesquieu, another vital influence on the founders, defined freedom in the same terms: "In order to have this liberty," he wrote "the government must be such that one citizen cannot fear another citizen."

Liberty, then, is a political concept denoting relief and refuge from the perils of nature. It is a garden, not a forest. It is achieved by the transfer of the sword from the burning will of the individual to the settled wisdom of the community. The power that a man formerly employed by his own authority, explains Locke, now serves the common good. The strength that was once disposed as a man saw fit is now engaged "to assist the executive power of the society, as the law thereof shall require." Now that we enjoy the benefits of living in a community, including "protection from its whole strength," we have to pay our way. We join the militia. The militia is to security what trial by jury is to justice: safety in numbers. It was the essence of the social contract, and an institution even more important in the new world than the old.

The founders of the American republic were no less preoccupied than Hobbes and Locke with the problem of passion and the need to baffle and diffuse it like the glare of the sun. "Power," sighed John Adams in a letter to Jefferson, "always thinks it has a great Soul . . . and that it is doing God Service, when it is violating all his Laws." But men do not know themselves. They do not see how insidiously their passions mold their thoughts. That is why "Power must never be trusted without a Check." Alexander Hamilton surveyed the history of mankind and concluded that the "fiery and destructive passions of war" held more powerful sway in the human heart than the "mild and beneficent sentiments of peace." "To model our political systems upon speculations of lasting tranquility," then, was "to calculate on the weaker springs of the human character." One had to think the worst of people to do the best for them. Man was the animal who must be saved from himself.

Jefferson was more optimistic about virtue. But he was no less clear that the political process exists to supply the defects of morality: to be reason where reason fails. In a democracy, he wrote, "the will of the majority" serves as "the Natural law" or "the general reason of the society." It is the parent to the impetuous child: a conscience for those who may have left theirs at home.

The point was made with almost comical vehemence in *Cato's Letters,* a volume of essays that left a deep impression on the founders. Humans were creatures that thought one thing, said another, and did a third. Indeed, "the greatest instances of virtue and villainy are to be found in one and the same person." The problem was egoism, or self-love—a passion that "makes a man the idolater of himself, and the tyrant of others." The art of government was "to erect a firm building with such crazy and corrupt materials"—judging men not by what they say they will do, but what they *will* do. The constitution that trusted more than it needed to any individual or body of men was "big with the seeds of its own destruction." The Caesars and Neros of history were not the worst of men—just men who were granted too much power.

People think of this as the age of reason and virtue, when power was wrested from kings by rugged, self-reliant individuals. Nothing could be further from the truth. The founders had a democratic theory of tyranny. They saw it in everyone. And it was to prevent a Hobbesian "war of all against all" that they designed the intricate structures of the Constitution. The formula was condensed into a few sentences by Thomas Paine, in a work that did more than any other to rally Americans to independence in 1776. "Government," he wrote, "is the badge of lost innocence." It covers our shame. "For were the impulses of conscience clear, uniform, and irresistibly obeyed, man would need no other lawgiver." Since that is not the case, governments are needed for protection and security. Britain had failed to provide it, justifying the colonies in forming a new political community, a new nation, in which the reign of force would give way to the rule of law. Let it be said, Paine concludes, "that so far as we approve of monarchy, that in America *the law is king*."

The founders were no libertarians or individualists, scorning government as a chain upon the soul. They understood its necessity and revered its ponderous mechanisms. "What is government itself," wondered James Madison, "but the greatest of all reflections on human nature? If men were angels, no government would be necessary. If angels were to govern men, neither external nor internal controls on government would be necessary." Such was the foundation of the American Constitution and the reasoning behind everything the founders wrote about the right to bear arms. There was no liberty outside the law.

Jefferson disclaimed all originality as he grafted these ideas into the Declaration of Independence, a text that glides seamlessly from the poetry of equality to the gristle of government. "To secure these Rights, Governments are instituted among Men, deriving their just powers from the consent of the governed." Liberty doesn't happen: it has to be secured. Precious among those securities was a well-regulated militia.

II

One of the catalysts of the Revolution was the goading presence of the British Army—carousing in the streets, crashing into homes, and killing civilians in what came to be known as the Boston Massacre. Republican theory had long disdained "standing armies" as engines of tyranny, and here was the proof. Jefferson excoriated the crimes of these "hostile bodies, invading us in defiance of law," protesting that every state had the right to judge for itself "the number of armed men which they may safely trust among them, of whom they are to consist, and under what restrictions they shall be laid." The complaint was renewed in the Declaration of Independence. The king had kept a standing army without the consent of the colonial legislatures, exposing the people to terrors. Troops had been quartered in private homes, and Americans had been seized in the coastal towns and forced to bear arms against their country on the high seas.

This was tyranny: a sumptuous outrage. The harder question was how to defeat a military power without becoming one. How do you drive off an army of professionals without drinking from the same well? The Second Amendment emerged from a tug-of-war between military realism and republican orthodoxy: between those who wanted a strong and efficient military, to stand up to the European powers,

and those who feared even the embryo of a military establishment and preferred to lean on the state militias. A contest
between Hamilton and Jefferson, in other words, with Madison caught in the middle.

The war was won, the Tories sailed home or fled to exile
in Canada, and reality reared its head. The states had been
bound together in a "league of friendship" under the Articles
of Confederation, and friendship was not enough to prevent
an armed rebellion raging for six months in Western Massachusetts under the retired military officer Daniel Shays. "Influence is not government," growled Washington in October
1786. It was time for a constitution worthy of the name.

What emerged from four months of deliberation was a
document that stunned an educated public: a formula that
struck some as an overcorrection, and others as a betrayal of
the principles of the Revolution. High among these anxieties was the power of the federal government to "raise and
support armies" and to provide for "organizing, arming, and
disciplining, the Militia"—two innocent-sounding statements that struck fear into the republican mind. "The common talk," reported the Philadelphia *Freeman's Journal*, "is,
'Well, what do you think of being surrounded with a standing army?'" Yet the Constitution said nothing about a *standing* army, and this power to raise armies was limited to a
period of two years. What was the problem?

Contrary to the doctrine established by the Supreme
Court in 2008, the militia was a vital institution in the eighteenth century and central to the American political creed.
Against those "hostile bodies" of professional soldiers, the
militia was lauded as the natural strength of the community:

local, accountable, and reassuringly transient. Madison's proposal seemed to imperil the ideal by giving a federal Congress the power to arm and call forth the militia, and by placing them under the president in time of war. The states would continue to choose the officers, but they were bound to train the men "according to the discipline prescribed by Congress." The federal government held all the aces. The fear was that the militias could either be absorbed into one de facto standing army or left to crumble while professionals were brought in, with the potential to take over the nation. That was the story of ancient Rome and a scenario Americans were desperate to avoid. The states wanted a guarantee that if Congress failed to arm the militias, they could do so themselves. That was the Second Amendment—a child of the eighteenth century, bullied by posterity.

Devotion to the militia was a legacy of the English Civil War, in which armies of mercenaries rode roughshod over the nation. The militia doctrine was codified in a work that became a classic of republican theory, John Trenchard's *An Argument, Shewing That a Standing Army Is Inconsistent with a Free Government,* written in 1697. The book was universally embraced by the founders, according to the historian Bernard Bailyn, and it must be the starting point for any quest for the meaning of the Second Amendment.

Trenchard was one of the authors of *Cato's Letters,* and his case for moderate and regulated force rests on the anxious realism expounded there. The book is an essay on the seduction of militarism: an appeal for clear lines of accountability between political and military power, based on the memory of the English Civil War when an army raised by parliament to defend liberty "made Footballs of that Parliament," establishing a dictatorship under Oliver Cromwell.

Trenchard did not create the militia doctrine. He was clarifying a consensus that strong armies under charismatic generals are the high road to tyranny. "I am afraid we don't live in an Age of Miracles," he writes, "for in the little Experience I have had in the World, I have observed most Men to do as much Mischief as lay in their Power." Professional armies placed intolerable temptations before men of power. They found wars where wars did not exist. The answer was to remove the temptation: to place the sword in the hands of the people so that military strength is always subject to the will of the community.

A well-regulated militia was like a horse reared to plod—loyal, reliable, and certain to protest if pushed beyond limits. It was an army of amateurs, innocent of conquest. As Trenchard eulogized the citizen militias of the ancient republics: "In those days, there was no difference between the Citizen, the Souldier, and the Husbandman, for all promiscuously took Arms when the publick Safety required it, and afterwards laid them down with more Alacrity than they took them up."

And afterwards laid them down. This was no blueprint for an armed society. It was an appeal for a citizen army that could be dispersed as quickly as it was assembled. And one that did not include everybody: "Arms," noted Trenchard, "were never lodg'd in the hands of any who had not an Interest in preserving the publick Peace." Training was confined to "the best of their People," and the authorities did not permit "a Deposition of their Arms in any other hands."

For a militia to provide any sort of inoculation against a standing army, it would have to be vetted and trained. "Seriously, Gentlemen, I assure you, that a Firelock, with a Bayonet fixed on the End of it, is a very awkward Kind of Instrument," advised one authority during a debate over the Militia Act of 1757. "It requires more Dexterity than you may be aware of." Many were the accidents involving regular troops. What could be expected from poorly trained or "half-disciplined Men, I need not inform you." Militiamen were required to train on given dates throughout the year, and they were subject to martial law when called into service. It sounded harsh, admitted the jurist William Blackstone, but this was "the constitutional security which our laws have provided for the public peace, and for protecting the realm against foreign or domestic violence."

Early militia laws anticipate the phrasing of the Second Amendment, describing "a well-regulated and well-disciplined militia" as the "only proper military force of a free country," and prescribing the terms of service, including arrangements for conscientious objection. The militias were even more important in the colonies, where regular troops were unknown before the Seven Years' War of 1756–63, and they involved all able-bodied males rather than the handful chosen by lot in the more populous mother country. Serving in the militia was not a choice. It was a legal obligation that only became a "right" when someone threatened to take it away.

In Pennsylvania, where pacifist scruples had long delayed the formation of a militia, the terms of the 1757 Militia Act were embraced with zeal, and the legalities of conscientious

objection were defined within the terms of the social contract. "In a state of *political Society* and *Government,* all men,
by their *original compact* and *agreement,* are obliged to unite in
defending themselves and those of the same community," declared a speaker in the Pennsylvania Assembly in 1775. Those
who withdrew themselves from the social compact could not
be entitled to protection. If men would not fight, they would
have to contribute financially. In a political community, "the
safety of the people is the supreme law."

When the colonies became states, nearly all of them codified their militias in terms of "common defense." It was "the
duty of every man who enjoys the protection of society to be
prepared and willing to defend it," declared the New York
Constitution in 1777. Exemptions would be confined to
those who "may be averse to the bearing of arms" from scruples of conscience. Such people would be required to pay a
fee "in lieu of their personal service."

New Hampshire's bill of rights spoke of service, surrender, and mutual protection. The right to bear arms was a tax,
paid in sweat and blood. Virginia's Declaration of Rights,
which became a model for many others, stated the doctrine
in one loaded sentence: "That a well-regulated militia, composed of the body of the people, trained to arms, is the
proper, natural, and safe defense of a free state; that standing
armies, in time of peace, should be avoided as dangerous to
liberty; and that in all cases the military should be under
strict subordination to, and governed by, the civil power."

The critical phrase is "in all cases." The militia will be the
norm, and professional soldiers the exception, in the work of
securing the state. Both would be held in strict subordina-

tion to the civil power. Both fall within "the state's monopoly on violence," in the language of political science—the difference being that a militia is a temporary and tractable guardian, less equipped to make footballs of elected bodies. Designed for defense, not attack, the militia is the healthy and stable portion of the military: loved for its limitations.

"The people have a right to keep and to bear arms for the common defence," asserted the Massachusetts Declaration of Rights, followed by a brisk reminder that all "military power" shall be held in "exact subordination to the civil authority." We are a long way from individual gun rights.

Indeed, the Massachusetts Constitution is notable for the clarity with which it distinguishes personal rights from those relating to "the people" as a body. Under the first heading are statements such as these: "Each individual of the society has a right to be protected by it in the enjoyment of his life, liberty and property, according to standing laws"; "No subject shall be hurt, molested, or restrained, in his person, liberty, or estate, for worshipping God in the manner and season most agreeable to the dictates of his own conscience"; and "Every subject has a right to be secure from all unreasonable searches and seizures of his person, his houses, his papers, and all his possessions."

Under the second heading are statements confirming that "government is instituted for the common good," and that "the people alone have an incontestable, unalienable, and indefeasible right to institute" it. Since all political power resides "originally in the people," and is "derived from them," the officers of the government must be regarded as "their substitutes and agents [who are] at all times accountable to them."

Such statements draw a sharp distinction between rights that belong to individuals and those belonging to the people as a whole. I have a right to life and liberty under the canopy of the state; I do not have a right to assemble my own militia. It is "the people" who hold the right to keep and bear arms— for "the common defense." "There can be no question," writes constitutional scholar Steven Heyman, that this right to arms "is one that belongs not to private individuals but to the people in their collective capacity."

III

Nobody asserted the principle behind the militia more clearly than George Washington. "It may be laid down as a primary position, and the basis of our system," he wrote in his plan for a "Peace Establishment" in 1783, "that every Citizen who enjoys the protection of a free Government, owes not only a proportion of his property, but even his personal services to the defence of it." All male citizens between the ages of eighteen and fifty, with a few legal exceptions, were to be borne on the militia rolls, provided with weapons and uniforms, and trained in such a way that "the Total strength of the Country might be called forth at a Short Notice on any very interesting Emergency." The training was critical and something to be standardized according to "a Plan that will pervade all the States." Without it, citizens would never develop the habits of soldiers—if indeed they ever could.

Washington was affirming the republican doctrine, trying to get all he could from a venerable institution, but his heart was not in it. Even as he spoke of turning citizens into soldiers, his doubts were palpable, and it was from such doubts that the controversy around the militias would grow.

The truth was that the militia was politically vital but woefully limited in the place that mattered: battle. Washington had previously testified to Congress that militiamen were somewhere between inept and useless in a theater of war—"timid, and ready to fly from their own shadows." War was bloody and brutal. The guns required skill and poise, none of which could be achieved by amateurs, "dragged from the tender Scenes of domestick life." Washington had been complaining about the quality of the "Draughts," as he termed the militiamen, since his time serving as a British officer in the Seven Years' War, when he reported that 114 of the 400 men drafted from the surrounding counties had deserted their posts. Men who eulogized the militias knew nothing of war. America needed a "standing force."

This was Hamilton's position as he defended the military clauses of the Constitution with boisterous eloquence. Thirteen independent militias, bumbling along with hunting rifles, were not going to keep the sea dogs of Britain and Spain at bay. For too long, he protested, Europe had plumed herself as "the Mistress of the World," considering "the rest of mankind as created for her benefit." These ambitions would not evaporate now that the United States was an independent nation. "It belongs to us," Hamilton declared, "to vindicate the honor of the human race, and to teach that assuming brother, moderation." "Let Americans disdain to be the instruments of European greatness!" he roared. "Let the thirteen States, bound together in a strict and indissoluble Union, concur in erecting one great American system, superior to the control of all transatlantic force or influence, and able to dictate the terms of the connection between the old and the new world!"

This was not the assurance anybody was looking for. It confirmed what many of the so-called antifederalists suspected: that this new model of "energetic" government was an empire-in-waiting, a surrender to the hubris of militarism. Thirteen commonwealths were being shoehorned into one European-style government. And nothing said "Europe" like a military establishment.

The antifederalists are known to historians as the losers of the constitutional debate, "men of little faith," but their insights were profound, and it is to them that we owe the Bill of Rights. Most of them felt that the Constitution compromised the republican values of locality and community for a forced unity: a union that did not exist. The thirteen states grew from proudly independent colonies, and to ask them to think and breathe as one was like asking a Protestant to become a Catholic. In the haunting words of a self-styled "Agrippa" in Boston: "It is impossible for one code of laws to suit Georgia and Massachusetts."

The militia debate encapsulated this anxiety. In the character of the militia, warned a writer in Pennsylvania, "you may be dragged from your families and homes to any part of the continent and for any length of time, at the discretion of the future Congress." There was no provision for conscientious scruples against bearing arms, and no protection against being "made the unwilling instruments of oppression" in other parts of the republic. This was an allusion to slavery, and a central theme of antifederalist dissent. Most of the anti-federalists could see the military advantages of a centralized system, but they feared a situation in which a citizen of one state could be dragged "like a Prussian soldier" to put out fires in another. Especially if the fire involved slaves.

In New England, the militia debate was inseparable from the abomination of slavery and the Constitution's cowardly deference to an institution it was too embarrassed to name. The Constitution, protested a New Hampshire antifederalist, made all Americans "partakers" in the sin and guilt of "man-stealing." It was one thing to accept that the Carolinas drew their wealth from "the detestable custom of enslaving the Africans." It was another to ask everyone else to uphold the crime. "Perhaps we may never be called upon to take up arms for the defence of the southern states, in prosecuting this abominable traffick," wrote three Massachusetts anti-federalists. Yet the prospect was real. Should the slaves unite to break their chains, Congress would surely call forth the whole force of the country to suppress the rebellion. Under the terms of the Constitution, anybody could be forced to bear arms in the service of slavery. For such reasons, the anti-federalists felt that every state needed the command of its own militia.

The argument could, of course, play out the other way. Virginians such as Patrick Henry warned of a federal super-state that could "liberate every one of your slaves," should it wish to. But the weight of antifederalist sentiment was against slavery and a federal system that bound everyone to the "national crime." It is no accident that two of the fiercest de-fenders of the militia system—Luther Martin of Maryland

and Elbridge Gerry of Massachusetts—saw slavery and standing armies as kindred evils: nurseries of tyranny.

The militia debate was an attempt to preserve a true republican relationship between military and political power: between the will of the people and the instruments of war. As a writer calling himself the "Federal Farmer" stated the demand in New York: a well-regulated militia "places the sword in the hands of the solid interest of the community." A centrally commanded militia was a contradiction in terms: it severed the cords of affection that held the sword and the civil power in close communion. The states wanted control over the means of violence, and they demanded it in the orthodox terms of the social contract.

The health of the militias, argued the incomparable "Brutus," was the difference between a genuine republic and burdening history with yet another military state. Brutus was perhaps the most penetrating of the Constitution's critics, matching Hamilton blow for blow in the bearpit of New York. His plea for state control of the militias was the clearest statement of the republican doctrine. Americans, warned Brutus, would not always be fortunate enough to have men like Washington to lead their armies, and they would pay as dearly as any European state for the creation of a permanent military. The price would be anarchy at home. While they were planning for armies and navies, the new political doctors seemed to have forgotten that government "was designed to save men's lives, not to destroy them." Internal peace, not military glory, was the state's first duty and care.

It was vital to remember that government was first conceived "to restrain private injuries," because individuals in a state of nature are prone to injure and oppress one another. The weak are prey to the strong. Such propensities do not mellow when societies come together. That is why societies form governments and governments create institutions, "in which the force of the whole community [is] collected . . . to protect and defend every one." Such was the militia. By centralizing military power to the degree proposed, the Constitution was tampering with this principle and gambling with liberty at the most basic level. It must "be left to the state governments," demanded Brutus, "to provide for the protection and defence of the citizen against the hand of private violence, and the wrongs done or attempted by individuals to each other."

Brutus was not trying to arm the individual. He was trying to secure the community against the armed individual. The difference is critical.

IV

Madison ran out of ways of saying that sovereignty would be shared between the states and the federal government, and that Congress had no power to disarm the militias. He began to see the wisdom of a bill of rights. Starting with Massachusetts, five of the last six states to ratify the Constitution did so on the condition that the First Congress would amend the Constitution to include a bill of rights—naming the liberties that could never be taken away.

Jefferson, observing the drama from France, nudged his protégé to retouch his "canvas." Writing from Paris in December 1787, Jefferson congratulated Madison on the draft Constitution before identifying some weaknesses: "First the omission of a bill of rights providing clearly and without the aid of sophisms for freedom of religion, freedom of the press, protection against standing armies, restriction against monopolies, the eternal and unremitting force of the habeas corpus laws, and trials by jury in all matters of fact triable by the laws of the land." Eight months later, Jefferson expressed his joy that the Constitution had been approved by nine states, and he renewed the request for a bill of rights as something desired by "the general voice" of the nation from North to South. The issues were so plain that Jefferson stated them in shorthand: "It seems pretty generally understood that this should go to Juries, Habeas corpus, Standing armies, Printing, Religion and Monopolies."

Jefferson didn't even name the militia or the right to bear arms, the force of his concern resting on what these things precluded: a standing army. Elbridge Gerry revealed the same emphasis when the discussion reached the House of Representatives: "What, Sir, is the use of the militia?" he challenged. "It is to prevent the establishment of a standing army, the bane of liberty." The words varied, but the idea was consistent. The aim, wrote Jefferson in 1789, was "freedom from a permanent military." Or, as he explained to a British correspondent some years later: "the substitution of militia for a standing army." That was the Second Amendment.

When the wording was debated in the House, the primary question was how to honor the rights of conscientious objectors without seeming to *invite* exemption. If Christians could refuse to serve, what about skeptics and freethinkers? What would be left if everyone discovered a conscience? Madison's first draft, submitted to the House on June 8, 1789, reads:

> The right of the people to keep and bear arms shall not be infringed; a well armed, and well regulated militia being the best security of a free country: but no person religiously scrupulous of bearing arms, shall be compelled to render military service in person.

In this cumbrous but revealing statement, "the people" refers to a body of people, and the individual is mentioned only in the context of exemption. For the state, this was a right. For the individual, it was a legal requirement.

The final version changed "country" to "state," to satisfy the antifederalist concern for locality, and it upgraded the potentially ambiguous "best" to "necessary" in stating the importance of the institution. It also reversed the order of Madison's draft so that the right followed a strong prefatory statement, anchoring it to the security of the state. Although the Senate struck the conscientious-objector clause, probably for the reasons raised in the House, the phrase that surfaced from two rounds of deliberation framed the military rationale even more firmly than the original:

> A well regulated militia, being necessary to the security of a free State, the right of the people to keep and bear arms, shall not be infringed.

There it was. Twenty-seven words, destined for torment. Nobody except Hamilton could see the danger.

In a stunning commentary on the subversive potential of a bill of rights, Hamilton warned that liberty could not be rolled into a sentence. Short, programmatic statements that seemed clear at the time, he said, would be targets for unscrupulous minds. "What is the liberty of the press?" he wondered. "Who can give it any definition which would not leave the utmost latitude for evasion?" It was better to leave these matters to the prose of the Constitution, and the deliberations of the legislature, than attempt to set them in amber. Hamilton may have been right about freedom of the press, but his warning cries out over the Second Amendment.

The right to keep and bear arms belonged to "the people" in their collective capacity, and it fell to the individual as a duty, not an entitlement. Private citizens did not form armies, and the militia was a state army. Since "the sword," in republican theory, follows "sovereignty," the right could only apply to the body of people that held the reins of power. "In democratic republics," affirmed the antifederalist "Cato," "the people collectively are considered as the sovereign—all legislative, judicial, and executive power, is inherent in and derived from them." The militia was the embodiment of the principle: the political community-in-arms.

While it was, in most cases, legal to keep a weapon in the home for hunting, that was not the matter under scrutiny or the right seeking protection. The use of firearms outside the home was subject to a welter of constraints, and the founders could not have annihilated them without a discussion. It would have violated the first principle of the liberal state to place the sword in the hands of the individual—the child of

passion whose "natural despotism" made government necessary in the first place. Republics do not vote for a state of
war. The very "idea of Government," wrote Hamilton, was
to substitute "the mild influence" of the law for "the violent
and sanguinary agency of the sword." This was a collective
right, and one that was strictly subordinate to the civil power.

But what was clear to a society in which the militia was
as familiar as death and taxes would be less clear when this
icon of liberty faded. Few could have predicted how quickly
the militia would drift into abeyance, leaving America with
a constitutional provision for an obsolete institution. Then it
was anyone's game. The trouble started in the South.

Chapter 3

THE PISTOL AND THE LASH

Whither will such contempt for the life of man lead us?
—*The New Orleans Bee*

A lexis de Tocqueville loved America—the energy of the people and the vigor of the culture. When he compared the poise and literacy of the average American, reared on "a thousand newspapers," to the debaucheries of the more learned classical republics, he said he was tempted to burn his books. America was the future, the bubbling cauldron of history. "No country administers its criminal law with more kindness than the United States," effused the Frenchman. "While the English seem bent on carefully preserving in their penal legislation the bloody traces of the Middle Ages, the Americans have almost eliminated the death penalty from their codes." The United States was, he thought, "the only country on earth where for fifty years no single citizen has lost his life for political offenses." And best of all: America had shaken the curse of militarism.

"The Americans," marveled Tocqueville, "have no neighbors and thus no great wars, financial crises, devastations, or conquests to dread. They need neither heavy taxes, nor a large army, nor great generals; they have almost nothing to fear from that scourge which is more terrible for democratic republics than all these put together, namely, military glory." America was "the least militaristic and, if one may put it so, the most prosaic [nation] in all the world." High praise in the nineteenth century.

But there were a few anomalies tugging at the Frenchman's homage to the humane, postmilitary democracy. One of them was Andrew Jackson—a bullying, "tyrannical" gun-toting ruffian, twice elected to the highest office in the land. For Americans to find something appealing in this "man of violent disposition and mediocre ability," a man destitute of "the necessary qualities to govern a free nation," was painful to behold. Tocqueville tried to explain it away: Jackson was a curiosity, a throwback. His "very commonplace feat of arms" at New Orleans was impressive only to a people who knew little of war.

It was an ingenious evasion. In 1839, four years after the appearance of *Democracy in America,* the abolitionist Theodore Dwight Weld addressed the subject head-on. Jackson's behavior, which included tavern brawls and a sequence of duels, was neither exceptional nor unusual within his milieu. It was consistent with a string of violent incidents involving Southern gentlemen in Congress—including stabbings, the drawing of pistols on witnesses, and threats to hang colleagues from oak trees. Who were these people, turning the national legislature into a battlefield? "All these bullies were slaveholders," observed Weld, "and they magnified their of-

fice." For Weld, and an army of abolitionists, a brawling president was not a vexing enigma. It was the price you pay for
inviting tyranny into a democracy.

Tocqueville, like many historians, saw slavery as the great
anomaly: a blemish, not a cancer. He had no hesitation in
describing one slave owner as "the most powerful apostle
democracy has ever had." Had he consulted the illustrious
Rousseau, he might have qualified his praise. He would have
known that slavery is a state of war: the coiled antithesis of
the social contract. For slavery, observed the philosopher,
rests on violence, not consent. It cannot be established without doing violence to human nature. When slave owners say
"that a man shall come into the world not a man," when
philosophers like Aristotle say that some are born for slavery
and others for dominion, they declare war on creation.
Whatever theology one might cast over the conceit, the tension is never resolved. Slavery is the war that is never won.

I take nothing away from Tocqueville's zeal for the new
republic, but this dream of the postmilitary society—a world
that moves by commerce and contract, not accident and
force—was never going to be possible in a republic that not
only tolerated slavery but rewarded it in its computations of
electoral power. Slavery, wrote Luther Martin, not only was
inconsistent with the doctrine of equality but also had "a
tendency to destroy" the principles of republicanism. It tramples on the slave, and it habituates us to tyranny and oppression. It was, feared three of the Massachusetts antifederalists,
"portentous of much evil in America."

One of those costs was the development of a civilian gun
culture—a tradition of arbitrary violence and instant redress

unknown outside the slave states. It was in the South that firearms first acquired constitutional protection outside the military, and it was from the South that such arguments began to spread. It was from slavery that the gun culture learned its basic grammar of human worth: the belief that some lives are precious, and others are not.

I

The fighting culture of the South was a source of lurid fascination in the North. Parson Weems, a writer best known for his story about George Washington and a cherry tree, wrote a jeremiad on the subject, *The Devil in Petticoats.* It told the story of Becky Cotton, a young woman from Edgefield, South Carolina, who drove an axe through her husband's skull for failing to defend her father against a mob. The real drama, however, centered on the courtroom, and a trial that smiled at her deed. Standing tall and radiant, with full bosom and "polished skin," Cotton charmed the jury and justified the killing. Acquitted of all charges, she went on to marry one of the jurors, who clearly weighed the benefits against the risks. Within months, however, she too was dead—murdered on the steps of the courthouse by her brother.

The South was an honor culture: a fiery compound of gentility and ferocity. As one writer explained the paradox, it paid to hold your tongue in a society where an argument could end your life. "They're mighty free with pistols down there," reported a runaway slave in 1842. They fought and killed over the smallest affronts.

The diarist Sarah Morgan lost her brother Harry to such an incident, after a dinner party descended into a quarrel. When one of the guests queried the choice of a folk song that may have offended his father, Harry scoffed at the complaint, causing instant offense. Within days, a challenge had been issued, a site confirmed, and Harry was killed when a bullet passed through his lung. The details of "this regrettable affair" were reported in *The Times-Picayune* of New Orleans: the weapons, the protocol, and the less-than-perfect weather. Only in the South.

Duels were not unknown outside the slave states, the most famous of them involving Alexander Hamilton, but they were rare and enjoyed none of the immunities of the Cotton Kingdom. In the category of killing, there was no comparison. The homicide rate in Florida's cotton districts was, according to the historian Edward Baptist, fifty times that of the Northeast in the 1830s. In some areas it was considered reckless to leave home without a weapon. This was not an American norm, a nonchalant reality. It was an idiosyncrasy of the South that did not penetrate the free states until the sectional crisis of the 1850s.

Before that fateful decade, legal wisdom was squarely opposed to the carrying of weapons in public. In most states, a version of the Statute of Northampton was still in place— a medieval law that criminalized "the offense of riding or going about armed with unusual and dangerous weapons, to the terror of the people." This law, explained William Blackstone, did not create the offense of going armed, which was long established in common law: it codified the crime and specified the punishment. A man could be guilty of affray—

from *affrir*, to cause terror—without raising a hand in anger: the mere presence of a dangerous weapon was enough to establish his guilt.

And the natural right of self-defense—so imperious in the abstract—had been trimmed and pruned by the wisdom of time. Whatever might have been permissible "in a state of uncivilized nature," wrote Blackstone, "the law of England, like that of every other well-regulated community, is too tender of the public peace, too careful of the lives of the subjects" to authorize violent retaliation as anything but a last resort. Though it would be cowardice, in time of war, to flee from an enemy, the law countenanced no such point of honor between fellow subjects. Outside the sanctuary of the home, an assaulted party had a duty to retreat from danger: he must flee as far as he could before he was entitled to the plea of self-defense. "For the law sets so high a value upon the life of a man, that it always intends misbehavior in the person who takes it away." The principle went back to Jewish law, which held that the death of a man, however it happens, will always leave a stain, and that even accidental killing requires "a solemn purgation." These, counseled Blackstone, are more than humane superstitions. They are the rudiments of civilization.

Until the emergence of the "true man" doctrine in the 1870s, which rejected the duty of retreat as an affront to "the American mind," a version of the English model held for most of the United States. Hunting was clearly legitimate, and military service came under a different heading. But pistols and bowie knives—the instruments of personal violence— were widely condemned. In 1835, Massachusetts amended

the Statute of Northampton to make an exception for anyone who could demonstrate a reasonable fear of an imminent threat. But the intention was not to normalize firearms.
As a venerable jurist explained the principle: trust in guns
was trust taken from the law. Societies that sacrificed law and
justice to "the passions of men" could not be called Commonwealths.

A number of states, including Maine, Michigan, and
Pennsylvania, passed laws modeled on the Massachusetts statute, sprinkled with warnings about the seduction of arms.
"Where," challenged an editorial in the *Philadelphia Gazette*
in 1835, "is the man who has so completely chained the
fiend in his nature that no incident will, even under the
maddening spell of liquor, call up the dark passions of his
bosom?" Even the most virtuous of men were capable of
deadly crimes. "No one knows himself," urged the writer,
with shades of the founders. "No one knows how easy it is
for the mildest nature, inflamed by liquor and passion, to
give a blow that may be fatal."

Americans, wrote Joseph Gales, a journalist who served
as mayor of Washington, D.C., from 1827 to 1830, were too
proud and sensitive to affronts to be trusted with deadly
weapons. Self-defense was a misnomer, for the decision to
carry a gun betrayed a willingness to kill. "The very possession of firearms," he argued, "incites to their bloody use."
Whatever the motive for carrying them in public, it "should
not be tolerated in any community which has emerged from
the condition of savages."

No statesman, jurist, or serious writer outside the South
endorsed the wearing of weapons as a legal entitlement or a

badge of citizenship. Duels were illegal, and pistols ran into a barrier more formidable than the law: social disdain. This, thought Massachusetts senator Charles Sumner, was the difference between the free states and the slave power. In the former, "violence shows itself in *spite* of law, whether social or statute; in the Slave States it is *because* of law, both social and statute. Elsewhere it is pursued and condemned; in the Slave States it is adopted and honored. Elsewhere it is hunted as a crime; in the Slave States it takes its place among the honorable graces of society." Why? Because slavery, like the fabled upas tree of the East, destroyed everything within its radius. A system born in violence lives by violence.

There was, argued Sumner, a dreadful symmetry between the culture of the plantation and the casual brutality of Southern culture. Regarding men as property, the slave master naturally adopts the revolver and the bowie knife as the tools of his trade. "Through these he governs his plantation, and secretly armed with these he enters the world." How could it be otherwise? "Slavery must breed Barbarians," argued Sumner, "in the individual and in the society to which he belongs."

Many people despised the institution, but few appreciated how systematically it was building a world in its own image, argued Sumner. Part of his challenge as an abolitionist was to alert Northerners to a catastrophe unfolding in their midst—one with the potential to consume them. The norms of American slavery, explained Sumner, were "not derived from the Common Law, that fountain of Liberty." Nor were they born of the old system of servitude "known as villeinage," which recognized the humanity of "the bondman" and "guarded his person against mayhem; protected his wife against rape; gave to his marriage equal validity with the marriage of his master." Slavery had grown outside that humanizing framework, creating its own "species of Common Law" along the way. Under slavery, "a person is withered into a thing," and all savageries are traceable to the principle.

One of them was the emergence of an armed society. Sumner's challenge is echoed by voices within the slave culture, and it must be the starting point for any attempt to unlock the paradox of a gun culture in a democracy: a world in which killing begins to lose its taboo.

II

"There must be an unhappy influence on the manners of our people produced by the existence of slavery among us," lamented a Southern writer in 1785—despotism on one side, abject humiliation on the other. Children see it and begin to imitate it. They are nursed and educated in tyranny: stamped by the "odious peculiarities" of the institution. A man would have to be "a prodigy" to retain "his manners and morals undepraved by such circumstances." The anguished moralist was Thomas Jefferson.

Frederick Douglass, whose ungovernable spirit propelled him on an odyssey of Southern homes, observed the process in real time: the corruption of initially reasonable individuals under "the blighting and dehumanizing effects of slavery." One of his enslavers was a kind lady who taught him to read and did not require the crouching servility demanded by others—until the "fatal poison of irresponsible power" began its work on her soul. Douglass watched her harden, until her "lamblike disposition gave way to one of tiger-like fierceness." "Slavery," he concluded, "proved as injurious to her as it did to me."

It was, however, another masterpiece of the genre that made the connection with guns. Solomon Northup was a citizen of New York and a gifted musician, kidnapped and sold into slavery in March 1841. Northup's account of the ordeal, *Twelve Years a Slave,* is one of the treasures of the nineteenth century and a critical window on the formation of a gun culture. Northup described a world of naked violence that spilled from the owner to the household to the culture of the planter class. Northup recalled the sight of his owner's son, a boy of ten or twelve, riding into the field to flog the slaves, including the beloved "Uncle Abram," a man in his sixties. Raised to look "upon the black man simply as an animal . . . to be whipped and kicked and scourged through life," the child was destined to grow into a cruel and unfeeling adult. It was no wonder that the slaves regarded their owners as "a pitiless and unrelenting race."

These cruelties, Northup observed, did not stop at the color line. The odor of slavery could be seen in the way his enslaver, Mr. Epps, treated his wife, and the way the planters treated each other. In one incident, a wealthy neighboring planter murdered a gentleman from Natchez during the sale of some land. When help arrived, the corpse of the buyer was found on the floor of the planter's house, and the killer was observed pacing back and forth, covered in blood. He evaded justice and returned to his plantation, "rather more respected, as I thought, than ever, from the fact that the blood of a fellow being was on his soul."

The story did not end there. Northup's master assisted the neighbor through what passed for a trial, "loudly justifying" the homicide, offending a kinsman of the murderer along the way. First, the men brawled over a gambling table. Then the man rode up to the house, armed with pistols, challenging Epps to come out and fight, "or he would brand him as a coward, and shoot him like a dog the first opportunity." Only the desperate intervention of Epps's wife prevented him from taking up the challenge, and the men later became friends.

"Such occurrences," remarked Northup, "which would bring upon the parties concerned in them merited and condign punishment in the Northern States, are frequent on the bayou, and pass without notice, and almost without comment. Every man carries his bowie knife, and when two fall out, they set to work hacking and thrusting at each other, more like savages than civilized and enlightened beings." This was the price of slavery. "The existence of Slavery in its most cruel form among them," he argued, "has a tendency to brutalize the humane and finer feelings of their nature." As daily witnesses of human suffering, accustomed to the sight of men "dying without attention, and buried without shroud or coffin—it cannot otherwise be expected than that they should become brutified and reckless of human life."

John Brown, another fugitive from slavery, made the same observation in his harrowing memoir, *Slave Life in*

Georgia (1855). Slavery had robbed a class of men of the capacity for dialogue. When a neighboring planter achieved higher yields by employing a waged workforce, he was driven from the land and finally shot at point-blank range by Brown's master, Thomas Stevens. Such incidents were so shocking to Northern opinion that they formed an essential part of the abolitionist platform. What clearer proof of the poison of slavery than a culture of killing?

Theodore Dwight Weld assembled an encyclopedia of incidents showing how slavery lived by violence and diffused it across the culture. He described masters hunting runaways through woods; a twenty-year-old shooting "a negro man in the road," without warning or motive; and an overseer shooting the most prized of his master's slaves over a moment of insubordination. The man had taken up a hoe to prevent his wife from being whipped by the overseer, who reached for a pistol and shot him dead in the blinking of an eye. The master rued the loss of a slave worth $2,000, reported a bricklayer who witnessed the scene, but the overseer was forgiven, and the body was "buried in a hole without a coffin." Stranger than fiction. "Slaves shall be considered as real estate," declared the Slave Code of Louisiana, with insouciant gravity. It was, then, "lawful to fire upon runaway slaves," should they refuse to surrender. The world has been turned upside down.

Weld's most disturbing material required no editing or comment. He simply copied notices for runaway slaves from the Southern press, letting tyranny speak for itself. I include only a handful, taken from the state of Georgia in the year Weld was writing his book:

Run Away—My man Fountain; has holes in his ears, a scar on the right side of his forehead; hes been shot in the hind parts of his legs; is marked on his back with the whip.

MR. ROBERT BEASLEY, MACON, GA.,
IN THE *MACON MESSENGER,* JULY 27, 1837.

Twenty five dollars reward for my man Isaac, he has a scar on his forehead caused by a blow, and one on his back made by a shot from a pistol.

MRS. SARAH WALSH, MOBILE, ALA.,
IN THE *GEORGIA JOURNAL,* MARCH 27, 1837.

Two hundred and fifty dollars reward, for my negro man Jim—he is much marked with shot in his right thigh—the shot entered on the outside, half way between the hip and knee joints.

MR. R. A. GREENE, MILLEDGEVILLE, GEORGIA,
IN THE *MACON MESSENGER,* JULY 27, 1837.

Ranaway a negro boy named Mose, he has a wound in the right shoulder near the back bone, which was occasioned by a rifle shot.

MR. JOHN MCMURRAIN, COLUMBUS, GA.,
IN THE *SOUTHERN SUN,* AUGUST 7, 1838.

My man. As Weld remarks, it is the cheerful candor of these advertisements, complete with the names of the aggrieved parties, that says most about the slave system. Here, wrote the abolitionist Sarah Grimké, who observed some of the brutalities firsthand, was a culture that had buried its conscience: a world in which violence had shaken all restraining stigma. Where, wondered the leading abolitionist

William Lloyd Garrison, in all the despotisms of Europe, could you open a newspaper and find offers of cash for human beings, returned "dead or alive!"—or an advertisement for the sale of a mother and an infant, "together or apart"? "Is it not a system of murder?"

When Charles Dickens visited the United States in 1842, he was gripped by the paradox of slavery and its creeping dominion within an emerging democracy. Slavery, in republican America, had produced a type of character more exacting and less responsible than any sultan of the East—a phenomenon visible in the brawls of Southern congressmen. Dickens was stunned by the absurdity of lawmakers lunging at one another with knives. He considered slavery the only credible explanation.

Was it any surprise "that the man who has been born and bred" among the worst deformities of slavery, wondered Dickens, "will shoot men down and stab them when he quarrels?" We would have to be "idiots," he said, "to close our eyes to that fine mode of training which rears up such men." "These are the weapons of Freedom," he thundered. "With sharp points and edges such as these, Liberty in America hews and hacks her slaves; or, failing that pursuit, her sons devote them to a better use, and turn them on each other."

As the historian Joanne Freeman observes, congressional violence was a weekly occurrence in the antebellum era and mostly a Southern game. A satire in *Vanity Fair* described "A Day in the House" as a long exchange of insults, followed by a brawl. *The New York Times* ran a piece describing a judge from Michigan arriving in the capital for the first time, not sure if he'd got off at the right station. The sight of a smartly dressed gentleman ferociously caning another man removed all doubt. "When I saw this," he said, "I knew I was in Washington."

Yet the violence was real. Having witnessed a congressman from Virginia biting the fingers of a newspaper editor to the bone, a British diplomat penned a memorandum advising that no foreign minister should ever go down to the floor of the chamber. It was not worth the risk. The slave men, lamented an abolitionist from Massachusetts, had turned Congress into "a field of blood." Charles Sumner refused to arm himself even after he was nearly bludgeoned to death in the most notorious of these incidents, in 1856. But the slaveholders applauded the violence, showering Sumner's assailant with new canes to replace the one he had broken on the senator's head. It should be no surprise that the first assaults on the Second Amendment came from the South.

III

The carnage of the Southern towns prompted a wave of gun control legislation, aimed in most cases at concealed weapons. Penalties included fines and imprisonment for up to a month, and in the early years of the nineteenth century, nobody questioned the constitutionality of the cause. These were housekeeping measures, falling within the police powers of the states, with no bearing on the health of the militias or the reach of the federal government. But as the militias began to lose prominence, the potential for mischievous readings of that constitutional right grew apace.

The republican ideal of a well-regulated militia had never

flourished as the founders intended. By the time he served as president, even Jefferson had to admit that a militia composed of men of all ages was "entirely useless for distant service." The trials of war were too much for ordinary citizens. The only viable compromise was a "select militia"—long feared as the first stage of a military establishment. To ask one group of men to carry the burden for everyone was a departure from the republican principle of "distributive justice," warned a congressman. And it was. But securing the nation was more important than preserving the militia, and after the humiliations of the War of 1812, the vision faded like a New Year's resolution.

In 1833, Supreme Court justice Joseph Story observed "a growing indifference to any system of militia discipline" and a general inclination "to be rid of all regulations." It would not be "practicable to keep the people duly armed without some organization," he warned. Or wise. Weapons without training could only bring trouble. As indifference turned to contempt, it was clear that "the protection intended by this clause of our national bill of rights" was in jeopardy—that is, protection against "foreign invasions, domestic insurrections," and the more insidious peril of a military establishment. By the 1840s, compulsory drills were a thing of the past.

As the militia drifted into memory, however, the Second Amendment's troubles were just beginning. What followed was a series of collisions between a Southern gun culture and the military substance of the right to bear arms. In all but two cases, the militia doctrine prevailed. But the vigor of these debates was a portent of trouble ahead.

The first challenge came in 1822 in *Bliss v. Common-*

wealth, when the Kentucky Court of Appeals struck down a ban on concealed weapons, which had been passed in 1813. In a 2–1 decision, the court declared that the right to bear arms predated the Constitution, and the right had "no limits short of the moral power of the citizens to exercise it"—a sweeping novelty. The ruling placed concealed weapons on the same footing as the bayonets of the militiaman.

The comparison prompted derision outside the state and outrage in the Kentucky House of Representatives, which bitterly protested the ruling. The fashion of carrying deadly weapons would have been "abhorred by our ancestors," asserted a joint statement. The constitutional right "applied only to the distinctive arms of the soldier, such as the musket or the rifle." It did not authorize a man to arm himself with "such detestable instruments" as a pistol or a bowie knife.

The same note of incredulity is apparent in one of the most important decisions of the period. In *Aymette v. State* (1840), the Tennessee Supreme Court dismissed the claim that a punishment for brandishing a bowie knife violated the constitutional right to bear arms. The scope and substance of the right, wrote the judge, could only be established by studying "the history of our ancestors" and their reasons for enshrining it in the Constitution. Chief among them was the republican animus against standing armies and a correlating faith in the militia as the natural strength of the community. This was a public and political right, "to be exercised by the people in a body, for their common defence." "No private defence was contemplated." This was clear from the language, as well as the history. For the words "bear arms" referred "to their military use, and were not employed to mean wearing them about the person as part of the dress." It could not apply to pistols or bowie knives, and it had nothing to do with hunting. "A man in the pursuit of deer, elk, and buffaloes might carry his rifle every day for forty years," explained the judge, "and yet it would never be said of him that he had borne arms; much less could it be said that a private citizen bears arms because he had a dirk or pistol concealed under his clothes, or a spear in a cane."

Finally, the provision for conscientious objection removed all doubt as to the public quality of the right. "Here we know that the phrase has a military sense, and no other," concluded the judge. To appropriate a right that existed for the preservation of the peace for weapons that violated that goal was an outrageous presumption. It was "to pervert a great political right to the worst of purposes, and to make it a social evil of infinitely greater extent to society than would result from abandoning the right itself."

A pattern was emerging. Southern individuals, charged and convicted for carrying weapons, reached for the weapon of the Constitution. The lower courts heard them. The higher courts slapped them down. In *State v. Reid* (1840), Alabama followed Tennessee, finding that a ban on concealed weapons violated no constitutional principle.

But the mother of all rulings came in Arkansas. A man called Buzzard had been convicted for violating an 1837 law prohibiting the carriage of concealed weapons. A circuit court quashed the conviction, accepting Buzzard's claim that his constitutional rights had been infringed. The state appealed to the Supreme Court, which responded with an essay worthy of John Adams. The regulations of 1837 were not only constitutional: they were the soul of good government.

The author of the opinion was Chief Justice Daniel Ringo, whose prodigious research and learned commentaries earned him the nickname "Old German Whig." Ringo was not content to elucidate the history of the militias. He wanted to grasp the meaning of liberty.

The goal of all free governments, wrote Ringo, with Locke and Montesquieu by his side, was to provide conditions of "peace and domestic tranquility," in which citizens could live without fear. The method was community—where power is shared, and individuals are protected by the aggregate force of their peers. Such freedom was not natural or spontaneous. It was purchased by resigning "many if not all of the rights" that might have been exercised in a state of nature. In particular: "the right of any individual to redress, according to the dictates of his own will or caprice, any injury inflicted upon his personal or private rights by another, is surrendered." In a political community, all questions of punishment are referred to the law. To refuse the regulation of weapons, therefore, was to touch liberty at its most fundamental level. It was to throw society "back to its natural state," threatening the very "object for which the government was formed." If firearms were not subject to regulation, the outcome would be "anarchy." It was inconceivable that the founders of the republic would have authorized "a principle pregnant with such dangers." And they didn't.

Were the founders seeking to protect individual force when they enshrined a constitutional right to keep and bear arms? "Certainly not," wrote Ringo. The right to keep and bear arms was designed with a view to "public liberty" and the security of the state. It was anchored to a well-regulated militia. All sources indicated "that this, and this alone, was the object for which the article under consideration was adopted." The right to bear arms had no salience outside the militia, and to extend it beyond the sphere of military service was like lighting a fire in a living room. States need to be able to protect their citizens, and few things threatened the welfare of the people like deadly weapons. The law would stand. And the rigor of the *State v. Buzzard* decision made it the standard authority on the right to bear arms for much of the nineteenth century.

But there was anxiety in the erudition: a palpable fear that republican verities could no longer be taken for granted. That feeling is apparent in another important ruling, delivered by the North Carolina Supreme Court in 1843. The decision has been travestied by modern gun activists and misquoted by the U.S. Supreme Court. Yet it reveals as clearly as *Aymette* and *Buzzard* how sharply the courts distinguished between the public and private uses of firearms.

A man called Robert Huntley armed himself with a double-barreled shotgun, with which he had threatened to kill several neighbors, demanding that one of them "surrender his negroes." Found guilty of affray under the Statute of Northampton, Huntley appealed to the state supreme court, which upheld the conviction, citing Blackstone on the presumptive criminality of the armed citizen.

What about the Constitution? Wasn't there a higher law that put these effeminate scruples in their place? No, declared the court. North Carolina's bill of rights secured to every man the right to "bear arms for the defence of the State," and in so doing, it deepened the guilt of those who would misuse them. "If he employs those arms, which he ought to wield for the safety and protection of his country, to the annoyance and terror and danger of its citizens," explained the judge, "he deserves but the severer condemnation for the abuse of the high privilege with which he has been invested." A gun that was legal in the context of hunting or military service became an "unusual weapon" when used to "terrify and alarm a peaceful people." The context was everything. Most people kept a weapon at home, but "no man amongst us carries it about with him, as one of his everyday accoutrements—as part of his dress—and never, we trust, will the day come when any deadly weapon will be worn or wielded in our peace-loving and law-abiding State, as an appendage of manly equipment." To do so was to attack "that public order and sense of security" that was the goal "of all regulated societies."

The clarity of the statement confirms that there was variety within the slave states, and the norms of the bayou—as Northup suspected—were probably the extreme. A migrant from North Carolina was appalled by the ubiquity of weapons in his new home of Alabama, estimating nine out of ten people carried a weapon as a matter of course. In North Carolina, it was considered disreputable to carry a dirk or a pistol, and murders were less common.

It is, then, all the more troubling that modern activists have fallen on one of the most radical statements of the period as representative of the whole: an 1846 decision of the Georgia Supreme Court, striking down the state's gun control law of 1837.

IV

Nunn v. State has become a proof text for the individual-gun-rights school of scholarship, quoted in *District of Columbia v. Heller* as a statement that "perfectly captured" the original meaning of the Second Amendment. It was, however, an outlier, even by the standards of the South, and a decision steeped in the politics of race.

Hawkins Nunn had been convicted for carrying a pistol in violation of the 1837 law, which banned openly or secretly worn weapons. Claiming that the law violated the Second Amendment to the U.S. Constitution, Nunn appealed and won. The opinion, written by Georgia's first chief justice, Joseph Henry Lumpkin, was an essay in natural law—defining the right to bear arms as a natural, not a political, right, and therefore immune to the slings and arrows of political fortune. By merging the right to bear arms with the natural right of self-defense, Lumpkin placed it on the same untouchable ground as freedom of conscience, absolving it from all bondage to the militia.

This was a bold move but not a convincing one. Sensing the difficulty of squaring his natural-rights theory with the actual wording of the Second Amendment, Lumpkin cuts it in two—asserting his thesis with a version that is both shortened and misquoted:

> "The right of the people to bear arms shall not be infringed." The right of the whole people, old and young, men, women and boys, and not militia only, to keep and

bear *arms* of every description, and not *such,* merely as are used by the *militia,* shall not be *infringed,* curtailed, or broken in upon, in the smallest degree.

Women and children. That was a first.

Lumpkin goes on to suggest that this general state of readiness is the key to the amendment's earlier reference to a militia, but regulation is not on the menu. Lumpkin has to kill the militia to extract his "natural right." The suggestion is that the militia language is nothing more than a gloss on an irrefragable natural entitlement: a gloss that cannot control the meaning. When the founders spoke about a well-regulated militia, proposes Lumpkin, they were taking one example of a much larger natural right, and we would be fools to get caught up in the details. Lumpkin is invoking the Constitution while ignoring its terms. He is using the Second Amendment to nullify the Georgia gun law, and he is using a natural law argument to nullify the actual terms of the Second Amendment. If he were right about natural law, every word of the Constitution would be reduced to ornamentation.

There was a reason the architects of the liberal state were so wary of human nature in the raw: the greedy clutch of pre-political man. For, in the real world, natural rights are almost instantly corrupted into the reign of the strong. As it was in Georgia. There was nothing natural about Lumpkin's natural law. Lumpkin was careful not to invalidate an 1833 law prohibiting "any free persons of color" from carrying firearms in Georgia, and his ardor for an armed society seems to have been inspired by the need to defend slavery.

Lumpkin was no disinterested judge. He was an intellectual chameleon who tailored his opinions to his ruling passion: white supremacy. As legal scholars have observed, when Lumpkin believed a decision "would undermine the slavery system, he defended the institution strongly, ignoring both court decisions and legislative enactments to the contrary." Lumpkin was notorious for denying due process to both slaves and free persons of color, and he larded his severities with quotations from the book of the Apocalypse.

Lumpkin upheld the use of bloodhounds in the pursuit of runaway slaves. He exonerated a man for brutally assaulting another man's female slave in the street. "When insults are given personally by a slave," he advised, "it is right to punish instantly; and the party offended need not delay until the owner can be consulted. The condition of our society demands this promptitude of proceeding." Dismissing the owner's claim of damages for the two weeks of labor that the assault had cost him, Lumpkin added: "We can hardly venture to consider the loss of a tooth as diminishing, either the actual or marketable value of the woman." That was the issue. Lumpkin's deliberations on the use of dogs, in a case where a boy drowned trying to elude the animals, turned on the cost. "The South has lost, already, upwards of 60,000 slaves, worth between 25 and 30 millions of dollars," he reported. "Instead, therefore, of relaxing the means allowed by law for the security and enjoyment of this species of property," it was imperative "to redouble our vigilance and to tighten the chords that bind the negro to his condition of servitude." The inference was therefore "irresistible, that dogs may be employed, prudently and properly, in the pursuit of runaways." That was also how he thought about guns: as tools of dominion.

On the only occasion that he addressed the question of firearms and race directly, Lumpkin justified the double standard with chilling equanimity. Whether slave or free, Lumpkin declared in *Bryan v. Walton* (1853), "the African" is not and "cannot become a citizen under our Constitution and Laws." For "the social and civil degradation, resulting from the taint of blood, adheres to the descendants of Ham in this country, like the poisoned tunic of Nessus." Once a slave, always a slave, in other words. "The argument is, that a negro is a man," he scoffed at the case before him, "and that when not held to involuntary service, that he is free." But to his mind, it was absurd to propose that "the mere act of manumission" could invest with all the dignities of manhood "a being" who had been held without name or title for so long—a being who had been held "*pro nullis, pro mortuis,* and for some, yea many purposes, *pro quadrupedibus.*" This was a classical expression that described slaves "as no men, as dead men, as beasts."

It was, then, in fidelity to the order of creation that, in Georgia, a man of color could not vote, bear witness against a white citizen, or preach without a license. And, Lumpkin adds: "He is not allowed to keep or carry fire-arms." These were divine mandates, but also very practical. For "the great principle of self-preservation, demands, on the part of the white population, unceasing vigilance and firmness," advised Lumpkin.

Sumner was right: the history of the gun is the history of slavery.

.   .   .

The judge who "captured" the Second Amendment was a man who likened humans to animals and used his office to uphold the cruelest of the era's oppressions. If there were a single jurist of the nineteenth century not to be trusted in these affairs, it would be Joseph Henry Lumpkin.

There is a reason gun enthusiasts lean so hard on such authorities, however. No one else saw the Second Amendment in such terms. In *Aymette, Buzzard,* and *Huntley,* Southern courts held firm against the pressures of a gun culture and the prerogatives of a planter class. Slavery poisoned everything, but not everything was poisoned by slavery. And far from representing even his own state of Georgia, Lumpkin's sweeping mandate of 1846 was quashed by the same court in 1874, as a position odious to the Constitution. The military interpretation of the Second Amendment held firm until the twenty-first century.

By then, however, firearms had acquired more eloquent advocates than the "peculiar institution." One of them was nationalism, a force that helped to conquer the slave power in 1865, yet inherited part of the mystique. Nationalism was the noble side of the gun culture, pure and beyond reproach. But it was no less capable of rewiring the republican mind than the slave power it defeated.

Chapter 4

PATRIOTS

There are many humorous things in the world, among them the white man's notion that he is less savage than the other savages.

—Mark Twain, *Following the Equator*

Three days before the fighting began at Fort Sumter, the Boston abolitionist Wendell Phillips made a desperate appeal for restraint. Nobody was more anxious to end slavery than Phillips, but he feared the consequences of a military conflict. A war could punish the Gulf states, but it could not deliver unity. Anyone who believed otherwise knew little of Southern pride or the miseries of warfare. It could take three years and "the death of a hundred thousand men" to bring the rebels back into the Union, and the nation would be more bitterly divided than before. Begin a war, he challenged, and "we know not where it will end."

The journalist Thomas Nichols pressed the point more directly: "Suppose we were to conquer—burn their cities, waste their fields . . . and finally overcome and subdue them.

What then? Can one portion of the Union hold the other conquered provinces? Can we hold the South as Austria holds Venetia, or as England holds Ireland? To do this, our Government must become a military despotism. It cannot be done under the Constitution."

The crucial insight, and one that would sharpen as the war progressed, concerned means and ends: Can freedom be won? Can unity be imposed? Can democracy grow in a furnace of nationalism? Among the legacies of the Civil War, it was the spirit of nationalism, this "sentiment mightier than logic," as Ralph Waldo Emerson termed it, that would build a home for the gun.

To say that Union victory did not establish a reign of democracy in the South is to say nothing new. The war ended slavery and conferred unprecedented rights on the freedmen, but these were paper promises, ruthlessly ignored. This was not the "second founding," as one historian has christened the era. It was a brittle, passing equality that quickly succumbed to Black Codes, the Ku Klux Klan, and a reign of terror in which a lynching occurred every two and a half days for over fifty years. Slavery was dead, but the spirit of Joseph Henry Lumpkin was not.

The legacy of the war, wrote the author and philanthropist Fanny Bixby Spencer, was "peonage, persecution and lynching" for Black Southerners, and "the bitterness of revenge" for an unmoved racial aristocracy. But the unspoken tragedy was the brutalization of the victors. Spencer admired the Lincoln who wanted to free the slaves but not the glazed captain of state who tried to unite a nation with guns. "The Civil War," she wrote, "has left us a heritage of American war traditions which have permeated the whole social life of the country. It has produced a ritual of patriotism which exalts force to a religious sacrament. It has created a war god, terrible and insatiable."

As these values were carried from the military to the fields of law, literature, history, and popular entertainment, the lineaments of a national gun culture began to surface. For men like Theodore Roosevelt, Frederick Jackson Turner, and Owen Wister, a gun was more than a tool: it was a symbol of freedom and the prerogative of "a vigorous and masterful people." Once defined in those terms, its status would be hard to challenge—even if the freedom in question was one that cut like a knife through the fabric of the Constitution.

I

Tension between the flag and the Constitution was as old as the republic. As early as 1787, John Adams fretted about the kind of patriotism that would lead Americans into dangerous places. There was nothing wrong with loving your country. Patriotism was one of the motors of the Revolution. But there was a type of pride that trampled on the political virtues. Any sense that Americans were blessed with providential immunities was an accident waiting to happen.

"There is no special providence for Americans," maintained Adams as he explained the Constitution's aversion to all swaggering monopolies on truth. We are, he once remarked, "all of the same clay." Adams complained to Benjamin Rush that he had been abused for this opinion many times, but nothing had convinced him of its error. When we fancy ourselves special, when we draw God into our quarrels, we draw ourselves into tyranny. "We may boast that we are the Chosen People," he sighed in another letter. "We may even thank God that we are not like other Men. But after all it will be but flattery, and the delusion, the Self-deceit of the Pharisee."

Adams was reacting against a Puritan tradition that burned witches and slaughtered Indians under the smiling mandates of providence, and he could see that the conceit persisted. Even the more secular founders were inclined to this way of thinking, conceiving America as the New Israel—an "empire of liberty," in Jefferson's awkward phrase. All men were created equal, but not all nations, it seemed. *We hold the keys to history.* Before you know it, all those checks and balances have acquired a flavor of absurdity. *If history is on our side, who could be against us?*

The War of 1812 showed glimmers of the problem when the so-called War Hawks hankered for an invasion of Canada, but it was the doctrine of Manifest Destiny and the dubious legalities of the Mexican War of 1846–48 that exposed the tension. Manifest Destiny was a winner's creed: the belief that success is its own justification. Advocates of Western expansion boasted of freedom and the special wisdom of our laws, noted the critics, but it was difficult to wage a war of aggression without violating those principles. The itch for expansion mocked the American ideal of "Liberty robed in law." It was a regression to the brutal logic of the state of nature.

To the disciples of Manifest Destiny, complained the editor of *The American Review,* "the restrictions of the Constitution are fetters to the free, its guidance useless and impertinent as a light-house to the mariner in the blaze of the sun." President James Polk spoke of "conquering peace" as he invaded the sovereign territory of the Mexican people. But history would not be fooled. Samuel Johnson was right when he called patriotism "the last refuge of a scoundrel."

Nobody pressed the point more fervently than a freshman congressman called Abraham Lincoln. Polk had listed the good of the Mexican people among his reasons for the war, noted Lincoln, framing aggression as virtue. But the words bore no relationship to the reality. "Let him answer with *facts,* and not with arguments," demanded Lincoln as he pummeled the president on the origins of the war. Arguments had become substitutes for facts; ideology, for truth. Polk was gambling that he could "escape scrutiny by fixing the public gaze upon the exceeding brightness of military glory—that attractive rainbow that rises in showers of blood—that serpent's eye that charms to destroy." The founders had regarded war as "the most oppressive of all Kingly oppressions," Lincoln wrote to his friend William Herndon, which was why they erected so many barriers against it. When the president authorized the invasion of another country without the approval of Congress, he betrayed this heritage: he stood "where kings have always stood." Patriotism was the new monarchy: a license to kill.

Lincoln had been sensitive to the tension since he entered the legal profession. His first public speech, delivered at the Young Men's Lyceum in Springfield, Illinois, in 1838, was a blistering critique of an American vigilante code and its disposition to hide violence beneath doctrines of national purity. Responding to a series of lynchings that had left bodies dangling from trees "to rival the native Spanish moss," Lincoln excoriated "the increasing disregard for law which pervades the country" and "the growing disposition to substitute the wild and furious passions, in lieu of the sober judgment of Courts." No crime could justify the law of the mob or the savage zeal of the vigilante. When justice is taken out of the courts, it is no longer justice. American democracy was premised on "reverence for the laws"; indeed, this was "the political religion of the nation." The vigilante threatened the project at its core.

The most perceptive part of the speech concerned one of the sources of those wild and furious passions: patriotism. Lincoln was conscious that men who hanged gamblers and lynched suspected rapists believed they were serving the community—ridding the nation of unclean elements. But the remedy was worse than the disease. A political community, he argued, cannot live on a soldier's diet of patriotism and valor. Indeed, the sentiments that enabled the United States to defeat the British and to establish her own institutions would be death to those institutions unless tempered by the rule of the law. "Passion has helped us," he advised, "but can do so no more. It will in future be our enemy."

This was a stunning insight, and a position Lincoln maintained twenty years later, when the eulogies were pouring in for John Brown and his botched insurrection at Harpers Ferry in 1859. "John Brown was no Republican," he thundered. "An enthusiast broods over the oppression of a people till he fancies himself commissioned by Heaven to liberate them." These were the ideas that set nations on fire.

Lincoln may have been right. But sympathy for John Brown was broad after a decade in which the federal government had thrown its weight behind the slave power. If there was a turning point for the political religion of liberty under law, a moment when its staunchest advocates began to lose faith, it was the passage of the Fugitive Slave Act of 1850, which bound citizens of the free states to assist in the capture of runaways—a law upheld by the Supreme Court in 1857. It was then that a number of abolitionists began to contemplate direct action against an omnivorous slave power, shipping rifles to the battleground of Kansas to beat the slaveholders at their own game. When Charles Sumner, the arch critic of Southern gun culture, found himself defending the rifles in his famous speech on "the Crime against Kansas" in 1856, a new era had begun.

In the course of a decade, a body of pacifists that included Harriet Beecher Stowe, author of *Uncle Tom's Cabin,* and William Lloyd Garrison rescinded their commitment to nonviolence, endorsing the war with the warmest epithets. From there, patriotism took over, swallowing the cause of antislavery in a surge of national feeling. "How does Heaven help us when civilization is at a hard pinch?" wondered Emerson. "Why, by a whirlwind of patriotism, not believed to exist, but now magnetizing all discordant masses under its terrific unity." It was what one sociologist has termed "collective effervescence": a moment of intensity in which minds are gripped by a kind of electricity. "Go into the swarming town-halls and let yourself be played upon by the stormy winds that blow there," urged Emerson. "I will never again speak lightly of a crowd. We are wafted into a revolution."

But this was a dangerous crowd. The war put a bit of John Brown into everybody—with or without the concern for slaves. By 1863, even Lincoln had exchanged the muscular solicitude of his political religion for higher laws and inscrutable destinies. The Union that was "saved" by the Civil War was closer to the military state that the founders had feared than the "prosaic" and commercial culture that excited Tocqueville in the 1830s.

And if Lincoln was torn and anguished in his descent to arms, the next generation was not. The Civil War not only armed America at the basic level of providing hundreds of thousands of guns: it invested liberty with a martial vigor. As the philosopher William James remarked in 1906, the Civil War came to be embraced as "a sacred spiritual possession worth more than all the blood poured out." It had seared the "military feelings" into the American mind. "Ask all our millions, north and south, whether they would vote now (were such a thing possible) to have our war for the Union expunged from history, and the record of a peaceful transition to the present time substituted for that of its marches and battles," he speculated, "and probably hardly a handful of eccentrics would say yes." To undo the work, to expose the "bestial side" of the mystique, would be no stroll in the park. Once established on imaginative and sentimental ground, it was apparently impregnable. To the poets of force such as Theodore Roosevelt, the horrors of war are a small price to pay to escape the miserable alternative: "a world of clerks and teachers."

Between the Civil War and the First World War, American culture was torn between the political religion and the religion of America: between the Constitution and the flag. James was with the clerks and the teachers. The gun culture grew from the war.

II

A wave of guerrilla and vigilante violence prompted a raft of gun control measures in the decade after the Civil War. The invention of the revolving pistol by Samuel Colt in 1835 had made handguns cheap and readily available, and the war put them into civilian hands. Within five years of Robert E. Lee's surrender at Appomattox, writes the historian Brian DeLay, "the War Department had decommissioned most of its guns and auctioned off some 1,340,000 to private arms dealers, such as Schuyler, Hartley and Graham." The dealers made fortunes selling them at home and abroad. Culturally and physically, the war had created a gun culture. And the courts were now fighting it.

In Texas, where gun-toting Confederate veterans made the state the most violent in the Union, fines of one hundred dollars were imposed on carriers of concealed weapons. The world had seen too much violence "cloaked under the name of natural or personal liberty," declared the Texas Supreme Court as it upheld the law in 1872. This wild and dangerous freedom was "exchanged under the social compact of States, for *civil* liberty"—something entirely different. Under the social contract, explained the judge, every individual has surrendered the right to avenge his own wrongs, and must look to the State for redress: "We must not," he warned, "go back to that state of barbarism in which each claims the right to administer the law in his own case; that law being simply the domination of the strong and the violent over the weak and submissive."

Decisions in Georgia and Tennessee echoed the sentiment. Overturning the infamous *Nunn* decision of 1846, the Georgia Supreme Court rejected the claim that the constitutional right to bear arms applied to personal weapons. "I have always been at a loss to follow the line of thought that extends the guarantee to the right to carry pistols, dirks, Bowie-knives, and those other weapons of like character, which, as all admit, are the greatest nuisances of our day," wrote the judge. He doubted whether any of the founders would have applied the word "arms" to pistols, revolvers, or any other "inventions of modern savagery." To have done so, they would have to have believed "that their whole scheme of law and order, and government and protection, would be a failure."

The founders, asserted the Tennessee attorney general in a similar case, had no intention of protecting "the claims of the assassin and the cut-throat to carry the implements of his trade." They would, he said, "as soon have protected the burglar's jimmy and skeleton key." To extend a military provision to the tools of casual homicide, affirmed a court in West Virginia, was to "make the Constitution defend lawlessness, tumult, and anarchy."

None of this was controversial. The difficulty was that the Civil War and the lurching course of Western expansion blurred the boundaries between military and civilian life. An editorial published in the *Abilene Chronicle* in June 1871 captured the ambiguity: "There's no bravery in carrying revolvers in a civilized community," asserted the editor, in support of an ordinance banning firearms within the town. "Such a practice is well enough and perhaps necessary when among Indians or other barbarians, but among white people it ought to be discontinued." That was the fatal rider. In the same breath, guns are condemned and authorized, disdained and approved. It all turned on the context, the contest, the blood.

If the Second Amendment held firm against the gunslingers, the same could not be said of the venerable "duty to retreat" from danger before exercising deadly force. This was a pillar of the common law and its unshakable commitment to the sanctity of life. Under common law, "all homicide is presumed to be malicious," until the contrary could be demonstrated, explained William Blackstone. Every "possible means" of escape had to be considered before a plea of self-defense could be recognized. Slowly, this principle began to crumble.

The process began with an affair that scandalized Boston in 1806—the shooting of Harvard student Charles Austin by the prominent lawyer Thomas Selfridge, after a bitter and prolonged feud between the families. In a case that captured the nation's imagination, Selfridge was acquitted, having argued that his honor was as precious as his life, and that honor was the lifeblood of the nation. "The greatest of all public calamities," argued his lawyer, "would be a pusillanimous spirit, that would tamely surrender personal dignity to every invader."

By arming himself with pistols and shooting his alleged assailant in the street, Selfridge had upheld the spirit that had conquered the redcoats and delivered independence a generation before. Without such a spirit, he archly contended, "we should soon deservedly cease to exist as an independent nation." Among the jurors who decided in his favor was an icon of the American Revolution: Paul Revere.

It all sounded so plausible, responded James Sullivan on behalf of the state. But to accept this line of argument was to allow a mysticism of national honor to "overset our Constitution." It was to throw us back into a state of nature, where every man is the avenger of his wrongs. "Where will these ideas carry us?" Sullivan wondered. If you prefer our democratic government to monarchy or aristocracy, he unsuccessfully appealed to the jury, you have to reject these doctrines. "If heroism and honor and chivalry are to return," he warned, this promised land of freedom will "be turned into a field of battle, and crimsoned by the blood of our fellow citizens."

It took sixty years and a Civil War, but these were exactly the ideas that began to coalesce in the 1870s, in what came to be known as the "true man" doctrine: the belief that the old duty of retreat was unreasonable because it forced a man into the posture of a coward. If it is cowardice for a soldier to flee from an enemy, asked the Ohio Supreme Court in *Erwin v. State* (1876), why not also for a citizen? The duty to retreat placed an unreasonable burden on a "a true man." In *Runyan v. State* (1877), the Indiana Supreme Court concurred, finding the English doctrine expounded by Blackstone odious to "the tendency of the American mind"—an intriguing criterion. American authorities, argued the judge, were increasingly impatient of any law that required a man to flee when assailed—"even to save human life." Both opinions exuded an enthusiasm, bordering on relish, for the prerogative of lethal force.

It was, protested Harvard law professor Joseph Beale, as though the courts were encouraging violence. Dealing with disagreeable people was "one of the penalties of life in society." We do not avoid this predicament by killing. It was always better "that one man should live rather than that another should stand his ground in a private conflict." Honor was creeping into the law. "Such thoughts," concurred a judge in Alabama, "are trash, as compared with the inestimable right to live." Another lawyer called it "the Jurisprudence of Lawlessness." When the "unwritten law" of honor supplants the actual law of the land, warned Thomas J. Kernan in a speech delivered before the American Bar Association, "liberty dies," and "all organized government is shaken to its foundation stones."

Yet the mystique was on the rise. In 1921, the true man doctrine finally gained the approval of the U.S. Supreme Court, when Oliver Wendell Holmes delivered an opinion shimmering with patriotic masculinity. "The law of Texas very strongly adopts these views," he wrote, and many "respectable writers agree" that a man should not have to flee from danger before exercising lethal force. As Holmes defended the principle in a letter that appeared to draw on his experience as a Union officer in the Civil War: "a man is not born to run away." The law, he maintained, "must consider human nature and make some allowances for the fighting instinct at critical moments."

The romance of war was rewriting the law. Scenes of ugly and incestuous violence were reconceived as patriotism. As the Canadian writer A. J. Somerset has observed, none of the killings that established the true man doctrine bore the slightest resemblance to the valorous pieties with which they were justified. One was an argument between a man and his son-in-law that escalated into a shooting for reasons that were never clearly established. The second was a political spat between neighbors, in which one man struck another before receiving a bullet in the chest. The third was a fight between two men who had fought before and almost certainly would have fought again, had one not decided to shoot the other. Yet these tawdry encounters were transfigured into noble assertions of American character. Who were these respectable writers, sending Blackstone into long-overdue retirement? One of them was the man who appointed Holmes to the Supreme Court in 1902: Theodore Roosevelt.

III

Roosevelt divided opinion like few American leaders before or since. For some, he was the walking embodiment of American manhood. For others, he was an "apostle of violence," steering a nation to the values of Prussian militarism. For Mark Twain, who was never an admirer, Roosevelt was "the most formidable disaster that has befallen the country since the Civil War." Roosevelt was "all that a president ought not to be"—proud, pretentious, and consumed by the glories of war. It is in Roosevelt that the dogmas of a gun culture take shape: a militarism in miniature; a nationalism aimed at unworthy parts of the nation.

Moving West, following the death of his wife and his mother on the same day, Roosevelt found strength on the frontier and built a career on its coruscating mandates. Life in the cities had become a purgatory of banality, a morass of materialism. But the arms of nature were open, summoning a nation back to its original virtues. The harmless side of the formula was delight in the beauty of the land. The dark side was the promotion of violence as the purging tonic of a broken society. "Unless we keep the barbarian virtues," he advised, "gaining the civilized ones will be of little avail." Roosevelt's sympathies were with the former.

Roosevelt's belligerence drew on a Darwinian division between the fit and the unfit, the holy and the damned—a category that starts with "savages" and ends with cattle thieves. Roosevelt's frontier was a testing ground for native ability, in which fighting did the revealing. The fact that Roosevelt, as a wealthy New Yorker, was able to invest $40,000 of his own money in the cattle trade was immaterial to his thesis that the land will find and disclose character. Roosevelt's narratives of ranch life in the Dakotas, and his sprawling histories of *The Winning of the West,* preach a message of struggle and survival, in which "the unfit are weeded out by a very rapid process of natural selection."

The first to go were the Native Americans. Responding to the "sentimental nonsense" of writers such as Helen Hunt Jackson, whose scorching exposé of American treatment of Native peoples, *A Century of Dishonor,* appeared in 1881, Roosevelt argued that the Native American was lazy and never asserted any real ownership of the land. It was only right that he, "who will not work, perish from the face of the earth which he cumbers." The doctrine seemed merciless, but Roosevelt believed the pioneers had history, and therefore justice, on their side. Without their unflinching remedies, the continent would have been "nothing but a game preserve for squalid savages"—scattered tribes, whose lives were "but a few degrees less meaningless, squalid, and ferocious than that of the wild beasts with whom they held joint ownership." Against these "wolf-hearted" enemies, the brutal and occasionally "inhuman" methods of the pioneers were necessary. In such circumstances, it was inevitable that "the whites, the representatives of civilization, speedily sink almost to the level of their barbarous foes." It was idle to judge these encounters by the rules of stable and cultured communities. Maybe so, but Roosevelt wants to bottle these energies and release them into the culture.

The cruelties that Helen Hunt Jackson calls tyranny Roosevelt calls decision and character. "In the long run civilized man finds he can keep the peace only by subduing his barbarian neighbor," he writes. Those who prated on "liberty" and the "consent of the governed" failed to appreciate what divides the races. "It is only the warlike power of a civilized people that can give peace to the world."

Roosevelt's ability to frame consent as the currency of women and cowards is a trademark of his writing and the Western genre he helped to establish. This is a racialized vision, openly committed to "white civilization" and the progress of "the higher races." But it is no less contemptuous of the unsuitable white—the losers within the master race. With nimble footwork and aching stereotypes, he steers the problem of crime into the politics of blood. Criminals were

savages: "cumberers of the earth." The good men had to police them.

Roosevelt presented the cowboys of the Dakotas as men
of skill and resolution, who "go armed" and are always "ready
to guard their lives by their own prowess." The practice made
them more courteous and chivalrous than the unarmed men
of the East. "When a quarrel may very probably result fatally,
a man thinks twice before going into it," explains Roosevelt
with excited gravity. A cowboy, he whispers, "will not submit tamely to an insult, and is ever ready to avenge his own
wrongs; nor has he an overwrought fear of shedding blood.
He possesses, in fact, few of the emasculated, milk-and-water
moralities admired by the pseudo-philanthropists; but he
does possess, to a very high degree, the stern, manly qualities
that are invaluable to a nation." Once again, it is the criterion
of nationhood that sustains the posture of aggression. Such
men are indispensable to the nation. Without them, America
would be a playground for criminals.

Among those manly virtues was a willingness to hang
thieves. Roosevelt felt that his foreman was getting above his
station when he objected to the lynching of "a certain
French-Canadian" who was suspected of being a horse thief.
Ranchers and cowboys were rarely constrained by such deli-
cacies, taking the law into their own hands when they knew
a man to be guilty. It was this intuitive knowledge, this natural sense of justice, that defined the frontier. "It is a noteworthy fact," reports Roosevelt, "that the men who are killed
generally deserve their fate." These were the men "who infest every frontier town," and the ranchers would come together to put them down, "often by the most summary

exercise of lynch law." Some were hanged, others were shot. One group of vigilantes, "known as 'stranglers,' in happy allusion to their summary method of doing justice," killed as many as sixty cattle thieves in one year. As a consequence, declares Roosevelt, "most of our territory is now perfectly law-abiding."

In *The Winning of the West*, Roosevelt continued his homage to the vigilante code. He conceded that mistakes were sometimes made, but maintained that such work was both necessary and generally "wholesome." Since virtue and virtuosity are linked, in Roosevelt's still-Puritan worldview, the good guys generally win. In one incident that clearly tickled the future president, "a party of returning church-goers" spotted a miscreant as they rode home on horseback. They chased him down, organized themselves into a court, and "hung him to a sycamore tree" before returning to their families.

That was how the West was won. Well-meaning citizens had tried to civilize the frontier "by simply passing resolutions of disarmament," he once recalled. "In every case the result was the same. Good citizens for the moment abandoned their weapons. The bad men continued to carry them." The details were not forthcoming. "No greater wrong can ever be done than to put a good man at the mercy of a bad," he admonished. The casual demonology that justified the killing of Native Americans has been transferred to the ordinary criminal. Nobody did more to frame the working philosophy of a gun culture, and nobody was more dismissive of the emasculating protocols of the law. Roosevelt's frontier was a morality play without a moral: a feast of violence, served as civilization.

As William James responded to Roosevelt's manifesto on "The Strenuous Life," the weakness of Roosevelt's philosophy was abstraction: a drama of righteousness in which monsters and demons stand in for real characters. Beneath the martial excitement and the effusions on national greatness, Roosevelt's speeches were "carnivals of emptiness," devoid of authentic detail. For Roosevelt, "one foe is as good as another," and real situations are drowned in a "flood of abstract bellicose emotion." This was Roosevelt's "crime" and the fallacy of the new imperialism. Roosevelt justified American control of the Philippines by pinning labels made thousands of miles away on the native population—declaring, in phrases of formulaic condescension, that the Filipinos were "unfit" for self-government. How could he know? Roosevelt was like a boy in adolescence, taunting his opponents for shrinking from strife; trivializing warfare as "a magnificent opportunity." Perhaps, advised James, it was not the Filipinos but Mr. Roosevelt's "abstract, aesthetic and organic emotionalities [that] need a policeman to keep them in check."

IV

It wasn't just Roosevelt, however. In a hugely influential lecture, delivered in Chicago in 1893, the historian Frederick Jackson Turner reduced the whole sweep of American history to the settlement of the frontier: a Homeric encounter from which a uniquely American personality emerged— tough, resilient, and pure. American history was the colonization of the West, the rush of American energy upon "this vast shaggy continent of ours," and it was here, not in the drawing rooms of Europe, that democracy was born. "American democracy," wrote Turner, "was born of no theorist's dream; it was not carried in the *Susan Constant* to Virginia, nor in the *Mayflower* to Plymouth. It came out of the American forest, and it gained new strength each time it touched a new frontier. Not the Constitution, but free land and an abundance of natural resources open to a fit people, made the democratic type of society in America for three centuries while it occupied its empire."

Turner, like Roosevelt, was thrilled by the clarity of frontier justice and he feels that something is lost when the frisson of vengeance is purged from the law. For Turner, democracy is action and will, and part of its spirit of adventure is a breezy defiance of the law. His idealized frontiersman had little patience with finely drawn distinctions. He was intolerant of men who split hairs or scrupled over the formalities of justice: "If there were cattle thieves, lynch law was sudden and effective." The pioneer was a man of "grim energy" and instant judgment. Andrew Jackson, "this expert duelist, and ready fighter," was the supreme embodiment. The frontier democracy of Jackson's time, writes Turner, "had the instincts of the clansman in the days of Scotch border warfare." These were men who got things done, and they built a nation in their own image.

This was not history. It was romantic nationalism, sprinkled with Social Darwinism. What Locke called a state of nature, and Hobbes a state of war, Turner calls democracy: a story of strongmen, staring down judges; mavericks, bending a world to their needs. And those solemn legalities that republican philosophy called the beginning of freedom are derided as the ghosts of fallen Europe. Turner's only mention of the Constitution is to dismiss it as an authentic source of democracy. His claim is that the frontier advanced "individualism, democracy, and nationalism," in dynamic unity. Yet these principles are at war. Turner's individualism is contemptuous of the rule of the law—a nonchalance vindicated on the higher ground of nation building. The irony is that when Turner eulogizes the imperious will of the duelist, he is taking America backward—to the honor code of the European aristocracy, to the values that the founders called tyranny.

While Turner was delivering his lecture on the grounds of the 1893 World's Fair in Chicago, Buffalo Bill Cody was performing his "Wild West" show outside the gates—an extravaganza of gunplay and horsemanship that blurred the boundaries between life and art by starring real Native Americans alongside Cody's "Rough Riders." Cody was a crack shot in the U.S. Army who made a career out of his reputation as the slayer of Native Americans, although his wife queried his claim to have been injured in combat 137 times. She said it only happened once. Cody magnified the mystique, reenacting battle scenes and displaying the dried scalp of one of his victims outside theaters. In the sultry saraband of history and fiction, militarism and entertainment, the truth of the frontier is dissolved in the myth, until the difference is no longer discernible. When Theodore Roosevelt christened his band of warriors "Rough Riders" during the Spanish-American War of 1898, the seduction was complete. Fiction was driving history—framing a military conquest in terms already established on Cody's stage. Gun culture was part of this circle of validation: this force field of history and myth. It had an advocate that would eclipse all others: the Western.

V

Owen Wister's novel *The Virginian* (1902) was the first of the great Westerns: the prototype of a formula that would dominate the early decades of cinema, cementing the image of the gunfighter as savior. *The Virginian* was the bestselling book in America for two years in a row, eventually lending its magic to five motion pictures and a long-running television series. It is the tale of a handsome cowboy moving the world to his will—a love story, a sermon, and an elaborate defense of a citizen's right to kill.

We meet the Virginian as a twenty-four-year-old who moves with the languid ease of a college quarterback, his muscles seeming to "flow" beneath his skin. Leaving home at fourteen, he travels widely before settling in Wyoming as the fixer and right-hand man of Judge Henry, a prosperous rancher. The Virginian is cool in all circumstances and possessed of a wicked sense of humor. He plays a trick on some merry-making parents by swapping their babies during a dance. The rage of the young mothers, who travel vast distances before discovering that their sleeping bundles belong to someone else, is defused with a wink and a smile. Here is a man who can get away with murder. And he does.

The Virginian's authority is charismatic, technical, and

physical. He is a magnetic character who always finds the right words. Wister's novel is a form of hero worship, in which the reader—like the Eastern schoolmarm Molly Wood—begins an awed infatuation. The Virginian, who is twice compared to George Washington, is an honest man whose violence is never casual or accidental. It is the extension of his being.

As the Virginian grows in stature, he drifts apart from old friends and adopts sterner remedies than practical jokes for the nonentities around him. As he rises, others fall, including his old friend Steve, who has fallen from "that particular honesty which respects another man's cattle." When the larcenies touch Judge Henry's head of cattle, the Virginian assembles a lynching party. Within days, Steve and his pals are left "dangling back in the cottonwoods," in a scene of ghastly intimacy. The doomed rustlers are confronted and left to brood on their iniquities for a whole night before being taken out and hanged. The Virginian has shown his mettle by dispatching his old friend and says he would "do it again" if he had to.

Disgusted by the affair, Molly confronts the Judge on the "hideous disgrace" of a lynching in "the United States." The real disgrace, responds the Judge, is the ineptitude of the courts. The Constitution put justice into the hands of "ordinary citizens," but the people of Wyoming had failed to enforce it. The courts were withered and weak. When an honest man sees this, he has no choice but to "take justice back into his own hands where it was at the beginning of all things." This was brutal, not barbarous. It proved that "Wyoming is determined to become civilized."

The most disturbing part of Wister's novel—dedicated to his old friend Theodore Roosevelt—is the interpretation of crime in terms of breeding and blood. The cattle thieves are described as men of "average rough male blood," whose sullen mediocrity is written all over their faces. The word "equality" is a term of reproach in *The Virginian:* the symbol of a crass and chimerical idealism. "All men are born equal," muses the Virginian as he rides with Molly during their courtship. He used to learn all about the Declaration of Independence. But life has taught him that "equality is a great big bluff. It's easy called." Fact is: some are good and capable. Others are not. Sooner or later, nature will have her say, bringing you back to the "old trail of inequality." "All America is divided into two classes—the quality and the equality," adds the narrator, and both "will be with us until our women bear nothing but kings." "Let the best man win! That is America's word. That is true democracy. And true democracy and true aristocracy are one and the same thing. If anybody cannot see this, so much the worse for his eyesight."

The book winds toward its grisly denouement with the final piece of the mythology: the quality never misses. Trampas, a louche and goading villain, escapes the lynching party and is now spreading slander about the Virginian. Holding his honor dearer than life, and confident that he will prevail in any encounter, the Virginian decides to kill Trampas. As he mulls over the insults, a rattlesnake slips into view. Before anyone sees it, the Virginian draws his pistol and blows its head off. Trampas would be next. "It had come to that point," muses the narrator, "where there was no way out, save only the ancient, eternal way between man and man. It is only the Great Mediocrity that goes to law in these personal matters."

Molly tells the Virginian that it would be murder to kill Trampas, that there is a higher courage than fear of outside opinion. It would show more strength to walk away. "There's something better than shedding blood in cold blood," she bitterly admonishes. The Virginian is unmoved, and a drably choreographed duel ensues. Trampas is dispatched with a single bullet and left bleeding in the road. "I have killed Trampas," reports the Virginian. "Oh, thank God!" says Molly, whose conversion is now complete. The young lovers marry, unmolested by the law, this singular act of violence putting an end to their quarrels. Wealth, love, and security flow from the barrel of the Virginian's gun.

"Life imitates art far more than art imitates life," wrote Oscar Wilde. Culture makes history as often as the other way round. The real West was a place of toil, hardship, and periodic violence, tamed by the rule of law. The mythical West was a place of dashing fortitude and redemptive violence—where the good guy always gets his man, where blood is spilled but not seen. The real West would have furnished weak credentials for a gun culture, because it involved a lot of rules and regulations. A monthlong imprisonment for "going armed" with a dangerous weapon would not have made an entertaining screenplay. But in the torrent of nostalgia that carried the gun into the twentieth century, it was the myth, not the history, that mattered. The Western, writes Richard Slotkin, was a story about America in which violence brings health and happiness. It bathed acts of brutality in a glow of innocence. As such, it was no less potent in the inversion of the realities of killing than the theologies of vengeance that it superseded. By the mid-twentieth century, even movie directors were poking fun at the process. "When the legend becomes fact," says a newspaperman in *The Man Who Shot Liberty Valance,* "print the legend."

Where Lincoln wrestled with the tension between the political religion and the demands of war, the frontier creed was openly hostile to the politics of consent and the dignity of the courts. It divided the world into two kinds of people, and it demanded force as the natural resolution. Violence is laudable because evil is legible: the fruit of inferior natures. But there was nothing natural about this law, either. The permission structure was patriotic: a doctrine of Americanism hardened by race.

"The whites," complained Big Eagle of the Santee Sioux, "always seemed to say by their manner when they saw an Indian, 'I am better than you,' and the Indians did not like this." Herman Melville called it "the metaphysics of Indian-hating," because it preceded any crime or wrongdoing. The Indian was a criminal before he opened his eyes. The next move, decisive for an age of immigration, was to transfer the curse onto the unsuitable white man: the invention of a criminal class. That was the gun culture, and it found a champion in another child of the Civil War: the National Rifle Association.

Chapter 5

THE BIRTH OF A GUN LOBBY

The pistol is the curse of America.

—William G. McAdoo

While novelists were preaching, the cities were bleeding. American cities were between ten and twenty times more dangerous than their European counterparts in the early twentieth century, not because Americans were more dangerous but because Americans had guns: handguns. Easily carried and easily concealed. Advances in gun-making technology had made pistols affordable and accessible, and America's patchwork of jurisdictions made their sale impossible to regulate. In Europe, the gun makers counted princes and government ministers among their clients. In America, they sold to civilians. This was the problem that threatened a democracy.

Gun control was a central concern of the Progressive Era, and it got off to a flying start in 1911, when New York passed the Sullivan Act, criminalizing the possession of a handgun by anyone who could not demonstrate a tangible need for self-protection. Under the new law, police had full discretion to grant or refuse a license, and public carriage of a handgun without a permit became a felony. "I wanted to make it hard for the desperate man to carry a gun and to accomplish this I began making it hard for him to get a gun," explained state senator Timothy D. Sullivan, who sponsored the bill. Take pistols off the streets, he told colleagues in the Senate, and you will "save more souls than all the preachers in the city talking for the next ten years." The bill sailed through both chambers.

Nobody could have foreseen the reaction. The Sullivan Act was greeted with dismay in the hunting and firearms periodicals, which called it "anti-American" and a step toward "national suicide." A cartoon in *Outdoor Life* depicted Uncle Sam crouching in terror while masked criminals point revolvers in his face. Sullivan was accused of being a traitor, an agent of a foreign power, and clinically insane. When the battle for regulation resumed after the First World War, the gun community was ready and waiting.

A tenacious myth holds that the National Rifle Association was a benign and apolitical body for most of its early life, innocent of the militancy with which it was later associated. The truth is quite the contrary. Not only was the NRA a dynamic presence by the 1920s: its opposition to federal regulation in that era was perhaps the most significant factor in the history of the gun in America.

The National Rifle Association was founded in 1871 by veterans of the U.S. Army to improve the quality of marksmanship in the civilian population. Led by a distinguished cast of retired generals, the NRA was a fervent advocate of military preparedness and the embodiment of Theodore Roosevelt's doctrine of "applied Americanism." By 1916, the NRA was an adjunct to the War Department and a valued partner of the government. The problems came when the doctrines of "Americanism" were applied to the dilemmas of peace. The NRA was one element in a wave of nationalism and nativist sentiment that swept the country in the second decade of the twentieth century. The gun debate played out on this harsh and unforgiving terrain. The gun was a symbol of America: pure and undefiled. Crime was foreign and dark. Those surging currents of nationalism and white supremacy came together in the organization that led the fight for guns.

I

Saving the Union, as we have seen, did not necessarily mean saving democracy. The painful truth of this era of migration and displacement was the diffusion of martial values previously associated with the South to the nation as a whole. The fact that Owen Wister named his protagonist "the Virginian" was one indication. *The Birth of a Nation,* a silent movie that took America by storm in 1915, was another.

The film, based on Thomas Dixon's novel *The Clansman,* told the story of the South's recovery from the supposed humiliations of Black rule after the Civil War: a recovery achieved by the cleansing violence of the Ku Klux Klan. This was more than the revival of the South, however. It was the renewal of a nation in the exclusion of "the Negro."

Some critics felt that the villains, played by white actors in blackface, looked more like European immigrants than Blacks. That was the subtext: a lesson from the South for an age of "impurity."

The director, D. W. Griffith, portrayed Reconstruction as a time of lawlessness and brutality, in which the freedmen lord it over whites. In a stunning inversion of history, we see Black men tying political opponents to a tree. Dark-skinned lawmakers are shown drinking, dancing, and eating chicken in the state house. Blacks are said to be lazy, lascivious, and eager for white flesh. But in an intriguing revision of the "lost cause" victimology, the reign of the Klan is nationalized, Americanized, and anchored to the awesome memory of Abraham Lincoln. "The Ku Klux Klan," we are told, "saved the South from the anarchy of black rule, but not without the shedding of more blood than at Gettysburg." The reign of the Klan was the completion of the war.

When a freedman called Gus presses his affections on the fair and defenseless Flora, he is hunted down like an animal and lynched in the red glow of a burning cross. In the bruising semiotics of the movie, Blacks move heavily and awkwardly, stooping and stumbling like newborn calves. The Klansmen move with grace and authority: strong, stately, and true. The Black characters cannot hold a gun properly. The Klansmen shoot like gods. When order is finally restored, we see cringing Black militiamen placing their weapons before a phalanx of Klansmen, who tower over them with Peacemakers. In a final scene of humiliation, mounted Klansmen supervise an election with weapons drawn, while despondent freedmen melt away. As Dixon confessed in the novel, the issue was not democracy—it was civilization: "Not whether a negro shall be protected, but whether Society is worth saving from barbarism." Dixon said he wanted "to demonstrate to the world that the white man must and shall be supreme." The message came across loud and clear.

"It's like writing history with lightning," said Woodrow Wilson, who hosted a private screening at the White House. This was a cultural event of some magnitude. *The Birth of a Nation* sold out the Liberty Theater in New York City for forty-four weeks consecutively at the unprecedented admission price of $2.20. A first-class stamp cost two cents in 1915; monthly rent averaged around $25. But the viewers kept coming. In Houston, audiences shouted "Lynch him!" as Gus pursued Flora. In Denver, a man pulled out a revolver and fired at the screen. Viewers cheered as the Klan swept in. As if to prove Oscar Wilde's point about life imitating art, a Methodist preacher used the film's premiere in Atlanta to launch the second wave of the Ku Klux Klan, with outfits and burning crosses to match the iconography of the movie.

This was redemptive violence on a national scale— a manifesto on firearms reducible to a single idea: Black people are dangerous; white men need to stop playing at democracy and assert their power. The film catalyzed latent and unspoken anxieties and organized them into a target. And like the billowing robes of the Klansmen, the guns were on the side of the angels. Researching America's "psychic investment" in firearms in the early 2000s, Joan Burbick found copies of *The Birth of a Nation* on sale "at most gun shows" she attended.

It was, however, the First World War and the fear of foreign subversion that unleashed the nativist storm. Radicals warned that entry into the war would exact a heavy cost at home: that the demands of a belligerent "Americanism" would be difficult to square with the democratic promise of liberty and equality before the law. So it proved. The war, wrote Randolph Bourne, made a kind of "white terrorism" acceptable: "almost a sport between the hunters and the hunted." For a certain kind of patriot, the pursuit of the enemy within was more exciting than the military conflict itself. The harassment of socialists, pacifists, and suspected traitors enjoyed the blessing of the state.

"The net gain of the World War," wrote Fanny Bixby Spencer in 1922, was not "democracy and international understanding, but intensified nationalism," palpable in red scares, lynchings, and the demand for "100 per cent Americanism in every community"—the dreary motto of the Ku Klux Klan. He was a lousy patriot, quipped one writer, who let "life, liberty and the pursuit of happiness" cloud the issues. Patriotism was the love that covered "any multitude of sins."

The Klan looked ridiculous and exotic, noted the polemicist H. L. Mencken. But what was terrifying about a movement that numbered nearly five million in 1925 was the familiarity of the hate. "If the Klan is against the Jews," he wrote, "so are half of the good hotels of the Republic and three-quarters of the good clubs. If the Klan is against the foreign-born or the hyphenated citizen, so is the National Institute of Arts and Letters. If the Klan is against the Negro, so are all of the States south of the Mason-Dixon line. . . . If the Klan lynches a Moor for raping someone's daughter, so would you or I."

This was a period in which members of the American Legion, a fraternity of worried veterans, burst into socialist meetings and forced speakers to salute the flag at gunpoint; a decade in which Benito Mussolini was twice invited to address the Legion's annual convention. The American Legion, declared its leader Alvin Owsley in 1922, "stands ready to protect our country's institutions and ideals as the Fascisti dealt with the destructionists who menaced Italy." Mussolini's anticommunist warriors were "to Italy what the American Legion is to the United States." It was a fight to the death.

This was the atmosphere in which the gun debate was born. In 1924, the national commander of the American Legion was General James A. Drain, who had previously served as president of the National Rifle Association and editor of its monthly journal, *Arms and the Man*. The Legion and the NRA shared ideas, personnel, and a nervous fidelity to what the economist Thorstein Veblen called "the patriotic animus"—"a spirit of particularism, of aliency and animosity between contrasted groups of persons." The patriot's mode of reasoning was "a work of preconception rather than of perception," wrote Veblen. He shoots first and asks questions later. If something is un-American, it is already condemned. That was the challenge facing those who would take guns off the streets.

II

The National Rifle Association had authority in target shooting and marksmanship. Its leaders were nearly all decorated soldiers. But on the travails of urban life or the vagaries of self-defense, they had little knowledge and even less expertise. When the demand for firearms regulation resumed after the war, it did not receive the hearing it deserved. It was tried and tested on the anvil of Americanism.

An Ohio congressman published a comparison of homicide rates between the United States and several other nations during the decade from 1911 to 1921. America's murder rate was nine times higher than England's, thirty-six times higher than Switzerland's, and more than double that of the second-most-violent nation, which was Italy. Why were Americans killing one another in such stupefying numbers? Guns. A fistfight in Europe was a murder in the land of the free. Seventy-two percent of all murders were committed with a firearm. It had to end.

The "outstanding fact of our deplorable murder situation," advised a prominent statistician, "is the large proportion of homicides by means of firearms." One writer called the prevalence of firearms "the paramount example of peacetime barbarism." Residents of Chicago fumed over a rash of killings in 1921, prompting a businessman to post a series of advertisements offering $1,000 to anyone who could give "one good reason why the revolver manufacturing industry should be allowed to exist and enjoy the facilities of the mails." The *Chicago Tribune* urged a campaign to rid the state of Illinois of all concealable weapons, and the American Bar Association recommended a countrywide ban on the manufacture and sale of pistols. "As a civilian's weapon," demanded one writer, "it ought to be forever outlawed." Others went further, proposing that even the police should be disarmed. "If nobody had a gun, nobody would need a gun" was the simmering contention.

The confidence of these demands was sustained by a consensus on the weakness of handguns in their chosen field of self-defense. "It has been proved time and again that a pistol in the house is no protection," maintained New York City coroner George P. LeBrun as he defended the Sullivan Act in *The New York Times*. "A man is awakened in the middle of the night, and even though he had a gun, it is probably in a closet or drawer," explained a senior police commissioner. "Even if he had it by his side, the crook has got the drop on him and he has no chance to use it. If he could use it, he probably couldn't shoot straight enough to hit the side of a barn door."

"The pistol is the curse of America," declared William McAdoo, chief city magistrate of New York City. These weapons were designed "to kill or maim human beings," a role in which they were far more effective than in protection. "Time and again," he observed, "bank messengers, loaded with pistols, have been shot down by robbers who had carefully planned the attack." As a defensive weapon, the pistol was "utterly and positively useless"; as a source of domestic tragedies, it was grimly efficient. "I would," he wrote, "as soon place a full-venomed cobra snake in my house as a loaded revolver."

It was easy to call out "the armed bandit," argued an editorial in the *San Antonio Evening News*. But the "so-called 'respectable' citizen who goes armed from cap to toe, ready to draw at the drop of a hat, is scarcely less dangerous. Many lives would be spared were both these elements denied the possession of revolvers."

This, however, did not happen. Surveying the crisis through the polarizing lens of national purity, the National Rifle Association resisted all attempts to ban revolvers and almost had the Sullivan Act abolished by promoting alternative legislation through allies in the New York statehouse. To the problem of crime and the trials of industrial labor it offered one unfailing response: guns. The NRA brought the psychology of war to straining nerves of the cities.

Taking issue with a 1924 newspaper article titled, "Let Philadelphia Be Disarmed," an editorial in *The American Rifleman* compared the menace of the criminal to the native insurgents of the Philippine-American War. The solution to crime in the City of Brotherly Love was not to disarm everyone but to take out the troublemakers, in the style of the U.S. Army. "The successful suppression of Aguinaldo's 'Little Brown Brothers' was possible," advised the writer, "because— to use the words of the old hiking song—we 'civilized 'em with the Krag.'" That is: with a repeating rifle. Another writer referred to "the Apaches of New York City," making a literal connection between the urban criminal and the fabled villains of the frontier.

The NRA's expertise on crime often sounded like white supremacy. An article published in *The American Rifleman* in 1924 ridiculed the theory of "the universal brotherhood of man," which made pacifists so squeamish about violence, and it rejected the concept of "the melting pot" as a surrender of white hegemony. "If there is to be but one race," warns the writer, "it won't be a white race, remember that." It was a law of nature that only the fittest survive, so why prepare a table for your enemy? "I have seen fine dogs that came from crossing breeds," mused the author, "but I never saw a mongrel that perpetuated race or type, because he *has* neither race nor type." Continue as we are, and in "a thousand years from now no American will be able to say with truth, 'I have no negro blood in me.'"

This was not an organ of the Ku Klux Klan: it was the monthly journal of the National Rifle Association.

An article warning about firearms prohibitions brewing in the capital was explicit on the need for white leadership. In such times, it fell to "the white American to make certain that whatever laws may be added to our already complicated code" are worthy of his "respect." In December 1923, the editors bemoaned "the anti-firearm movement which has been disturbing the country for the past few years" under the defiant heading "Truth Is Mighty and Shall Prevail." The subtitle was more revealing: "An Editorial for White Americans."

Another said what others had implied: "The growth of murder in America" is the price we pay for foreign blood. In recent years, "we have had drained in upon us in an unselected stream of immigration a vast number of ignorant and vicious newcomers," seethed the writer. "We have taken in a stream of criminal material from nations where the climate, the racial background or centuries of oppression has provided explosive, passionate or sneaky natures." This was the true source of the killings that humiliated America. It was, the writer maintained, "the foreign killer behind the gun, and not the gun itself that is at the root of our troubles."

The honest patriot, on the other hand, was described in terms usually reserved for the deity: "Our old native stock are law abiding, sane, slow to anger," he ventured, "distinctly the sort that are fit to be trusted with weapons." And they needed them to deal with the "vipers" arriving with every boat from Europe. "Out with them!" concluded the jeremiad. "They soil our hearthstone!"

This was what the reformers were up against. The mastermind behind the Sullivan Act was the coroner George LeBrun, who studied thousands of cases of domestic violence and later founded the League for the Preservation of Human Life. Convinced of the dangers of pistol ownership, and grimly conversant with the consequences, LeBrun was qualified to take a stand. Rather than engage any of these arguments about the insufficiency of handguns in real-world conditions, or the risks they posed in the home, *The American Rifleman* poured out Rooseveltian verities about good men trouncing scoundrels and living happily ever after.

The American Rifleman routinely endorsed extralegal violence. "The vigilante method is short and very much to the point," advised an article of 1928, and it leaves "no work for the jury." Crime, argued one editorial, could be "stamped out by an aroused armed citizenry"—"as in the days of the Old West," when rugged patriots, disgusted with corrupt police officials, organized "their own law-enforcement groups—the Vigilantes." Our "pioneer forefathers," fulminated an editorial of 1934, would find it hard to believe their eyes if they could see what was happening in the state of California, where legislators were proposing to prohibit the possession of all concealable weapons. Such attempts to "emasculate California's free citizenry" could only result in more crime. Proponents of such measures had forgotten how these lands had been so recently civilized—"when the pioneer vigilantes with the aid of the Peacemaker established law and order." "Crime is a disease," declared an article titled "Thug Medicine" in 1926. "It is like certain tree diseases and can only be cured by pruning." And that meant killing. The writer was "of the firm belief that one thug in the morgue is worth ten in prison."

In 1932, the magazine launched the Guns vs. Bandits column, which institutionalized the formula around clean, liturgical encounters between good and evil. Even its more erudite apologists such as Karl Frederick, an Olympic gold medalist who later served as president of the NRA, offered a theology of division that bordered on caricature. Explaining the NRA's hostility to pistol regulation, Frederick began with a grand statement about the human depravity that had existed since the time of Adam—before confining it to what he termed "the predatory classes." The honest Americans represented by the NRA had apparently escaped the curse. To say that anyone who owned a pistol was a "potential murderer," protested Frederick, was a slander on the redoubtable patriots who used guns "in entirely legitimate and desirable ways." And this was the American heritage. It was well known that "the late President Roosevelt often went armed and that he placed a loaded pistol at the side of his bed at night."

Criminals, meanwhile, belonged to another region of existence: the predators. "Here, and here alone," Frederick maintained, "is the pistol put to an improper use. Here, and here alone, is it harmful to society." Every building had pests under the floorboards. Gun control was akin to burning down the house to get rid of "the rats." Frederick offered no evidence for his perfect division, except to draw on racial fear. "Two negro burglars, attempting to force their way into a store" in Washington, D.C., he reported, "were put to flight" when the female proprietor "opened fire on one of them with a .38 caliber revolver." Progressive reformers, who would disarm such a woman, were not much better in Frederick's eyes. They reminded him of "the negro who was elected in reconstruction days to a Southern legislature"—naïve, "childlike," and hopelessly adrift from reality.

When the reformer was no different from the criminal, dialogue was impossible. Firearms advocates like Frederick assumed an aura of realism and responsibility, but their sage and loaded assessments bore little resemblance to the quotidian realities of gun violence. Racial stereotypes are substitutes for considered reflection, and summary violence is preferred to caution and restraint. Rooted in nationalism and xenophobia, the gun creed was the militarization of social policy—a militarism without the training. It gained a hearing thanks to the prestige of the National Rifle Association as a patriotic institution led by high-ranking military officers.

As other states aimed to pass their own versions of New York's Sullivan Act, the NRA promoted alternative legislation that increased penalties for gun crime but quietly eliminated the licensing requirement for buying a handgun. When

Governor Franklin D. Roosevelt discovered in 1932 that such a law had been passed by the New York state legislature, abolishing the Sullivan Act by default, he vetoed the measure on the advice of his police commissioner.

"There are very few people," he believed, "who desire to have revolvers in their homes for theoretical self-protection." The safety of the community could not be sacrificed to such a minority. Besides, he added, "the value of a revolver for this purpose is very problematical." He found it hard to understand "the interest of sportsmen in pistols," and harder to appreciate their refusal to submit to licensing. With glimmers of the fireside manner he would perfect as president, Roosevelt implored gun owners to take an "unselfish" view of the question. There was nothing insulting or degrading in being photographed and fingerprinted, and the willingness to do so assisted the state in its struggle against crime. This was a test of democracy. A government that failed to take every reasonable measure to protect the lives of its citizens, he warned, "is out of step with modern thought."

Roosevelt's convictions were not mellowed by a close shave with an assassin's bullet in February 1933, in an attack that killed the mayor of Chicago. The weapon was a revolver bought in a local pawn shop. As president, Roosevelt was determined to establish a federal system of gun control, to put an end to the patchwork of laws that enabled firearms to flow like water from one state to another.

This time, however, the NRA came out on top, in an episode that foreshadowed the politics of the 1960s. As introduced, the National Firearms Act of 1934 would have required a permit to purchase a pistol or revolver anywhere in the

United States. The proposition induced panic within the gun fraternity. The NRA campaigned furiously against the measure and shifted the conversation from handguns to the tommy guns of the gangsters, which had been terrorizing American cities during the unsuccessful experiment of Prohibition. For the NRA, this was not a crime-preventing measure or an attempt to save lives. It was an assault on the honest American. The National Firearms Act, raged an editorial in *The American Rifleman,* was an attempt "to crucify the interests of ten million or more sportsmen on the cross erected by gang-controlled politicians." The bill would "leave the criminal the only properly armed man in America." By now, the NRA operated a legislative reporting service that alerted members to imminent catastrophes and encouraged them to write to their legislators. And they did.

The NRA belief was that criminals will find guns, whatever laws you pass, and that prohibitions on gun sales only punish the righteous. Since the criminal will always get his gun, open access for the honest citizen is a moral necessity. But as he grilled NRA president General Milton A. Reckord in Congress, Senator Royal S. Copeland of New York posed the million-dollar question: "How are we going to know?" When you speak of arming honest citizens, "how are you going to know who they are? . . . If I can freely ship a gun to you, I can ship one to Dillinger," he said, referring to the notorious gangster and public enemy number one.

No, replied the general. Dillinger would be excluded because he had a conviction for violent crime.

Copeland was incredulous. Did that mean it was safe for everyone without such a conviction to buy a gun? "Under that provision," observed Copeland, "[Al] Capone, who never was convicted of a crime of violence, could ship a gun to Dillinger." Here were men who shuddered at the mention of Dillinger, men who saw themselves as the nation's defenders against crime, blissfully unaware that they were arming every criminal in the land. Copeland could not get the NRA president to see that his sense of detachment from this dark and vicious "underworld" was an artifice and a delusion. And he resented the sinister motives ascribed to his efforts in the firearms press. All they were trying to do was "protect the men and women and children of America, and one of the ways to do it is to make it more difficult to get pistols."

Copeland was mystified by the encounter, but his next move was even stranger. Sensing the organization's grip on his colleagues in the Senate, Copeland met with NRA representatives privately and asked them to help draft an acceptable bill. The result was a law that taxed machine guns out of circulation but failed to touch the weapons responsible for the groaning mass of American homicides: pistols. It was, said one official, like "playing Hamlet with Hamlet left out."

The same drama played out four years later, when the Roosevelt administration pressed for the registration of all firearms. A poll conducted by George Gallup established overwhelming popular support for the measure, 84 percent of respondents answering yes to the question "Do you think all owners of pistols and revolvers should be required to register with the government?" In the New England states, the percentage exceeded 90, and what was most promising to the Department of Justice was that even in those parts of the country "fondly known to generations of . . . Americans as 'the Wild West,'" 82 percent of respondents supported registration. "Show me the man who does not want his gun registered," said Attorney General Homer Cummings, "and I will show you a man who should not have a gun."

But in a prelude of things to come, the project failed. Having initially tried to block the publication of the survey, alleging "unethical behavior" on behalf of Dr. Gallup, the NRA mobilized its members to protest the measure in the strongest terms. The ensuing "barrage of letters and telegrams," writes the historian Patrick Charles, was decisive in persuading members of Congress to drop it.

The NRA had every reason to be proud of its role in the passage of the Federal Firearms Act of 1938: it was another drama in which the guns eluded their persecutors. The law imposed some bureaucratic burdens on dealers, but it did nothing to interfere with individual access to firearms. Roosevelt's dream of a Sullivan Act for the nation was over. It would take another thirty years, and the murder of a president, before the opportunity would arise again.

Chapter 6

GUNS AGAINST AMERICA

One act of real political leadership could break the thrall of the gun in American life.

—Henry Fairlie, "Our Fetish of the Gun,"
The Washington Post, August 7, 1966

In February 1963, Lee Harvey Oswald clipped a coupon from *The American Rifleman* and ordered an Italian carbine from Klein's Sporting Goods in Chicago, adding a handgun and a telescopic sight for good measure. Nine months later, he murdered a president before an astonished world.

As the simplicity of the operation became apparent, grief turned to rage. This was no foreign incursion, no poisoned dart from the KGB: it was an all-American affair. Kennedy was the fourth president in a hundred years to fall to an assassin's bullet. What kind of nation would tolerate it? Where else were public figures exposed to such effortless savagery?

The Kennedy assassination was the first of a wave of gun-related traumas—a crescendo of slaughter that included deadly riots in New York, Los Angeles, and Detroit; the murder of civil rights leaders; and the first of the modern era's mass shootings, at the University of Texas in 1966. Together, these events catalyzed an unprecedented mandate for gun control, as the nation "climbed toward unanimity" on the senseless reign of the gun.

"What is at stake here is America's place among the civilized nations of the world," declared Joseph Clark in the Senate. "Let us throw over this idol and build for ourselves and our children a decent, safe, and sane society." *The Washington Post* ran editorials on gun violence for 77 consecutive days in 1965, doubling its energies with 166 the following year. *The New York Times, The Boston Globe,* and the *Los Angeles Times* were not far behind. "It is past time that we wipe out this stain of violence from our land," said Robert F. Kennedy. It was time "to put away childish things"—before one more life was lost.

But an aroused nation faced a resolute opponent: a National Rifle Association representing less than 1 percent of the population but commanding formidable powers in the places that mattered. Senators in the South and West did not feel that the opinion polls reflected the true sentiments of the nation. They liked their guns, and they did not like to be told what "conscience" and "civilization" demanded of them. When a bill aimed at handguns in the mails was expanded to include rifles, in the wake of President Kennedy's death, the old engines of resistance began to stir.

Thus began a bruising five-year battle between a nation and a gun lobby, one that set the terms by which all future battles would be fought. Would America master the gun—or be mastered by it?

I

The trauma of President Kennedy's assassination and the prospect of federal legislation precipitated a storm of journalistic activity. The firearms press dismissed it as hysteria and "emotionalism," but this was no transient protest. "For over thirty years approximately 85 per cent of all Americans and 65 per cent of gun owners have favored registration," observed a letter to *The New York Times.* "Rather than whimsical or hysterical, support has been long standing and overwhelming, and ignored by a supposed system of representative democracy."

Most Americans abhorred the concept of "preparatory armed carriage," and shuddered at the sight of a firearm in public. In 1959, an opinion poll conducted by George Gallup revealed that 59 percent of Americans would support a total ban on handguns outside the police, and 65 percent believed that a permit should be required before the purchase of any firearm—including shotguns. The American public, reported the *Los Angeles Times,* was willing to support drastic measures to prevent the shootings that kill fourteen thousand Americans a year. And "even hunters" favored these restrictions. The survey found that while 50 percent of American homes contained a firearm, the concentration was in the South and, to a lesser degree, the Midwest. And while it was no surprise to learn that gun ownership was lowest in the Northeast, where only 20 percent of homes contained a gun, readers were stunned to discover that only 24 percent of households in the far West possessed a firearm. Why were Americans prepared to ban handguns? Because few cared for them. Only 16 percent of all American homes contained a pistol or revolver.

"Public Would Outlaw All Pistols Except for Police," reported the *El Paso Times.* "Pistol Ban for All but Cops Backed," announced *The Tampa Tribune.* "Public Favors Outlawing Pistols," reported the *Orlando Sentinel.* "No Guns Without Permit," ran the headline in the *Los Angeles Times.* The Kennedy assassination brought this latent antipathy to the surface.

For over a century, protested a series of editorials in *The Washington Post,* revolvers had been marketed as peacemakers and equalizers: icons of freedom. The truth was more prosaic. The only equality they delivered was the "sterile equality of death." Following news reports of four children shot by a parent, and a birthday party that ended with the fatal shooting of a sixteen-year-old, the editor wondered if "sacrifice" was the more appropriate word: "What paralysis of feeling, what hideous complacency, what failure of will and understanding allow this kind of human sacrifice to be continued without an effort to prevent it!" It was a strange freedom that was unmoved by "the daily record of senseless, needless shootings of human beings."

Gun enthusiasts were fond of that word "freedom," but their obduracy went far beyond "the Nation's basic concepts of individual liberty." Democracy was at stake. "In a civilized society based on law," argued an editorial in *The Atlanta Con-*

stitution, "the very first principle is that citizens disarm themselves and entrust their protection to the state. Until the day comes when this principle reigns in America, the least we can do is to establish firmly that the ownership and the sale of guns is a regulated privilege, not a right." John Locke could not have said it better.

And what of that Second Amendment? Did the Constitution authorize every American to possess the instruments of violence? Not at all, maintained a Harvard professor in *The New York Times.* The right was limited to a state-controlled militia, which was really an army. The only prohibition imposed by the Second Amendment on Congress, argued Senator Thomas J. Dodd, was against interference with the state militia forces. The private use of firearms enjoyed no such immunity. It was a "privilege" not a "right." So had the Supreme Court established on several occasions. It was hard to see how the prohibition of concealable handguns, argued a writer in the Baltimore *Sun,* would "weaken the security of the state."

If we want to talk about a well-regulated militia, argued another journalist, the example of Switzerland was worth pondering. Firearms activists often cited the Swiss—a nation with a high rate of gun ownership and one of the world's lowest crime rates—in support of the belief that guns are not the problem. But the devil was in the detail. "In that country, which maintains a citizen militia system of able-bodied males who keep their guns at home, every gun is registered," noted the journalist, "and the ration of ammunition must be accounted for down to the last bullet. The soldier may not use his gun except with specific permission for military-training exercise." That was the tradition enshrined in the Second Amendment and the one so recklessly violated by the gun lobby. Guns had taken more lives since 1900 than all the wars America had fought in the same period. Was this the price of liberty?

In a series of influential articles later published as a best-selling book, the journalist Carl Bakal bemoaned the military rhetoric that framed gun rights as Americanism and liberty as force. Bakal quoted an article written by Karl Hess, a lifetime member of the NRA and speechwriter for Republican presidential candidate Barry Goldwater: "The question of freedom," wrote Hess, "when stripped to its steel center, is just this: Who has the guns?" "Ours," he continued, "is the sort of freedom which . . . was born in gunfire, preserved in gunfire, and which is, even today, maintained by a ready strength of arms." Hess defined American character as the smoldering intensity of "men who suddenly tire of palaver and reach for the rifle on the wall."

No, thought Bakal. This was not freedom. It was the infusion of martial values and rabid anticommunism into the democratic game. It was a "pseudopatriotism," because it trampled so many American principles in its quest for mastery at home and abroad. Men like Hess and Goldwater made civilian firearms an adjunct to the nuclear arms race, demonizing the skeptic as a traitor to a besieged nation. But it was their philosophy, not the gun control movement, that represented the political heresy: a philosophy of force.

Bakal's most profound contribution was his critique of the master narrative of the gun culture: the myth of the cool and flawless patriot. For decades, the National Rifle Association had resisted firearms controls by pinning gun violence on a despised class of criminals. *Punish the criminal, not the law-abiding citizen* was the phrase that launched a thousand telegrams. *Guns don't kill people; people kill people!* was another. But these dogmas had no basis in fact. Gun owners boasted of mastering criminals. Many were incapable of mastering themselves.

Bakal chronicled a "Day of Death" in America, a melancholy sequence of "angry shootings by average citizens," including a six-year-old girl, killed by her stepfather at her own birthday party. "The names are real. The incidents described did happen. The day was fairly typical of any of the others on which guns now claim, on the average, nearly 50 lives, or about one every half hour." The only thing unusual was the date—November 22, 1963—the day a president of the United States was murdered. Contrary to widespread belief, most murders were committed by persons who were law-abiding citizens until the moment they were not. These included the knight errant who killed a dishwasher in a restaurant in Arlington, Virginia, because he objected to the man's foul language toward the waitresses. These were the people who demanded guns for self-defense, people who thought of themselves as the solution. And they were responsible for the vast majority of American homicides. If "murder were left to only the hardened hoodlum," our murder rate would drop to "a mere fraction" of the current level, noted Bakal. The terms of the debate had to change.

"There is a great deal of crime in the streets," wrote Ralph McGill in Atlanta, but "by no means all of it is in the streets." The very concept of "law and order" seemed to mask an inherent, unacknowledged aggression. An editorial in the Baltimore *Sun* pressed the point. In a complex society, it was impossible to determine who was law-abiding and who was criminal—or whether the concepts had any validity. "One of the disturbing oversimplifications of opponents of gun control legislation and of those who advocate law and order," challenged the writer, "is that society is naturally divided into these separate camps." Realtors practice discrimination. Businessmen fiddle their taxes. In what sense were such people better, more trustworthy than a thirteen-year-old looter? Yet these were among the people itching for guns, clamoring for guns: demanding them as security against a criminal underclass. Wouldn't it be better if none of these people were armed?

The Washington Post agreed, complaining that whenever the paper reported on gun violence, a "bevy of letters" would arrive explaining that "the only real remedy is to be found in harsher punishment of criminals and less concern for the niceties of due process." But who was the criminal? The striking feature of a recent wave of shootings was that "none of them seem[ed] to involve anyone who was ordinarily criminal." One of the killers was a man who objected to some youths loitering around his car. Was he a law-abiding citizen?

Even the policy of licensing, based on character and criminal record, missed the point about human nature, argued a letter to the *Post*. It implied that there was a body of citizens who never succumbed to anger. The truth was that even the "most estimable citizens" lacked the poise and experience to handle a weapon in a crisis. "Few of them have real appreciation of what is likely to happen beyond their pious and righteous intentions." And what is done with a firearm is not easily undone. It was time to rethink the "sacred right" of citizens to own firearms of any kind. "Put simply," wrote one journalist, "private citizens should be disarmed."

If there was disagreement on the solution, there was a robust consensus that the gun-rights community had failed the nation. "Those who cry, 'Law and order,' but oppose gun control," protested Senator Joseph Tydings of Maryland, sponsor of several unsuccessful bills, "are accomplices to the murder of police officers and innocent citizens." Such people had no idea how intimately their values as well as their policies sustained the carnage.

The fact that Kennedy's assassin acquired his murder weapon via an advertisement in *The American Rifleman* captured the absurdity. Here was a body of patriots, providing a clearinghouse for the world's unwanted guns—including a "Submachine Gun for Father's Day," almost certainly of Soviet provenance. Even more than the guns, however, it was the values: the relentless advocacy of violence as a way of life and a way out of trouble. "We cannot wash our hands of Oswald so easily," contended an editorial in *The Nation* in response to a speech describing him as "a stranger to the American heritage." The same was true of another ex-Marine, Charles Whitman, who killed fourteen and wounded forty-five from the observation deck at the University of Texas in 1966. Whitman, observed a profile in *The New York Times,* had been "the typical American boy," who went to church, sold newspapers—and grew up with guns. Where was the real madness, wondered a writer in *The Washington Post:* in the mind that perpetrated the massacre or the society that made "a private arsenal so accessible to its citizens"?

Finally: the National Rifle Association—the gladiator that posed as the Socrates of the gun question—came in for a withering critique. Why, wondered *The Washington Post,* should men expert in war hold authority in domestic politics? What did they know that the doctors, police commissioners, and criminologists did not? A column in *The American Rifleman* on how to train women to shoot criminals was the final straw. The blithe admission that "there are psychological quirks to overcome" in preparing civilians for self-defense, and that most women are reluctant to take a human life even to save their own, sent *The Washington Post* into orbit. Here was the poverty of the gun creed in a sentence. When reluctance to kill is a "quirk" to be overcome, a scruple to be navigated, a nation is in trouble. "There is a savagery behind this twaddle that makes it worse than irresponsible," thundered the editor. There was nothing but madness in the goal of equipping Americans to kill other Americans. "The time is long overdue for an end to this nonsense and for the beginning of a program of disarmament at home."

The case for federal reform was clear: local laws were effective as far as they went, but if guns could be purchased through the mail or in a neighboring city, the strongest measures were reduced to an inconvenience. It was like trying to heat a building with the windows wide open. Contrary to the claim that criminals find guns, whatever laws are in place, police reports from New York and Massachusetts showed that most weapons recovered from crime scenes had been bought in neighboring states, where gun laws were weaker. Very few had been stolen. A commission on crime in the District of Columbia reported that murders were committed with handguns five times more frequently in Washington than in New York City, where the Sullivan Act strictly regulated their possession. It recommended a "licensing law aimed at severely curtailing the purchase and possession of handguns."

The critical insight was that gun violence had to be understood as an ecology: a web of interconnections and unintended consequences rather than the simple binary encounters imagined by the gun community. Guns bought for self-defense were more likely to be used on family members than on intruders. Guns intended for the home had a habit of slipping their collars. The division between the public and the private sphere was, therefore, something of an artifice. Guns, argued Thomas McDermott, president of the Police Chiefs Association of Southern Pennsylvania, encouraged the violence they were supposed to contain. Not only were Americans sloppy and undisciplined with their firearms, he argued in an editorial later submitted to Congress, but few appreciated the dangers inherent in the possession of lethal force. "The revolver," he suggested, "is, in itself, an urge to kill."

Marvin E. Wolfgang, a professor of criminology who later directed the firearms task force on President Johnson's Violence Commission, was no less emphatic: "I am one of those persons who believe that violence and instruments of violence breed violence," he said. "Legislation which makes more restrictive the manufacturing, sale and distribution, and licensing of firearms is, I think, desirable in almost any form. If pushed to the wall, I would probably support the Japanese ruling that no one except a police officer should be allowed to possess or carry a pistol." What could possibly go wrong?

II

A gun fraternity that had resisted regulation for two generations had a way of turning defense into attack. Just as the gangsters of the 1930s had taken the heat off the revolver and the "ordinary" killer, the assassinations and riots of the 1960s deepened the binary categories on which the gun culture thrived. Challenged by reports of a death toll inching toward twenty thousand in 1966, NRA chief Franklin Orth responded that many of these shootings were "justifiable" and should not be held against guns. From the thirties all the way through the sixties, the NRA advised members to regard opinion polls as propaganda, bought and paid for by antigun elites. A basic flaw in the Gallup report of 1959, advised *The American Rifleman,* was that 51 percent of respondents were women. If people were better informed about the positive side of firearms, and the fact that violent crimes are also committed with "belt buckles" and "broken soda bottles," they would not rush to such judgments. "We, as a people," cautioned the NRA's executive director, Louis Lucas, "must not be deceived by public opinion polls and other propaganda aimed at destroying our basic right to keep and bear arms."

Within days of John F. Kennedy's assassination, the NRA was portraying the demand for gun control as a witch hunt. If the assassination was a tragedy for the nation, it was a "calamity" for "those who treasure the right to keep and bear arms," reasoned an editorial in *The American Rifleman*. It was vital that Congress was not swayed by "this highly emotionalized reaction," insisted the editors. "The President's death demands that a scapegoat be found," complained another journal, and the "victim for revenge apparently is the honest, law-abiding citizen."

The consistent reading of the moment was that something bad had happened in Texas, but any incursion into the domain of gun rights would be worse. "The unfortunate incident at Dallas on November 22, 1963," reported the New York State Rifle and Pistol Association, an NRA affiliate, had "created new problems" for gun owners. But the storm had passed, and 1964 had left members in "good cheer." Every harmful antigun bill introduced in the state had been defeated. Challenged, in a CBS interview, on record levels of gun violence, NRA president Bartlett Rummel shrugged his shoulders. He didn't think everybody's rights should be taken away "just because a few people misuse things."

Unfortunate. Misuse. In the garden of innocence, violence is dissolved in euphemism. Attempts to prevent it are the real acts of aggression. Not once in all the pages of *The American Rifleman* do we find an acknowledgment that gun control is inspired by a concern to save lives. It is the gun that matters, the gun owner who is under attack. "Mr. Kennedy was not killed by a gun," declared the military historian Robert A. Murray, in testimony submitted to Congress. "He was killed by a man, a man who only happened to use a gun rather than any one of the many other instruments that might have served his criminal purpose." Murray didn't say what those other instruments were.

The language says everything about gun rights and why the reform project was destined to struggle. Men used to fight duels because their "honor" was more precious than life. By the 1960s, honor had been buried in an object, a symbol, an icon. The gun zealot is not offended by gun control: he is wounded. When *The American Rifleman* tells him that sinister elites in Washington are preparing to confiscate his weapons, the forces are visceral. The combined circulation of newspapers advocating gun regulation was forty-two million, according to a Senate subcommittee. The readership of journals editorializing against it was three million. But this was a determined minority, armed with a weapon that never ran out of ammunition—fear.

If the assassinations strengthened the hand of the reformers in the court of public opinion, the riots worked the other way. In the Great Migration of the mid-twentieth century, more than five million African Americans had fled the stifling conditions of the South to seek freedom and economic opportunity in Northern, Midwestern, and Western states. Some found success; most walked into an icier version of Jim Crow—distrust, denial, exclusion. The riots, prompted in many cases by police brutality, were like the crashing pendulum of history: a century forced into a day. But it was difficult to take the long view, to feel the pain beneath the mayhem. Sometimes it was easier to buy a gun.

An article in *Guns & Ammo* magazine appeared to welcome the deadly riots of 1965 as a gift to the cause. "In the final analysis," ruminated the editor, "rampaging hoodlumism such as experienced in Los Angeles, Chicago, and other major cities may yet be a blessing in disguise which will do a great deal to preserve our precious right to keep and bear arms." The image of a Black rioter, set against the smoke and shattered glass of a burning city, was the gift that kept on giving. It was the vindication of a worldview.

One dealer offered a .45-caliber semiautomatic rifle as a "Long Hot Summer Special," in clear allusion to the riots. A gun dealer in Fern Park, Florida, offered a "Nigger Getter" promotion on a 12-gauge shotgun: "Shoot a nigger with it, bring it back and we'll give you your money back," ran the blurb. The NRA's demand for armed citizens to serve as community stabilizers after the Detroit riots of 1967 felt like an appeal for white posses, argued Ben A. Franklin in *The New York Times*. Joseph Tydings had no doubt that the phrase "law and order" was a tribal summons: "code words for race." Placards waved at a Ku Klux Klan rally in Montgomery, Alabama, bellowed the mantras of the gun movement: "Register Communists Not Firearms." A cartoon in *The Washington Post* showed a hooded Klansman clutching an assault rifle next to a quotation from Mississippi governor Paul Johnson: "I wish to assure all Americans that Mississippi will continue to be the most law-abiding state in the nation." This was the rock that met the storm of protest.

In California, Governor Ronald Reagan branded racial strife in Detroit as an assault of "the mad dogs against the people," a brutal but hardly exceptional turn of phrase. Newspapers reported that white communities were stockpiling weapons in anticipation of more trouble. One dealer admitted to selling guns to citizens who had never handled a weapon, including a woman who bought a shotgun without knowing which end of the barrel to load the shells. A Senate subcommittee found that of more than four thousand guns sold in a single day, only thirty-seven were bought by Blacks. "I'll be frank," said Fred O'Rourke, owner of the Sportsman Gun Shop in suburban Bethesda, Maryland: "Many of our customers have been white Montgomery county residents who know little about guns and want protection."

Reporting on the domestic arms race for *Esquire* magazine, Garry Wills confessed his embarrassment that it took him so long to perceive the racial subtext of this "Second Civil War." "We are," he lamented, "two nations, white and black, strong and weak; and the stronger side wants to keep things that way." The Black man lay at the periphery of white sympathy and the center of white fear. It was hard for some Americans to think of him as a person. When the white man thinks of "*my* country," observed Wills, "the Negro is clearly not part of that country." Racism was the bullet. Patriotism was the grease in the barrel.

Just as a portion of Americans believed in the integration of schools while objecting to the busing policies aiming to bring it about, one could believe in gun control without surrendering their gun. "It is in the realm of behavior," observed a report on *Trends in White Attitudes Toward Negroes,* "that we find . . . the limits of white tolerance." It was an awesome understatement. For all the pieties of the polls and the liberal press, Americans were arming themselves with nervous alacrity. In 1964, nearly 2,500,000 weapons were sold. In 1965, over 3,000,000. In 1966, nearly 4,000,000. In 1967—the year Robert Kennedy asked Americans to put away childish things—Americans bought 4,585,000 firearms. And membership of the National Rifle Association grew and grew, from roughly 600,000 in 1964 to just short of 1 million in 1968.

When Bobby Seale led a group of armed Black Panthers into the California State Assembly in May 1967, nobody gained more than the NRA. "The real issue over gun control," asserted a pamphlet cited in a government report titled *Firearms & Violence in American Life,* was not the Second Amendment to the Constitution. It was "whether or not White Americans will be able to defend themselves against an uncontrollable, well-armed Black army as soon as the summer riots turn into all-out race war." This was to state what others thought. "The fact that this domestic arms race is partially integrated," wrote the journalist Ben A. Franklin in *The New York Times,* "that many equally frightened Negroes are known to have guns and that more have been urged to get them by such black ultras as Stokely Carmichael— does not seem to have enhanced the chances of regulation aimed at civil disarmament. In fact, it may have finished it."

The gun debate was not about guns. It was not even a debate. It was about who controls whom in a world turning upside down. While reformers talked about saving lives, the NRA talked about saving America. And that was the more persuasive idiom. The gun debate was an example of what the conservative writer Peter Viereck called "metapolitics": a war of principle to which facts are supremely irrelevant. The gun control bills introduced in Congress by Senator Thomas Dodd in 1964, and every year thereafter, were innocuous compared to the measures demanded in the newspapers. But in the Manichaean drama, even the right to send a gun through the mail was ground that could not be surrendered. It was well known that Hitler began by confiscating guns. Resisting the reformers assumed the urgency of a war.

III

Armed with such beliefs, the gun fraternity brought an unprecedented ferocity to the corridors of Washington. Disinformation and intimidation, it seemed, were two sides of the same coin. The relationship was explored in a long article in *The New Yorker*, explaining the failure of Congress to move on a cause supported by most Americans. It described the desks of congressmen piled high with letters protesting measures that no bill had actually proposed—threatening violence against anyone who would lay a finger on their guns. Many of them began with the preamble "I have just received a bulletin from the National Rifle Association," followed by accusations of a conspiracy to disarm every American. "What are you catholics and commies trying to do?" began one cheery missive. "Take our guns away, and niggers will break into our houses and rob and rape and kill. . . . You might as well give up this unpatriotic way of life," advised the writer, "as we will outvote you and when you buck up against the NRA, you have something to beat." The letter was signed: "True American."

"I'd rather be a deer in hunting season than a politician who has run afoul of the NRA crowd," said a senator from a Western state, who preferred not to be named. "Most of us are scared to death of them. They range from bus drivers to bank presidents, from Minutemen to four-star generals, and from morons to geniuses, but they have one thing in common: they don't want *any*one to tell them *any*thing about what to do with their guns, and they *mean* it."

Many public servants received death threats. Maryland legislator Leonard S. Blondes received several for proposing safety instructions for buyers and the limitation of sales to persons whom police could determine were of good character. "What really concerns me," he remarked, "is that a person who would make such threatening phone calls is exactly the type that should not be allowed to buy guns."

The success of the machine gun ban of 1934 proved that gun control is effective when the government is serious about it. But with the relentless contention that regulations never work, and that registration is the first stage of confiscation, the firearms periodicals worked their readers into a frenzy. In 1965, Senator Dodd confronted Franklin Orth in Congress over a memorandum sent to NRA members that had misrepresented his bill and encouraged members to protest it on the basis of those inaccuracies. Some of the NRA's claims were outright falsehoods. Orth admitted there were errors but insisted they were innocent. Yet the damage was done. In a similar exchange, Dodd forced Thomas Siatos, editor of *Guns & Ammo* magazine, to concede that an article on one of his bills contained errors in twenty-seven out of twenty-eight paragraphs.

"All I can say is this is what we call editorializing," offered Siatos.

"Some people call it lying," replied the senator.

The Washington Post likened the contribution of *The American Rifleman* to the "deliberate yelling of 'Fire!' in a theater"—a stream of falsehoods "directed to an increasingly unstable audience." "The NRA's lies," mourned Tydings, "have had a very great effect—so great that I don't know whether we can ever reverse it."

The discussion in Congress proved his point. Robert Sikes, a congressman from Florida who sat on the NRA's board of directors, claimed that "New York State has the toughest gun laws in America and probably the highest crime rate" in the nation. The truth was that his own state had a crime rate 25 percent higher than that of New York, and a homicide rate nearly double. Paul Fannin, a former governor of Arizona who succeeded Barry Goldwater in the Senate, made a long speech on the futility of Sullivan-style gun laws and the burdens they would place upon the "honest, law-abiding citizens" of states such as his own. Dodd replied that New York City, with its "much-maligned Sullivan law," had one of the lowest rates of murder-by-firearm of all American cities, while Phoenix, where regulations were practically nonexistent, was second only to Dallas in that uncoveted category.

Yet the slogans seemed to stiffen in the breeze. Dodd was

accused of communism for advancing policies that would only "keep good people from being able to buy a gun." "Congress might as well try to outlaw the silk stocking used by the Boston strangler," offered one legislator. In one hearing, opponents of a gun control bill introduced Arizona's senior state senator, Carl Hayden—"the rootingest-tootingest sheriff that Arizona ever had"—as a specialist on firearms. Hayden's first contribution was to pick up a .38 Colt revolver (placed before the committee as part of an exhibit of confiscated arms) and aim it at senators, asking, "Who shall I shoot?" Strom Thurmond of South Carolina ducked in playful solidarity. A member of the Arizona delegation admitted that he hadn't read the bill that he was disputing—but he would use any of his twenty-five guns on any government official who tried to record its serial number.

While it was disappointing to think that the belligerence could change anyone's mind, noted several journalists, the fear and loathing took its toll. *The Washington Post* reported that a candidate for governor of Maryland had renounced his commitment to registration and licensing after a Baltimore rifle club threatened a television campaign against him. The group contained 750 members. Where, raged the editor, were the leaders prepared to stand up to the bullies?

One man willing to try was Robert F. Kennedy, who contended at a public meeting in August 1967 that the National Rifle Association "must take a share of the responsibility for the deaths of many Americans." By campaigning against every proposal to address the problem, he asserted, the NRA had done a grave disservice to the country. Kennedy could not have anticipated the reaction from one member of the panel. As he appealed for legislation to spare thousands of families the grief that may come from the loss of a husband, a son, or a friend, a voice cut in from the side. Joseph Modugno, a Republican from Queens, asked Kennedy if his brother's assassination "could have been prevented by this type of legislation." Kennedy turned to the moderator and asked if he had to answer the question. No. But the exchange left him shaken.

A few months later, Franklin Orth accused Kennedy of pursuing a "vendetta" against the NRA and orchestrating a smear campaign against a "great American organization," after a speech at the University of Buffalo in which Kennedy called out the NRA for opposing all reasonable firearms controls. In May, Kennedy was heckled as he pressed the subject in a campaign speech in Oregon. When Kennedy said that refusal to regulate guns amounted to complicity with "all the violence and murder," a man in a cowboy hat booed, telling him that criminals would "get them anyway." Others murmured that "Nazi Germany started with the registration of guns." Kennedy looked down, and that was his last word on the subject. Ten days later, he lay dying on the floor of a hotel in Los Angeles as a seventeen-year-old boy cradled his head.

Kennedy's death came weeks after the murder of Martin Luther King, Jr., and less than five years after the assassination of his brother. In two months, America had lost a beloved apostle of nonviolence and one of the only men in Congress willing to confront the intransigence of the gun lobby.

"WRITE YOUR SENATOR," screamed a series of ads commissioned by an Emergency Committee for Gun Control, ". . . WHILE YOU STILL HAVE A SENATOR." Next to the words was the shocking image of Kennedy's body. If a vote were taken now, averred a lobbyist in a private memo, "a majority of Americans probably would prohibit private ownership of guns." Surely Congress would finally act.

IV

One version of the events of 1968 is that the National Rifle Association read the room, sensed the mood, and finally agreed to a federal gun law. The truth is less salutary.

The NRA orchestrated a boycott of companies represented by the agency behind the "Write Your Senator" ads, a policy likened by *The Washington Post* to the darkest instincts of the McCarthy era. Even after the assassination of a man who had spent five years warning of the suffering caused by firearms, *The American Rifleman* editorialized against the hysteria. "Can three assassins kill a civil right?" challenged the editors, as if only three Americans had fallen to gunfire since 1963. "The rights of 200 million law-abiding Americans to own and use firearms legitimately are gravely threatened because of three assassins, all of them possibly Communist tools," protested the editors, claiming the will of the people for the stance of a minority. Were the guns committing the crimes? These assassins "had struck a staggering blow to the American tradition of firearms ownership that has stood since the first settlers landed gun in hand." The staggering blow was not the one that killed King or Kennedy: it was the prospect of gun control.

It is difficult to overstate the indifference with which both the King and Kennedy assassinations registered in the gun fraternity. "Do Americans Really Want New Gun Laws?" was the headline in *The American Rifleman* twelve days after King was murdered. The following month, the magazine published a bullish apologia titled: "Happiness Is a Warm Gun." Although the organization subsequently agreed to support a vote in Congress, the bill that emerged was a shadow of what the nation demanded.

The NRA's influence was one factor. The structure of Congress was another. It was not just that a number of strategically placed senators were either members of the NRA or sympathetic to its project—enabling them to kill most of Dodd's bills in committee. The electoral geography of the Senate gave disproportionate power to sparsely populated Western states, such as Idaho, which joined Southern states in resisting federal controls. It was all check and no balance.

In the South, gun rights were about white hegemony and the mortal dread of racial equality. In the West, the gun was a symbol of independence from Eastern elites. The more eloquently the case for gun control was made, the more firmly it was resisted. For Senator Frank Church, explaining why the people of Idaho could not submit to licensing requirements, the "inconvenience" of applying for a license was really an insult. We should not be forced to pay for your problems, he calmly asserted. "Idaho does not ask to write the gun laws for California or Illinois," he said. "We ask only to be left the master of our own house."

Church's position might have been tenable, were Idaho an independent nation. But this refusal to be bullied by metropolitan elites amounted to a veto over the cities. Gun control, as Franklin D. Roosevelt always said, was the test of whether Americans could think and act as a community. That moment was some way off. When President Lyndon Johnson demanded registration and selective licensing as the patent necessity of the hour, Dodd advised him that it might not be within the "art of the possible." The policies recommended by his Crime Commission, which reported in 1967, and supported by an overwhelming majority of the American people, were politically unfeasible. And so it proved.

"Today the nation cries out to the conscience of the Congress," declared Johnson within twenty-four hours of Robert Kennedy's death. "Criminal violence from the muzzle of a gun has once again brought heartbreak to America." It was time to put an end to "the terrible toll inflicted on our people by firearms." It was time to pass a law governing the full range of lethal weapons. We cannot expect irresponsible people to be prudent in their use of firearms, said Johnson, "but we can expect the Congress to protect us from them." Weapons of destruction could be purchased as easily as baskets of fruit. "So today, I call upon the Congress in the name of sanity, in the name of safety—and in the name of an aroused nation—to give America the gun control law it needs."

Congress refused. The Senate rejected the administration's demand for the registration of all firearms and the rigorous licensing of handguns but agreed to ban the interstate sale of rifles, shotguns, and ammunition—expanding a measure recently applied to the sale of pistols through the mail. Sales of ammunition would be recorded by dealers, but no government agency would have access to the records.

And that was the Gun Control Act of 1968. We could call it an act of symbolism, but first we'd have to apologize to symbols. *The Washington Post* called it "a crimp in the mail order gun business." In a country where guns could be bought almost anywhere, a ban on interstate sales was not likely to achieve much.

Signing the bill into law in October 1968, Johnson did not hide his disappointment. The law "falls short," he said, "because we just could not get the Congress to carry out the requests we made of them. I asked for the national registration of all guns and the licensing of those who carry those guns." But the zealots would not be moved. "The voices that blocked these safeguards were not the voices of an aroused nation," he maintained. "They were the voices of a powerful lobby, a gun lobby, that has prevailed for the moment in an election year." For the moment. That was the hope.

Johnson had been calling for "strict firearms control laws at every level of government" since he inherited the office from a man who had been killed by one. He called it "a measure of a civilized society" and a test of whether the United States is a "Government of law" or a "Government by lobby." But the moment had passed, and everyone knew it.

"A nation that could not devise a system of gun control after its experiences of the 1960s, and at a moment of profound popular revulsion against guns," mourned the historian Richard Hofstadter, "is not likely to get such a system in the calculable future. One must wonder how grave a domestic gun catastrophe would have to be in order to persuade us. How far must things go?"

The answer was: a long way.

Chapter 7

A STATE OF WAR

Is the accuser always holy now? Were they born this
morning as clean as God's fingers?
—Arthur Miller, *The Crucible*

Richard Nixon did not like guns, and he despised the
NRA. "I don't know why any individual should have
a right to have a revolver in his house," he said in a taped
conversation in the Oval Office in 1972. Never mind licensing; why couldn't they go after handguns, period? He knew
the National Rifle Association would be against it, and so
would the gun makers. But "people should not have handguns," he insisted, with the usual flood of expletives. A version of the conversation took place several times during his
presidency, typically ending with an aide reminding him that
gun control was a losing issue for the party. But Nixon persisted. When White House special counsel Charles Colson
told him that the House of Representatives had stalled on a
bill to curb the sale of cheap handguns known as "Saturday
night specials," Nixon was enraged. "Goddamn it!" he said.

"That ought to be passed." Years later, in that special freedom of disgraced retirement, he repeated his conviction: "Guns are an abomination."

Nixon was not alone in loathing guns, or resenting the Republican Party's captivity to them. In April 1971, Nixon's attorney general, John N. Mitchell, appeared on *The David Frost Show*, where he told the British broadcaster that he was "diametrically opposed to anybody having a gun, except law enforcement officers." Two years later, the Department of Justice instructed the Federal District Court of Indiana to reject a challenge to the 1968 Gun Control Act under the Second Amendment, advising that "the Amendment applies only to the organized militia of a State and not to individuals."

For all his cynicism and will to power, Nixon was a traditional Republican who had served as Eisenhower's vice president and enjoyed few of the prophetic certainties that drew his successors into the arms of a gun lobby. Had the Republican Party retained these instincts, the gun rights revolution that began to unfold in the 1980s would not have been possible; names like Columbine and Sandy Hook might never have been seared into our collective memory. But the Republicanism that replaced it was a radical departure from the instincts of the conservative tradition and its reverence for the rule of law. This new conservatism, personified by Barry Goldwater and Ronald Reagan, was really a form of nationalism, fueled and fired by anticommunism. Insatiable and omnivorous, it attacked anything that smacked of compromise with the enemy—even if it happened to be the Constitution. This was a revolution cast as a restoration. At its core was a politics of violence centering on access to deadly weapons. Americanism was once again at war with the American promise.

I

Postwar conservatism had started on an entirely different path. In a brilliant article published in *The Atlantic* in 1940, a twenty-four-year-old Harvard graduate called Peter Viereck issued an appeal for the traditional conservative values of humanism and restraint to combat the "crashing panaceas" of the modern age. The free market was an empty vessel. Military wisdom had evolved into "glorified lynch law." And self-styled libertarians "give us only the negative liberty to starve and be unemployed." It was time, he said, to recover the "non-economic values of the spirit" from the broken vessels of militarism and materialism.

Viereck's conservatism was inspired by his father's sympathy for Hitler, a quiet infatuation that convinced him that it could indeed happen here. The conservatism he envisioned would be obsessive over the rhythms of the law—impervious to those instinctive, unwritten notions of justice so appealing to nationalists everywhere. The true conservative, urged Viereck, "will everywhere answer illegal force with force-in-law," meeting aggression with restraint. For you "weaken the magic of all good laws every time you break a bad one, every time you allow mob lynching of even the guiltiest criminal." It was Lincoln's Lyceum Address, all over again.

For fellow travelers Russell Kirk and Richard Weaver, it was the atomic bomb that delivered the final blow to the myth of progress and the chimeras of liberalism. "We are the barbarians within our own empire," Kirk wrote to a friend when news of Hiroshima reached him in 1945. "We have dealt more death and destruction in the space of ten years than the men of the Middle Ages, with their Devil, were able to accomplish in a thousand." Kirk's conservatism was a plea for moderation and maturity against the "terrible simplifiers" of Left and Right. His models were Edmund Burke, John Adams, and the sacred principle of "liberty under law."

So much for the preamble. It is fair to say that every goal, every aspiration, of this new conservatism was disappointed by the political apocalypse that assumed its name. If Viereck and Kirk were offended by the arrogance of ideology and the hubris of nationalism wherever they found it, men like Barry Goldwater and William F. Buckley, Jr., narrowed the complaint to communists and liberals. Their conservatism was shrill, Manichaean, and uncompromising—the punitive zeal that Arthur Miller exposed to such caustic scrutiny in *The Crucible*. Their zest for guns flowed from these habits of mind.

Men like Buckley and Goldwater, wrote Viereck, failed to appreciate the tragic paradoxes of the human condition. That was why they were always on the attack. Buckley liked to include God in his politics, but his theology was a firing squad. His conservatism was a crusade. Liberty had lost its sense of humor, and with it the virtues of balance. The poet T. S. Eliot had a similar reaction to Buckley's journal, *The National Review*, which came fizzing through his mailbox every week. To Eliot, the whole thing felt like a vehicle of prejudice, where all the issues were decided in advance.

None of it augured well for the emergence of "a sane Conservatism in American life."

Eliot was right. When Buckley chastised Lyndon Johnson for failing to deploy nuclear weapons in Vietnam, describing the United States as "the good guys" and comparing North Vietnam to Hitler's Germany, the conservative renaissance had turned full circle. The messianic vigor that had driven Viereck and Kirk in search of cooler remedies was the working philosophy of the new movement. The unbridled individualism that Kirk called "the road to hell" was an unblinking orthodoxy. The angry thrust of anticommunism had taken conservatives into strange places.

There was nothing, from watershed management to gun control, that could not be outed as a communist plot. When libertarians framed government as "the great oppressor," heaping opprobrium on the ordinary workings of the state, warned Kirk, they were not attacking communism. They were attacking the constitutional tradition itself. True conservatives knew "that the state is natural and necessary for the fulfillment of human nature and the growth of civilization; it cannot be abolished unless humanity is abolished." The true conservative knew that the "primary function of government is restraint," because people are flawed. When that insight is lost, freedom is lost. The new conservative's urgency to be rid of all regulation was closer to the natural liberty that devastated Europe after the French Revolution than the civil liberty enshrined in the Constitution.

This was fair comment, and something that had been clear to observers such as Richard Hofstadter when the movement began to surface in the 1960s. Here was a conservatism that seemed to derogate every ideal of its own tradition: the caution, the skepticism, the belief that Rome is not built in a day. Seeing politics as "a conflict between absolute good and absolute evil," the new conservative preferred fires to deliberation. He tolerated no compromises, understood no defeats. Goldwater was the rough draft, crass and abrasive. Reagan was the friendly face, genial and convincing.

II

Reagan's arrival in the White House, remarked a writer in *The New York Times,* was one of the darkest hours for the cause of gun control in America. With his election as president, "the battle shifted from winning passage of stiffer handgun control legislation to trying to keep the conservative tide in Congress from sweeping away laws already on the books." That is what happened. Reagan's gun policy was an extension of his foreign policy: good and evil, light and darkness, "peace through strength." With Watergate, military defeat in Vietnam, and the Iranian hostage crisis of 1979, the seventies had been a decade of humiliation, a mood in which Reagan's predecessor, Jimmy Carter, seemed to wallow. For Carter, the problem always seemed to be "us." For Reagan, it was "them."

"We know that living in this world means dealing with what philosophers would call the phenomenology of evil or, as theologians would put it, the doctrine of sin," Reagan reflected in a widely quoted speech of March 1983. But "we," he proceeded to argue, are not the sinners. Any reasonable observer would have to agree that America had "kept alight the torch of freedom" in a dark and fallen world. It was, therefore, essential that the United States remained armed and alert against "the aggressive impulses of an evil empire." America's strength was her virtue. As Alexis de Tocqueville had famously warned: "if America ever ceases to be good, America will cease to be great."

Only, Tocqueville never said this. It was not the kind of thing he would say. Tocqueville was as caustic as John Adams on the stupefactions of national pride and the "vainglorious" patriotism that plumed itself on "the corruption of all other nations." Vanity in a nation, he wrote, was like vanity in a person: "it wearies even those who are disposed to respect it." Reagan was deaf to this insight as he divided the world into the chosen and the damned, describing the armed opponents of Daniel Ortega's Sandinista government in Nicaragua as "the moral equal of our Founding Fathers," and refusing to believe reports that they were committing atrocities with American weapons. When the Speaker of the House, Tip O'Neill, confronted the president with photographs of an extrajudicial execution carried out by the Contras, Reagan was unfazed. "I saw that picture," he replied, "and I'm told that after it was taken, the so-called victim got up and walked away." Such was the thinking that poured weapons into Central America, in defiance of international law, and launched a new era of gun rights at home.

In his speech to the National Rifle Association in 1983, Reagan situated the struggle for gun rights within the crunching dialectics of the Cold War. The theme was innocence. The tone, astonishment that anyone could see the world differently. "We're a free people, a democratic people; we believe in God and we love peace." But as George Washington always said: to be prepared for war is "the best means of preserving the peace." We needed the guns, at home and abroad. Reagan felt that he was dignifying gun owners by identifying them with soldiers. What he was actually doing was putting domestic policy, and the delicate terrain of crime and punishment, on a war footing—nonchalantly equating the "career criminals" of America's cities with "the guerrillas . . . destroying El Salvador's economy."

For Reagan, criminals occupied another plane of existence. He had no qualms about praising a civilian outfit called the Sun City Posse, "a group which has had great success roping in the bad guys." We are back on the frontier. And as "we crack down on criminals," Reagan reported, he was working with the NRA leadership to write a bill that "truly protects the rights of law-abiding citizens." In a dark and uncertain world, the least a government could do was allow the honest people to buy guns.

But who were the honest people? Reagan's beaming host, Harlon Carter, executive vice president of the NRA, had recently been exposed as the killer of a Mexican teenager, Ramón Casiano, many years earlier. Carter's murder conviction had been overturned on a procedural technicality, and there was no suggestion that he had acted in self-defense. Carter changed the spelling of his name to cover up the incident, and he initially denied all knowledge of it when *The New York Times* broke the story in 1981, claiming it must have been another person. This was, at the very least, an episode that embarrassed the doctrine of the law-abiding citizen. But Reagan plowed on with his "bill of rights for America's gun owners," against the recommendation of his own Task Force on Violent Crime.

"Only a madman could look at the problem we have in this country," wrote Michael Beard, head of the National Coalition to Ban Handguns, "and then say that what this country needs is to weaken our handgun control laws." Incredible as it sounded, that was what the bill proposed. In 1980, 14,287 Americans were murdered with firearms, 11,520 of which were handguns. A Gallup poll in 1981 showed that six out of ten teenagers favored an outright ban on the weapons. Gripped by the fantasy of patriots mastering villains, the Reagan administration pressed on with a bill to make firearms more accessible, abolishing some of the bureaucratic burdens created by the 1968 Gun Control Act.

Nixon had been careful not to offend the cranks and extremists, but he never doubted that was what they were. Reagan offered them a seat at the table. "You recall, when Moses came down from Mount Sinai, the command was, 'Thou shalt not steal,'" ventured the lobbyist Neal Knox during congressional hearings on a bill proposing to eliminate some of the record-keeping requirements and transportation restrictions imposed by the Gun Control Act. "It did not say, 'Thou shalt not carry a rock with which to steal,'" he earnestly reported. Gun control was an attempt "to control the rocks." Knox would go on to write articles speculating that the assassinations of Martin Luther King, Jr., and Robert F. Kennedy had been orchestrated "for the purposes of disarming the people of the free world." His belligerence was ultimately too much for the NRA. But Knox was one of the architects of the Firearm Owners' Protection Act of 1986. This was the world Reagan embraced.

III

The gun debate, which had always operated at a distance from the ugly realities of killing, had entered a new phase: a culture war in which political partisanship was added to the racial and patriotic compulsions that had long protected firearms from rational scrutiny. Gun rights joined abortion among the untouchables: something so important, it could not be discussed. In the culture war, conflict between the parties assumed the intensity of the struggle with communism. As a symbol of that conflict, a gun was never just a gun. It was a shield and a defense against the malice of time: against the terror of being forgotten in your own country. It was America, compressed into an object. When a president says your gun is your birthright, a right imperiled by treacherous liberals, it is difficult to see gun violence for what it is.

When Patrick Purdy murdered five schoolchildren and injured thirty-two others in Stockton, California, in January 1989, it was the same response: How do we protect the guns? The murder weapon was an AK-47, designed in the Soviet Union and manufactured in China. Many Americans had no idea that such weapons were available to civilians. But defending them was now a patriotic necessity. "What are they going to do," wondered a retired U.S. Army colonel, "shoot down the trees?" John Hanlon, a former FBI agent who lost two colleagues in a similar attack, supported a ban. "There's always going to be a Purdy out there," he said. "It's the guns we can do something about."

Support for a ban on assault rifles was broad, if not over-whelming, running at around 70 percent of all Americans. One of them happened to be First Lady Barbara Bush, whose public appeal for such a measure put her husband, President George H. W. Bush, in an awkward position. Bush had stated his opposition to gun control as a condition of election, but his heart was not in it. This groping orthodoxy, from the son of an establishment Republican, is another indication of how novel these dogmas were. Bush compromised with an executive order to ban imported assault rifles, leaving domestically manufactured models untouched. He continued to oppose the Brady Bill, which would have established a waiting period for the purchase of a handgun, but Bush's standing with the NRA never recovered from this gesture of compromise. In the politics of purity, hesitation was an unforgivable sin.

The Brady Bill, first introduced in Congress in 1987 and named after Reagan's press secretary, James Brady, who was permanently disabled during an assassination attempt on the president in 1981, was a measure supported by 89 percent of Americans, including a solid majority of gun owners. It seemed to ignite a special fury within the NRA, however, and it was not until the presidency of Bill Clinton that a modified version of it was passed, followed by the long-awaited ban on semiautomatic rifles the following year. Both of these measures, however, were throttled by "sunset clauses" that limited their powers and ultimately prepared the ground for a Republican counterattack. The Brady Bill's five-day "cooling-off" period would be replaced after five years by an instant background check, and the assault weapons ban would expire in ten years. Both laws were weaker than even the modest proposals of the 1980s, and light-years away from the robust demands of the sixties. And it was here, in partisan revolt from Clinton's symbolic victories, that a debate already starved of dialogue entered the abyss.

The cover of the October 1994 issue of *The American Rifleman* depicted a liberal politician grabbing the Statue of Liberty from behind while covering her mouth. The headline: "Stop the Rape of Liberty." Two years later, Congress voted to defund research on gun violence at the Centers for Disease Control, a violation of academic freedom justified as the protection of a constitutional right. A nation was at war with itself.

IV

When the gun debate entered what might have been its endgame, after two schoolchildren slaughtered twelve of their peers and one of their teachers at Columbine High School in 1999, the new normal revealed its brutal terms. The Columbine massacre devastated the community and horrified the nation. But the gun fraternity held firm against another storm of grief.

With the NRA's annual meeting scheduled to take place in Denver only a month after the massacre, the mayor of the city asked the organization to consider relocating. The NRA refused. Charlton Heston, the actor turned NRA president, opened the meeting in a mood of defiance. "Tragedy," he said, "will always be with us." Such events should not become "an axe for opportunists" to cleave the Bill of Rights from the American people. "America must stop this predictable pattern of reaction," he demanded. "When an isolated terrible event occurs, our phones ring demanding that the NRA explain the inexplicable. Why us?" he protested. "Because their story needs a villain."

The NRA was the victim. The liberal media was the aggressor. It was time to fight for the American heritage.

But Heston was making history, not defending it. A slaughter conducted by children was an unprecedented calamity. The weapons had not been stolen. They would not have been accessible had the gun lobby cooperated with attempts to regulate them. It was no complex chain of causes that connected the tragedy to the NRA.

In a culture war, the charges could always be reversed. In a sneering riposte to liberal hysteria, William Buckley even managed a dig at "the Big Guns of the ACLU," as he attempted to relieve actual guns of responsibility in the affair. "Guns are valuable hobgoblins in the scene," he wrote, as he prepared to pounce on the fallacy. "Guns were used, after all, to kill students and a teacher. . . . If only we could just blame it all on guns," he continued, with aching irony. But the guns didn't fire themselves. The real cause was in the heart. "The little monsters of Littleton" would have used bombs if they hadn't found rifles. In this tortured train of thought, the guns that left fifteen people dead, and many more injured, are etherealized as the hobgoblins of the liberal imagination, and the writer's fury is turned on a liberal culture that would tamper with an American tradition. Yet worse was to come.

Explaining why his party would oppose any regulation of firearms, House majority whip Tom DeLay, a devout evangelical Christian, began a speech that was really more of a sermon. The Columbine massacre was not caused by guns but by the moral turpitude of a godless society—a point he attempted to prove by quoting a letter from a concerned citizen. "Yeah, it must have been the guns," began the jeering homily. "It couldn't have been because half our children are being raised in broken homes. . . . It couldn't have been because we place our children in daycare centers where they learn their socialization skills among their peers under the law of the jungle." So it continued—listing television, contraception, the teaching of evolution, and a lack of conversation with adults among the maladies of the age and the probable causes of the tragedy. "It couldn't have been because we teach our children that there are no laws of morality that transcend us, that everything is relative and that actions do not have consequences," perorated DeLay: "Nah, it must have been the guns."

Molly Ivins, a columnist reporting from the gallery, was lost for words. She thought the speech, which included a swipe at President Clinton's infidelities, was one of the worst she had ever heard: a glib and heartless evasion. Ivins described the pain etched on the faces of gun control advocates as one after another speaker chimed in with comments like "Guns are a two-edged sword," meaning they save as well as destroy. Carolyn McCarthy, a congresswoman from Long Island who ran for office after her husband was killed in a mass shooting on a commuter train, was a picture of grief by the close of the session. For Ivins, there was cruelty beneath the banality of the debate. A body of men had concluded, to their own satisfaction, "that guns had nothing to do with the deaths in Littleton." That was the culture war. Under the scrambling gaze of partisanship, your opponent is wrong before she has opened her mouth. Truth is tribal. Reality is negotiable.

"What is the Cold War now about?" wondered the great historian E. P. Thompson in 1982. "It is about itself." A war that had started with a coherent set of causes was now self-sustaining, and self-consuming. The same was true of the culture war that inherited its molten energies: a war that assaulted democracy in the name of an implacable freedom. The terrible irony was that when conservatives defended the private uses of military firepower, they could not have been further from the Constitution if they tried. This was the final stage of the counterrevolution: the shattering of the Second Amendment.

Chapter 8

DEATH BY DICTIONARY

> We keep summoning the founders to testify against what they founded.
>
> —Garry Wills, *A Necessary Evil*

Molly Ivins, who lost her father and an uncle to gunshot wounds, was no casual observer of this American malaise. She had never understood the connection between preventing death and "the death of liberty." Her position was not improved by the hate mail. "I've been writing in favor of gun control for years," she reported, "and people always threaten to shoot me in response." As the letters poured in, questioning her fidelity to the Constitution, Ivins went on the attack: "Let me say that I am indeed a strong supporter of the Second Amendment," she declared in *The Seattle Times*. "I firmly believe we need a well-regulated militia," she insisted. "So let's regulate and regulate well."

The Second Amendment, she argued in *The Washington Post*, was a pill that had to be swallowed whole. To read it, rather than invoke it, was to see that the right to bear arms was tethered to a well-regulated militia and the security of the state. "Fourteen-year-old boys are not part of a well-regulated militia," Ivins insisted. "Permitting unregulated citizens to have guns is destroying the security of this free state." She was intrigued by those who claimed to follow the judicial doctrine of original intent but turned pale at the word "militia." "It says quite clearly that guns are for those who form part of a well-regulated militia, i.e., the armed forces," she noted. "The reasons for keeping them away from everyone else get clearer by the day. . . . 'A well-regulated militia' surely implies both long training and long discipline," she continued, "because a gun is literally the power to kill." Yet this was exactly what the "noisy minority" in the National Rifle Association refused, forcing everyone to live with the carnage. "No sane society would allow this to continue."

So argued another barnstorming columnist, Tom Teepen. If you can appreciate why drugs require a prescription, or why doctors need accreditation, you can understand the concept of a well-regulated militia, he insisted. No one could deny that the Constitution recognized a right to bear arms. But the right was linked to a militia: a locally governed alternative to a professional army. The NRA's position was a perfect inversion of the constitutional principle. America was now burdened with leaders indifferent to the sanctity of life. Events had shown that there was no "magical body count" that could precipitate action, and Congress seemed to be divided between those who subscribed to the fictions of the NRA and those who were merely scared of them. And the nation was bleeding. "On average," raged the journalist, "we're sacrificing 13 kids a day to keep the NRA happy. It's political paganism."

Ivins and Teepen were right about the Second Amendment and their position consistent with two hundred years of settled law. But the gun culture was not going to be appeased by eloquence or history. A movement that had claimed one of the two political parties now had eyes for the Supreme Court. What followed was more of a coup than a battle. It produced one of the strangest and least convincing decisions in the Court's history.

I

On the three occasions that the Supreme Court had addressed the question, it ruled against any private interpretation of the right. *United States v. Cruikshank* (1876) defined the Second Amendment as a limitation on Congress, not the States, who were free to regulate weapons as they saw fit. In *Presser v. Illinois* (1886), the court decimated the contention that laws against private weapons infringed a constitutional right. The right belonged to "the people" in their capacity as servants of the state. To claim such a right, a man would need to be a member of "the regular organized militia of the state," and to exercise it within that body, in conformity with the state's "Military Code." It was preposterous to suggest that an individual could establish his own militia, or claim constitutional protections for activities that clearly threatened the security of the state. It would be like a lynching party claiming the status of a grand jury. Laws against the private use of weapons were indispensable "to the public peace, safety, and good order," and matters that fell "especially under the control of the government." "The Constitution and laws of the United States will be searched in vain," declared the court, for any indication to the contrary.

Finally, in *United States v. Miller* (1939), the Supreme Court upheld the constitutionality of Roosevelt's National Firearms Act in the clearest possible terms. Finding that the "obvious purpose" of the Second Amendment was to assure the continuation of the state militias, according to the division of labor set out in article 1, section 8, clause 15 of the Constitution, the court asserted that the right "must be interpreted and applied with that end in view." The sentiment of the time strongly disfavored professional armies, explained the opinion, preferring to entrust the security of the nation to a militia manned and officered by the people—"civilians primarily, soldiers on occasion." These militias were set in contrast to the professional troops that could not be employed without the consent of Congress, and the states were expected to maintain them. The goal was "the common defense." This was the background to the Second Amendment and the right that it protected—as elucidated by the Tennessee Supreme Court in *Aymette v. State* (1840). Once again, there was a note of exasperation as the court spelled out what should have been obvious. A sawed-off shotgun, transported illegally across state lines, had no relationship to a well-regulated militia and no protection under the Second Amendment. The decision was unanimous.

No federal court, observed the president's Crime Commission in 1967, had ever interpreted the amendment "as a guarantee of an individual's right to keep or carry firearms." "The argument that the Second Amendment prohibits State or Federal regulation of citizen ownership of firearms," added the authors, "has no validity whatsoever." It was going to take some sorcery to turn the ship around.

Even the NRA, for much of its existence, was constrained by the transparency of the history. Addressing the subject in *The American Rifleman* in 1932, Karl Frederick, the NRA's preeminent legal mind, warned that the Second Amendment held no powers against the menace of "Pistol Regulation." The Second Amendment applied only to the federal government, and it had no bearing on laws passed in the states "for the regulation or abolition of pistols." Much as he regretted the clarity of the issue, gun owners had to "recognize the fact that constitutional provisions which set forth the right of citizens to keep and to bear arms will not protect us against vicious and undesirable statutes affecting pistols." Protection lay in educating the public on the benefits of owning a gun: "It is not to be found in the Constitution."

This was no crushing revelation. It was an admission of a consensus, and a warning not to go down the rabbit hole. One man who did was Jack Basil, a young lobbyist commissioned by Merritt Edson, executive director of the NRA, to scan the history for proof of an individual right to bear arms. The year was 1955. Basil went away and started to read, and Edson's plan quickly unraveled. "From all the direct and indirect evidence," Basil wrote in a confidential memorandum, "the Second Amendment appears to apply to a collective, not an individual, right to bear arms. So have the courts, Federal and State, held. Further, the courts have generally upheld various regulatory statutes of the States to be within the proper province of their police power to protect and promote the health, welfare, and morals of their inhabitants." It was what scientists call a negative finding.

Infuriated by the verdict, Edson penned a jittery editorial on "The Right to Bear Arms" in *The American Rifleman,* castigating the follies of " 'expert' opinion," and urging readers to embrace the right at face value: "We prefer to believe that the simple, straightforward language means exactly what it says." Unfazed by the rebuke, Basil decided to study for a master's degree in political science at Georgetown University. His dissertation doubled down on the claim that "the keeping and bearing of arms is a collective and not an individual right." The regulation of private or nonmilitary weapons, therefore, was entirely consistent with the Second Amendment. So much was apparent from "the history of the construction, interpretation and administration of the right to bear arms." Basil continued his work as a lobbyist, but he was honest enough to acknowledge that the Second Amendment was not his friend.

A quantitative analysis of editorials in *The American Rifleman* shows that the Second Amendment ranked bottom on a list of regular topics in 1960, behind such themes as Americanism, gun regulation, and crime. From there, it began to rise, pulling clear in the 1990s as the preeminent concern of the National Rifle Association: the Constitution under attack. A critical factor was the emergence of aggressive new scholarship that claimed to have unearthed the truth of the Second Amendment: an individual right, long buried under the lies of a liberal establishment. The quality of the work was low, and much of it was written by lawyers who had represented either the NRA or other pro-gun organizations. Nobody could have foreseen that its blunders and guesswork would one day surface in a ruling of the Supreme Court.

II

Much of this revolution was achieved with a single weapon: Webster's English Dictionary. By taking each word of the Second Amendment separately and defining it with the help of the dictionary, lawyers such as Stephen Halbrook and Don Kates announced with triumph that the word "bear" means "to carry" or "to wear" and cannot be confined to a military context. In a passage headed " 'To Bear Arms in a Coat': The Legacy of Noah Webster," Halbrook reported that contemporary uses of the words, listed in the dictionary, included the phrase "to bear arms in a coat." This proved that the phrase "bear arms" meant "carrying weapons on the person."

Except it didn't. As Garry Wills responded in an incredulous review, the phrase had nothing do with weapons: it referred to a coat of arms, the art of heraldry. To bear arms in a coat was not to carry a gun in a jacket: it was to display the family colors on a badge or a shield. This was no isolated blunder. Forgetting that the power of "organizing, arming, and disciplining, the militia" was defined in the main body of the Constitution, the lawyers went to work on the phrase "well-regulated militia," concluding, with Webster's help, that the militia meant everybody, and "regulated" meant "skilled" or "trained," which anyone could do at home.

In a 1983 article later cited by the Supreme Court in *Heller,* Don Kates argued that a "detailed exploration of the Founding Fathers' attitudes [toward firearms] . . . powerfully supports an individual right interpretation." The jewel in the crown, and a source he would quote on many occasions, was a letter from Jefferson to Washington in which the former seemed to profess his love of guns. As Kates revealed his treasure: " 'One loves to possess arms,' Thomas Jefferson, the doyen of American intellectuals, wrote to George Washington on June 19, 1796. We may presume that Washington agreed."

Or not. A glance at the letter reveals that Jefferson was not referring to guns but to some documents that he needed to defend a decision he had taken as secretary of state. In the original, the word "one" is not capitalized, and it comes in the middle of a paragraph discussing these papers. Having come under attack from Alexander Hamilton for his refusal to sanction military action against a French vessel called the *Little Sarah,* Jefferson was asking for a copy of the reasons he had submitted to Washington at the time. "While on the subject of papers permit me to ask one from you," the passage begins. The "arms" Jefferson sought were simply arguments. No honest reader could claim that the allusion was to guns. And the fact that the incident was an example of Jefferson's pacific temperament, as he defended his refusal to fight against a hawkish Hamilton, is an irony lost on the author.

In another article, Kates proposed that Montesquieu had been among the first to argue that "when guns are outlawed, only outlaws will have guns," which seems improbable and turns out to be false. In the passage cited, Montesquieu made a very different point. In an Italian republic "where bearing firearms is punished as a capital crime and where it is no more dangerous to make bad use of them than to bear arms," argued the Frenchman, the prestige of the law suffers, because the punishment is out of proportion to the crime. When the crime of carrying a weapon is punished with the same severity as using it to kill, the law reeks of tyranny. Montesquieu does not suggest that republics are wrong to criminalize firearms: his objection is to the severity of the punishment. These are not errors. They are fabrications. The author of *The Spirit of the Laws* was no friend of the armed citizen.

Next we are told that "Locke, Trenchard, [and] Rousseau" extolled "personal arms possession as both the hallmark and the ultimate guarantee of personal liberty," which will be news to anyone who has read them. Kates does not quote an original source, and when the claim is traced through the notes to Trenchard, the larceny is immediately apparent. Trenchard is praising the militia against the specter of a standing army. In the very passage cited in support of an individual right, Trenchard makes the contrary point that this was a public duty and that "Arms were never lodg'd in the hands of any who had not an Interest in preserving the publick Peace."

None of this literature could be described as scholarship in the traditional sense, and much of the material was circular, repetitive, and cluttered with references to the work of like-minded gun advocates. This gave it the appearance of substance without the weight. But by the 1990s, advocates of the individual-rights perspective had christened it the "Standard Model" of Second Amendment interpretation, and Supreme Court justice Clarence Thomas was praising the "growing body of scholarly commentary" that rejected the military interpretation of the right to bear arms. The myth was on the march.

In 1970, Richard Hofstadter, the leading American historian of the day, had scoffed at the suggestion that the Second Amendment protected private gun rights against state or federal regulation. "Plainly it was not meant as such," he wrote. "The right to bear arms was a collective, not an individual, right," confined to service in the militia, and vital in a republic sworn against a military establishment. The notion of an individual right was a flagrant anachronism, "largely confined to the obstinate lobbyists of the National Rifle Association."

In 1991, Warren Burger, a former chief justice nominated by Richard Nixon to the Supreme Court, struck an angrier note as he inveighed against the ambush of a constitutional right. "This," he said in a PBS television interview, "has been the subject of one of the greatest pieces of fraud, I repeat the word fraud, on the American public by special interest groups that I have ever seen in my lifetime." "Now, just look at those words!" he demanded. The right pertained to "a well-regulated militia," and the militia was "the state army." It was not an army of individuals. There was not a whisper of an individual right. "The Second Amendment doesn't guarantee the right to have firearms at all," Burger maintained in subsequent articles and speeches. The concern was "to ensure that the 'state armies'—'the militia'—would be maintained for the defense of the state." If the history felt abstruse, the words spoke for themselves. The very language proved that this was no private right—still less an "unfettered" one. Sixteen years later, the fraud was the law of the land.

III

The election of George W. Bush in 2000 was as portentous for gun rights as Ronald Reagan's in 1980. "If we win, we'll have a Supreme Court that will back us to the hilt," said NRA vice president Kayne Robinson before the election. "If we win, we'll have . . . a president where we work out of their office. Unbelievably friendly relations." He did not exaggerate.

The expiry of the Assault Weapons Ban was followed by legislation to protect gun manufacturers from liability, and whispers of anticipation about a ruling on the Second Amendment. That was the real prize: a Supreme Court decision that could set the claims of the gun owner in the granite of the Constitution. In 2008, Vice President Dick Cheney signed an amicus brief urging the court to overturn a handgun ban in Washington, D.C., on constitutional grounds. In June, the court struck down the measure with a 5–4 majority, finding the true meaning of the Second Amendment in "the right of law-abiding, responsible citizens" to own weapons for self-defense.

Even the words sounded modern. Argued under the banner of "originalism," the *Heller* decision marked a revolution in the jurisprudence of firearms. Justice John Paul Stevens called it "a dramatic upheaval in the law." Others called it "hubris." *Heller* was nothing less than the substitution of the mythology of a gun culture for the truth of the Second Amendment.

The law in question stretched back to 1975, when the district moved to ban residents from owning handguns (with exceptions for law enforcement personnel and guns already registered), and required other firearms in the home to be kept "unloaded, disassembled, or bound by a trigger lock or similar device." The decision reflected the criminological wisdom that gun violence is an ecology, and weapons acquired for self-defense are central to the problem. In 2002, a group of libertarians began vetting plaintiffs for a Second Amendment lawsuit that they would personally finance. The list of candidates was reduced to six, who filed a claim against the District of Columbia in 2003. The claim was dismissed by the district court but upheld by the court of appeals, in a 2–1 decision citing the "individual right" protected by the Second Amendment. Among the appellants, only Dick Heller, who had been denied a handgun permit, had legal standing, so it was on his shoulders that the case climbed through the courts. In her dissent from the majority decision, Circuit Judge Henderson cited the Supreme Court ruling in *United States v. Miller*, which confined the right to bear arms to "the Militia of the States." It was on such grounds that the District of Columbia appealed to the Supreme Court, which debated the issue on March 18, 2008.

It is said that you should never meet your heroes, because the experience will fall short of the expectation. The same could be said of reading the debates of the Supreme Court. When the court met to establish whether the Constitution enshrined a personal right to own a gun, it floundered. Several justices felt that the Second Amendment could not have been inspired by concern for the state militias, because the Constitution had already granted Congress full power to control them—a ludicrous assumption that begged the entire question. To declare the matter moot, because Congress was already in charge, was to suggest that men like Brutus were wasting their time as they exhausted their erudition defending the state militias. Mostly, the judges ignored these debates, assuming a tone of intelligent speculation as they steered the text into the terrain of the law-abiding citizen.

When Walter Dellinger, counsel for the District of Columbia, articulated the military rationale for the Second Amendment, he was peppered with questions about self-defense: "It had nothing to do with the concern of the remote settler to defend himself and his family against hostile Indian tribes and outlaws, wolves and bears and grizzlies and things like that?" wondered Justice Anthony Kennedy. That, Dellinger responded, was "not the discourse" that produced the amendment. When you read the debates, he advised, "the only use of the phrase 'keep and bear arms' is a military phrase." There was nothing about "the use of weapons for personal purposes."

But Kennedy pressed on with questions about the needs "of people living in the wilderness to protect themselves," sticking to his conviction that self-defense "must have been foremost in the framers' minds" when they established the right. "Must" is a strong word for a groundless speculation.

Justice Antonin Scalia, meanwhile, was happy to talk about the militia, as long as everybody could agree that it wasn't an organized body. "The militia that resisted the British was not state managed," he ventured. "Doesn't 'well regulated' mean 'well trained'?" he wondered, before answering his own question. "It doesn't mean—it doesn't mean 'massively regulated.'"

Such were the minds entrusted with the Constitution in 2008. Amicus briefs estimated that one million Americans had been wounded or killed by gunfire over the previous decade. But the court struck down a law designed to curtail some of that violence with a higher truth that turns out to be a tissue of errors.

The majority opinion, authored by Justice Scalia, consists of four fundamental claims.

The first is that the right to keep and bear arms applies to all individuals, unconnected to military service, and centers on self-defense. The right is larger and more expansive than the narrow remit of military service, and it authorizes personal "confrontation."

The second is that the militia was a latent and amorphous, rather than a state-controlled, phenomenon, whose military effectiveness rested on personal skills and a general familiarity with weapons. A well-regulated militia meant simply a body of armed citizens.

The third was that this personal, demilitarized right was a bedrock of English law, predating the American Revolution and codified in the influential commentaries of William Blackstone.

The fourth was that this individualist interpretation of the right to bear arms was adopted by "virtually all" legal authorities in the nineteenth century and is consistent with the Supreme Court's previous rulings on the Second Amendment.

Each of these claims is mistaken. The only silver lining is that the errors are so profound, so poorly substantiated, they make their own case for revision. *Heller* did not restore an ancient liberty: it created one, striking down a public health measure with a false and invented history.

Scalia's first move is to divide the Second Amendment into "prefatory" and "operative" clauses, defining the latter as the meat in the dish. His analysis therefore begins with the second half of the amendment, where he establishes his individual right, before turning to the opening phrase. With this arbitrary division, Scalia takes the discussion away from the historical axis of standing armies and well-regulated militias and into his preferred territory of self-defense. Only after he has established an individual right, detached from all military obligation, does he turn to the opening words in what is by then a victory lap. How does he do it? With a dictionary.

"Before addressing the verbs 'keep' and 'bear,'" he writes, "we interpret their object: 'Arms.'" And he cheerfully reports: "The 18th-century meaning is no different from the meaning today." Samuel Johnson defined arms as "weapons of offence," and "Timothy Cunningham's important 1771 legal dictionary defined 'arms' as 'any thing that a man wears for his defence, or takes into his hands, or useth in wrath to cast at or strike another.'" The term was applied, "then as now," writes Scalia, "to weapons that were not specifically designed for military use and were not employed in a military capacity." Although one founding-era thesaurus limited arms to "instruments of offence *generally* made use of in war," he concedes, even that source stated that all firearms constituted "arms."

So he proceeds with the words "bear" and "keep." This, he insists, is the only way to establish their natural or ordinary sense, as opposed to the "technical meaning" that confines them to the militia. "At the time of the founding, as now, to 'bear' meant to 'carry,'" he asserts. "From our review of founding-era sources," he writes, "we conclude that this natural meaning was also the meaning that 'bear arms' had in the 18th century." To bear arms is to carry a gun. History is easy when you have the right tools.

Scalia then moves to the word "keep," a term Johnson defined as "to retain; not to lose," and Webster defined as "to retain in one's power or possession." These are Scalia's founding-era sources. These are the authorities for the claim that the right to keep and bear arms was personal, not public: a private choice, not a military obligation.

As we burrow into dictionaries, all connection with the text is lost. We are not reading the Second Amendment: we are toying with words. The rhythm and flow of the sentence has been broken, and with it, the meaning. Apart from the infelicity of defining a text without reference to the authors or context, the method fails its own test of studious literalism. Scalia's insistence on addressing the words "keep" and "bear" separately leads him to misquote the text. "Thus," he concludes, "the most natural reading of 'keep Arms' in the Second Amendment is to 'have weapons.'" But the Second Amendment does not contain the words "keep Arms." Scalia heaps scorn on Justice Stevens for insisting that the phrase "to keep and bear Arms" is a "term of art" that must be taken as a whole. Yet he is misquoting the Second Amendment when he reaches his triumphant conclusion. Under the banner of originalism, Scalia is dismantling a fluent and coherent statement, and pouring his own meaning into the scattered parts. The result is a disaster of anachronism as cavalier toward the text as the hurried history of the Standard Model.

A quantitative analysis of the use of the phrase "bear arms" in books and pamphlets from 1690 to 1800 found that 96 percent of the uses were "unambiguously military and collective." The same search on early American newspapers found that 98 percent of sentences containing the phrase were "clearly related to rendering military service or performing militia duty." Whom would you trust?

The *Heller* opinion describes the military interpretation of the right to bear arms as "idiomatic" and one that would turn every man into a soldier, something that Scalia finds ridiculous. "Giving 'bear Arms' its idiomatic meaning," he warns, "would cause the protected right to consist of the right to be a soldier or to wage war—an absurdity that no commentator has ever endorsed." Yet this is *exactly* what bearing arms entailed: war. Why? Because the founders wanted to preclude the establishment of a professional army. Absurd as it may have seemed to the Roberts court in 2008, that is what it meant to bear arms in the eighteenth century, and that is what the Supreme Court correctly adduced in the *Miller* decision of 1939. These bursts of scorn reveal how far the court has traveled from the history. Scalia simply does not engage the republican philosophy behind the text.

This idiomatic meaning, which would tie the bearing of arms to serving in the militia, he advises, "fits poorly with the operative clause's description of the holder of that right as 'the people.'" For the people, he assumes, means everybody, and not everybody could go to war. True. But rather than resolve the tension by recognizing that the militia was indeed limited to able-bodied males of good standing in the community—as clearly and thoroughly documented—he refutes the suggestion with another appeal to the inherent force of words, as he understands them. Taking "people" to mean "person," he confidently infers that the phrase could not refer to military service because it would involve sending ladies into battle. But "the people," as we have seen, did not refer to the individual in the eighteenth century, and certainly not in the context of military service. It was a single from a plural: a body from a mass. And it was clearly distinguished from the "person" described in Madison's original draft of the Second Amendment: the "*person* religiously scrupulous of bearing arms," who would not be "compelled to render military service *in person*."

Sweeping all of this aside, Scalia presents his verdict on the "operative clause" of the Second Amendment: "Putting all of these textual elements together, we find that they guarantee the individual right to possess and carry weapons in case of confrontation."

Possess and carry. Confrontation. We have just reinvented an entire era. No legal authority of the eighteenth century supports the claim. The truth is that prohibitions against carrying weapons were firmly established in common and statutory law, going back to the fourteenth century. It is inconceivable that either Madison or the First Congress would have dissolved them at the stroke of a pen. In his defense of the soldiers responsible for the Boston Massacre of 1770, John Adams appealed to a long-established distinction between the military and personal uses of weapons—and won the case. The men were acquitted of murder because they acted as soldiers and servants of the state. Both English law and early American culture frowned upon the carrying of weapons in public, and Scalia's claim that it was a practice not only tolerated but enshrined in constitutional law reveals a grave misunderstanding of the period. He constantly tells us that phrases "then" meant exactly what they mean "now"— yet he studiously avoids the one phrase that matters: the Second Amendment, read from beginning to end.

Only after he has annihilated the historical meaning of the right to keep and bear arms does he turn to what he considers an ornamental "preface." "We must determine," he writes, "whether the prefatory clause of the Second Amendment comports with our interpretation of the operative clause." Naturally, it does. Because behind this august language of comportment is a palpable aggression to make the text mean exactly what he wants it to.

With the same unblushing certainty, Scalia tells us that the "militia" named in the Second Amendment cannot be identified with "the organized militia," what he terms "congressionally-regulated military forces." Far from it. That is the narrow and idiomatic sense that he has already described as an absurdity. The individual right established in the operative clause is, Scalia declares, "fully consistent with the ordinary definition of the militia as all able-bodied men."

The militia, he insists, was not an army: it was a "pool" of armed men. Regulation did not mean government control, the stern hand of the state. It meant "training." How do we know? Johnson's dictionary defined "regulate" as "to adjust by rule or method." And you don't need officers, musters, or courts-martial to do that.

These are desperate maneuvers. We are still waiting for the originalist to provide some history. The opinion proceeds to argue that the "security of a free state" was established by this motley aggregate of armed citizens. *How* is not explained. What we are told is that "preserving the militia" was not "the only reason Americans valued the ancient right [to own a weapon]; most undoubtedly thought it even more important for self-defense and hunting." "Undoubtedly" is another strong term for an unsupportable claim. The fear that prompted the Second Amendment was the fear of a military establishment. The right that needed protection was the right of the people to maintain a militia. Not once in that raging national symposium around the Constitution in 1787–88 do we find a demand for the private, individual right that is now asserted as the real issue on the table.

Scalia found evidence of an individual gun right in a demand, issued by the minority report of the Pennsylvania constitutional convention, that "the people have a right to bear arms for the defense of themselves and their own state." This is his strongest source from the Revolutionary era. But the context reveals that, even here, the demand is collective, not personal. As a group of historians explained in a strongly worded brief: the concern in Pennsylvania was not "an individual's right to defend his home." This reference to "the defense of themselves and their own state" is one that had particular connotations in a region where "the colonial government's failure to organize effective militia units prior to independence" had been an ongoing grievance. And the fact that the statement refers to the defense of "the United States," with the usual warnings about "standing armies," and the need to keep the military in subordination to the civil power, confirms that the concern in Pennsylvania was not for individual gun rights. Scalia finds it "peculiar" that anyone could infer military service from phrases that do not mention the militia explicitly. But this was an eighteenth-century code, clear and legible at the time. And none of this potentially ambiguous language made its way into the Second Amendment.

Is it a problem that Scalia cannot quote Madison, Jefferson, or Adams on the necessity of guns for self-defense? Does it matter that we don't have a single quotation from the Revolutionary era to substantiate the private right? Not if you appreciate, as the *Heller* opinion now argues, that the battle had been won in the seventeenth century, and the privilege safely embalmed in the English Bill of Rights.

But the history, once again, is not up to code. Few scholars would entertain the idea that English law sanctified a private right to bear arms, and the passages Scalia quotes from Blackstone clearly describe a political or public right of resistance to "tyranny and oppression"—the fifth and final of his "auxiliary" rights. Far from the personal right Scalia suggests, it is a mechanism that comes into play "when the being of the state is endangered, and the public voice proclaims such resistance necessary."

It would hardly govern the meaning of the Second Amendment if Blackstone had in fact equated the natural right of self-defense with a right to own a weapon. But he said nothing of the kind. And this is a basic flaw of the *Heller* opinion: the conflation of *natural* liberty—the liberty Blackstone calls "wild and savage"—with the *civil* liberty that demands the surrender of those terrifying impetuosities as the price of civilization. Scalia does not appreciate the political nature of these rights: their suspension in webs of civic duty and reciprocity. The freedom he is contending for is the freedom Blackstone defined as savagery. The British history he invokes is a history unknown to specialists of the period.

If the British were so zealous for individual gun rights in the seventeenth century, why are historians unaware of them? Why did they not catch on in the mother country? The answer is that Britain, which did most of its slavery and imperialism overseas, did not develop a civilian gun culture on the American model. A society divided by class, not caste, did not possess the visceral certainties that grew in America from slavery. Which is why a gun-friendly court, seeking flesh for its historical fictions, pitched its tent in the cotton fields of Georgia. There was nowhere else to go.

Having turned the people into a person, and the militia into a metaphor, Scalia attempts to square his individual-rights approach with the facts of history and the verdicts of the courts, claiming that "virtually all interpreters of the Second Amendment in the century after its enactment interpreted the amendment as we do." This is categorically false. His embrace of Joseph Henry Lumpkin's infamous *Nunn* decision of 1846 as one that "perfectly captured" the original meaning of the Second Amendment, "in continuity with the English right," does not enhance the claim.

Nunn, as we have seen, was crafted by a notorious white supremacist with the aim of controlling runaway slaves, and it was considered extreme even by the standards of a brutal, slaveholding South. Far from expressing a stable nineteenth-century consensus, as Scalia claims, the *Nunn* decision was not even representative of Georgia, which rejected its sweeping mandate in 1874. But Joseph Lumpkin was clearly a vital source for the Roberts court, which quoted him two years later in the case that struck down a handgun ban in Chicago. Can it be right that the jurisprudence of slavery is guiding the legalities of gun ownership in the twenty-first century?

Having leaned on the *Nunn* decision, and dexterously avoided the body of law that contradicted it, Scalia addresses *Aymette v. State,* a case that had become synonymous with the military interpretation of the right to bear arms, and one that was cited by the Supreme Court in *United States v. Miller* to that effect. "Those who believe that the Second Amendment preserves only a militia-centered right," he writes, "place great reliance on the Tennessee Supreme Court's 1840 decision in *Aymette v. State.*" But the case, he calmly advises, "does not stand for that broad proposition." The opinion "does not mention the word 'militia' at all, except in its quoting of the Second Amendment," he notes.

This is a rotten subterfuge. The singular finding in *Aymette v. State* was that the right to bear arms had "a military sense, and no other"; a right "exercised by the people in a body, for their common defence." So, while it didn't use the actual word "militia," as Scalia eagerly reports, it did apply the adjective many times, establishing the military substance of the right with scorching clarity. Scalia betrays his profession when he seizes on a nuance of grammar to suggest the opposite. But worse is to come.

Scalia argues that some states actually encouraged "individual arms-bearing for public-safety reasons," and this was "the connotation" of the right adopted by the North Carolina Supreme Court in *State v. Huntley* (1843). This, however, was another opinion that defined the right to bear arms in terms of "the defense of the State," and one that condemned the kind of nonmilitary carriage of weapons that Scalia thinks it endorsed. "A gun is an 'unusual weapon,' wherewith to be armed and clad," asserted the judge in *Huntley*. "No man amongst us carries it about with him, as one of his everyday accoutrements," he continued, and he hoped the day would never come when such weapons would be worn "in our peace-loving and law-abiding State" as a matter of course. To cite the case in support of the view that private carriage was encouraged in the nineteenth century suggests that something has been lost in translation. Scalia misspells the name of the case, and both the spelling error and the exact page references match a brief submitted by GeorgiaCarry.org.

Whether or not the amicus brief was the source of the error, it is hard to avoid the conclusion that this was a court playing in a game it was employed to referee. America deserves better.

The final blow is the attempt to square the individualist reading of 2008 with the *Miller* judgment of 1939. The words have to be emptied to be brought into agreement.

. . .

Locke had a phrase for those who would confuse the savage freedom of nature with the cultured liberty of civil society: "patrons of anarchy." With its relish for "confrontation" and studious aversion to the ideas behind a well-regulated militia, the *Heller* decision did not advance the democratic virtues: it attacked them. This was culture war, not justice: the Reagan revolution in robes. The court failed on so many levels, but to neglect the principles behind the amendment, and to play with dictionary entries as a substitute for that work, seems nothing less than scandalous. The fact that Dick Heller, the model citizen handpicked to serve as the Rosa Parks of the movement, has since blamed gun regulations on "communists" within the government does not enhance the credibility of the episode.

The gun culture won, in the highest court in the land. The real casualty is not the Constitution: it is the lives that are sacrificed to the myth.

THE FUTURE OF FREEDOM

> Any man's death diminishes me,
> Because I am involved in mankind.
> —John Donne

In February 1956, William Faulkner gave an interview to a British journalist on events in the South, including the Montgomery bus boycott, then entering its third month under the leadership of Martin Luther King, Jr. Faulkner was an American literary icon: a Nobel laureate, a Pulitzer Prize winner, and a major coup for the British reporter. Faulkner was sympathetic with the civil rights movement, but he didn't think anything should be forced. "The South is armed for revolt," he observed with perfect ambiguity. The gunsmiths sold out after the Supreme Court decision on school integration in May 1954, and Faulkner knew people who'd never fired a gun in their lives who were now stocking up with rifles and ammunition. "Go slow," he told the history makers, because the "the Southern whites are back in the spirit of 1860." The tone began to harden. "If that girl goes back to Tuscaloosa," he said of Autherine Lucy, the student at the center of an admissions standoff at the University of Alabama, "she will die." Then Faulkner got personal. He didn't like segregation, and he knew that one day it would have to end. But if the government was going to force it, he would pick up his own rifle: "I'd fight for Mississippi against the United States even if it meant going out into the street and shooting Negroes. After all, I'm not going out to shoot Mississippians."

That is why America has a gun culture: the curse of second-class citizenship. "The central question," wrote William F. Buckley, Jr., the year after Faulkner's interview, "is whether the White community in the South is entitled to take such measures as are necessary to prevail, politically and culturally, in areas in which it does not predominate numerically." The sobering answer was yes—"because, for the time being, it is the advanced race." Buckley did not say what he meant by advanced, but the candor of the statement says everything about the chemistry of the new conservatism and its affinity for force. To modify Faulkner's most famous aphorism: The past is not dead. It is still killing us.

What the history shows, what history can achieve, is clarity about origins. To confront these origins is to demystify the gun: to bring an icon down to earth. "What has once become ridiculous," wrote Voltaire, "can never more be dangerous." It was an exaggeration, but it made a point: the first stage of resistance is to cut your problem down to size; to see it for what it is; to pull it from the canon of untouchable truths. When the origins of an institution like the monarchy are known, it is hard to bend the knee. There comes a point when a king can hurt you, but no longer hold you in awe. And this is the beginning of the end. As the philosopher Simone Weil argued in a famous essay on violence: when force loses its "prestige," it loses "three quarters of its strength." Revolutions can happen quickly when the glitter fades.

Gun rights are claimed as an American birthright and clothed in the dignity of the Constitution, but this is a false and fabricated history. To believe in the gun, you have to subscribe to a series of fantasies about the American past. You have to believe Theodore Roosevelt when he says that guns civilized the West and that the men who died "generally" deserved their fate. You have to believe Supreme Court justice Clarence Thomas when he writes that firearms brought "possibilities of salvation" to African Americans after the Civil War. You would have to believe that, for two hundred years, every court in the land got the Second Amendment wrong, until Antonin Scalia rode in with his dictionaries in 2008. For me, the question is aesthetic as much as moral or political. When I see a handgun, I do not see freedom. I do not see possibilities of salvation. I see an open wound. I see the hole in the American promise. I see a failure of imagination.

We would, as Charles Dickens wrote nearly two hundred years ago, be fools not to see the connection between firearms and slavery. And having seen it, we cannot see guns in the same way. This is not to say that the militias, which fought and subdued Native Americans, were beacons of light. But there is a difference between violence perpetrated under the auspices of the state and the arbitrary, sustained, privatized terrors unleashed by slavery. The work of the militias was controlled, and it ceased when danger passed. The phrase that leaps out from the Militia Act of 1792 is the clause that refers to duration. The rules of discipline, indeed the right to bear arms itself, applied to the militiamen "during the time of their being under arms." The implication was that military service is finite, contained, and set apart from civilian life. This was the tradition protected by the Second Amendment, and the one that was slowly undone by a jurisprudence of confrontation—"these bastard laws of violence and wrong," as Thomas J. Kernan put it in a speech before the American Bar Association in 1906.

I say "slowly" because it was not until the twenty-first century, as we have seen, that the personal rights demanded by slave owners such as Joseph Lumpkin gained a hearing in a federal court. Offensive as these ideas remained for most Americans, however, the Civil War began to diffuse them, drawing the North into an economy of honor and redemptive violence. Even though it was the U.S. Army, commanded by Lincoln's triumvirate of generals, that actually conquered the West, in the frontier mythology that came to speak for the history, it was rugged individualists like Theodore Roosevelt who did the work. The message would have been less harmful had it remained a literary phenomenon. But when Americanism met the age of immigration and industrial labor—when the frontier came to Chicago—a modern gun culture came into being.

The sensation caused by *The Birth of a Nation,* and the spread of the Ku Klux Klan far beyond its Southern heartland, showed that the values of the Confederacy had traveled. In the nativist imagination of the twenties, the American-born Black man is as prominent as the unwelcome immigrant. Both offend a sense of purity, and it is within this soil of entitlement that the myth of the law-abiding citizen begins to grow. The divine right of kings was reborn as a handgun.

As I have argued, the notion that the founders intended to enshrine a personal right to own a firearm in the Constitution is not only flawed at the level of the law and the history: it reveals a profound ignorance of republican philosophy and its quest to transfer the sword from the individual to the community. This was not a right that could be relieved of its public duties, divorced from service to the state. It is one thing to find NRA-funded lawyers trying to do this in the 1980s, slicing through the history with dictionaries; it is quite another to watch the Supreme Court perform the same maneuver, striking down vital public health measures in the process. I am not advocating originalism. I agree with those who argue that the right dies when the militia dies, and that the Second Amendment is therefore obsolete. But if we are going to justify gun rights under this sacred charter, we have an obligation to study the sources. *Heller* fails that test. It talks over the text in phrases that could have been written by gun lobbyists and, in some cases, almost certainly were.

To say that America has a gun culture, however, is not to say America *is* a gun culture, as I have tried to argue on every page of this book. If one of the powers of history is to relativize the present—to provincialize what seems fixed and permanent—another is retrieval: the recovery of voices that tell another story. In the history of firearms, the other story happens to represent the majority of the American people, over most of their history. The triumph of a gun culture, in politics and law, has been the triumph of a minority. And while the gains have been dramatic, their novelty would suggest vulnerability. Historians have already begun to compare the *Heller* decision to the infamous *Dred Scott* ruling of 1857, as an example of the prostration of justice before a special interest group. To see that is to know that something can be done. It is surely significant that one of the four leading advocates of the individual-rights interpretation of the Second Amendment in the 1980s has since changed his mind, endorsing the military interpretation that is, in truth, the only authentic one.

And history need not wait for the historians. When people tell me that the gun problem will never be solved, I think of a time when the same was said of the "free market" and the winds that turned Oklahoma into a "dust bowl" a hundred years ago. "While they prate of economic laws," charged Franklin D. Roosevelt in his nomination speech of 1932, "men and women are starving. We must lay hold of the fact that economic laws are not made by nature. They are made by human beings." The same is true of gun laws. I want to finish with two challenges: one to those fighting for stronger laws, and one to those who would oppose them.

The first is that we need a more robust narrative than "common sense" and "gun safety"—phrases that risk endorsing what they oppose. We need to reclaim the concept of freedom from the weapons and the values that violate it. We need to recover the larger question explored by the Violence Commission of 1969, when it advised that "no society can remain free, much less deal effectively with its fundamental problems, if its people live in fear of their fellow citizens." This was to define liberty in almost precisely the terms that John Locke and the founders defined it. The Violence Commission identified firearms as a central threat to "our democratic society," recommending federal policies that would drastically reduce their availability. One of its strategies was to expose the ambiguities of self-defense and to challenge Americans to recognize what a "dangerous investment" a loaded gun represents in any hands.

This clarity is lost when the aim is reduced to keeping guns out of "the wrong hands." Not only does the policy fail in the real world of imperfect people, the ideal of responsible ownership risks legitimizing the violence it aspires to arrest. As the historian Joanna Bourke has argued, codes of conduct and good practice have sometimes accelerated atrocities in theaters of war. By creating the notion of the "humanitarian war," these ennobling mandates have sometimes facilitated acts of savagery—because we are saving the world. Anything that distracts from the fact that guns are designed to kill adds to the glow of legitimacy—which is why popular culture is such a potent collaborator. Like William James, in the early twentieth century, Bourke regards our infatuation with weapons as an aesthetic and cultural problem: one that starts with words and begins in the home.

While I am hugely indebted to the rigor and professionalism of the public health literature, I wonder whether the pursuit of a neutralized discourse, which compares the risk of owning a gun with the dangers of smoking or driving, takes us further into undeserved legitimacy. A gun is not a cigarette. It is not a car. We need a more robust conversation about the realities of lethal force. "Here's my commentary," said Jodie Foster in an interview of 2007: "I don't believe that any gun should be in the hand of a thinking, feeling, breathing human being. Americans are by nature filled with rage-slash-fear. And guns are a huge part of our culture. I know I'm crazy because I'm only supposed to say that in Europe. But violence corrupts absolutely." Abigail Adams could not have said it better.

And this is what I would say to my friends in the gun fraternity: if you're a patriot, read the history. This is why the American Revolution succeeded where the French Revolution failed: it understood human nature. It did not unleash the wild and savage freedom of nature, because it knew that men are not angels, and all men would be tyrants if they could. As James Sullivan explained the contrast between the French and the American revolutionaries: "They talked loud of liberty," he wrote of the Europeans, "but liberty in its natural extent, and complexion, has nothing to do with civil society." Natural liberty was as far from the cultured liberty of civil society as "the untouched clay of the earth" from "the finer vessels of China." Everything the founders taught about the right to bear arms fell under this paradigm of civil liberty. Nothing could be more patriotic than gun control. Nothing could be more foreign to the founders' vision of democracy than unregulated force.

And what of that word, "freedom"? Do guns deliver on the promise? Real freedom, wrote the German philosopher Friedrich Nietzsche, must always rest on a peace of mind, which is impossible in an armed society, where "one trusts neither oneself nor one's neighbor." When the power to kill is among our options, it enters our thoughts and begins to possess them. Nobody is less free than the man who sleeps by his sword. To break the sword, and to do it of our "own free will," on the other hand, is to reclaim our humanity. "Rendering oneself unarmed when one has been the best-armed," advised the philosopher, "that is the means to real peace."

After his home was bombed in 1956, a young civil rights activist was advised to hire armed protection for his family and to keep a gun in his car. He went down to the sheriff's office and applied for a license. But he never felt comfortable with the idea, and having talked the matter over with his wife, he decided that arms were no solution. Instead of more guns, they got rid of the one they owned, investing in floodlights and unarmed security. "From that point on," he reported, "I no longer needed a gun nor have I been afraid." "I was much more afraid in Montgomery when I had a gun in my house."

The young activist was, of course, Martin Luther King, Jr., and his decision to renounce firearms changed the course of American history. If a man whose house was bombed can do it, so can we.

Acknowledgments

B ooks are collaborations, and this more than most. There is nothing I have that I did not receive. My first thanks are to my editor, Kevin Doughten, for taking this on and turning it into something more potent than it could have been without his passion, insight, and patience. Next, I would like to thank my agent, Laurie Bernstein, for taking me on and steering me through every stage. Thanks also to the incredible production team at Crown, from the copy editors to the designers. The professionalism and attention to detail have been extraordinary.

I would like to thank Meredith Artley and Rich Galant for publishing the op-ed from which this book grew, and for confirming my belief that the ideas do not belong in the academy. Having said that, I could not have done this without the support of Patrick Allitt and Joe Crespino at Emory University, and the immense resources I have enjoyed as a visiting scholar. For that, I'd like to thank Jan Love, Jonathan Strom, Ted Smith, and Myron McGhee. It's strange to describe a book like this as a pleasure to write, but the hours I have spent in the electronic archives of *The Washington Post* and other newspapers are among the most rewarding of my career. This would not have been possible without the generosity of the Candler School of Theology. Thanks also to Ethan Shagan and Brian DeLay for hosting me at Berkeley and helping me to believe in the project. The list of scholars I would like to thank is too long to name, but I will mention Jill Lepore, Michael Kazin, William Merkel, and Patrick J. Charles for decisive contributions.

The same is true of friends. Special thanks to Jeff Arvin, Sarah Arvin, Tom Ptacek, Matt Molchan, Brent Wyper, Andy Tooley, Christine Carter, Ryan Cooper, Lee Miller, John Merlino, Jonathan Glass, and my (almost) daily visitor, Teddy Hodgins, for getting me over the line. Finally, my family. We have lived this story, these past few years in Atlanta, and I cannot overstate my gratitude to my children Connie, George, and Emma for showing me the difference between the critic and the cynic. The biggest thank you is to my wife, Meara, for retaining her sense of humor throughout this incredible journey.

—DE. Atlanta, June, 2023

Notes

PROLOGUE

xv **"the real war"**: William James, *The Works of William James*, vol. 11: *Essays in Religion and Morality*, ed. Frederick H. Burkhardt, Fredson Bowers, and Ignas K. Skrupskelis (Cambridge, Mass: Harvard University Press, 1982), 165.

xv **no such thing as an "accident"**: "Accidents?" *The Washington Post*, November 16, 1965.

xv **all murders are "political"**: Martin Luther King, Jr., *The Autobiography of Martin Luther King, Jr.*, ed. Clayborne Carson (London: Little, Brown and Company, 1999), 235.

xv **"the one who masters the art of shooting"**: Ibid., 237.

xv **"arms to be purchased at will and fired at whim"**: Ibid.

xv **Violence was a "plague"**: Ibid., 235.

xvi **"aroused nation"**: Lyndon B. Johnson, "Remarks Upon Signing the Gun Control Act of 1968," October 22, 1968, The American Presidency Project, https://www.presidency.ucsb.edu/documents/remarks-upon-signing-the-gun-control-act-1968.

xvi **"the curse of America"**: William McAdoo, "Causes and Mechanisms of Prevalent Crimes," *The Scientific Monthly* 24, no. 5 (1927): 417.

xvi **"we say no to the amateur gunslingers"**: Jan Reid,

"Richards Sets a Politically Fateful Course on Guns," *The Texas Tribune,* October 4, 2012.

xvii **"as a place where gun-toting vigilantes"**: Ibid.

xvii **"spirit guns"**: Pamela Haag, *The Gunning of America: Business and the Making of American Gun Culture* (New York: Basic Books, 2016), 105.

xviii **"A government which cannot preserve the peace"**: Thomas Paine, *The Writings of Thomas Paine,* ed. Moncure Daniel Conway (New York: G. P. Putnam's Sons, 1894), 96.

xviii **"Not everything that is faced"**: James Baldwin, *The Fire Next Time* (New York: Knopf Doubleday Publishing Group, 1992), 78.

CHAPTER 1

3 **"bitter, clinging types"**: Richard Venola, "Uncertain Ground," *Guns & Ammo,* February 1, 2009.

3 **"a person of substance and responsibility"**: Richard Venola, "Have Gun, Will Travel: A Wanderer's Notes on the Trials and Tribulations of Traveling with Long Guns," *Guns & Ammo,* November 1, 2011.

3 **"John Wayne position"**: Richard Venola, "Empowering the Euros," *Guns & Ammo,* October 1, 2009.

4 **"An extremely drunk man"**: Jim Seckler, "Venola's Second Trial Gets Started," *Mohave Valley Daily News,* February 26, 2013.

4 **"He had so many possible options"**: Suzanne Adams-Ockrassa, "Hung Jury, Again: No Verdict in Golden Valley Shooting Death," *The Miner* (Kingman, Ariz.), March 3, 2013.

5 **"That's a little over my head"**: Dave Hawkins, "Ex-Editor Relieved Arizona Murder Charges Dropped," *Las Vegas Review-Journal,* March 22, 2013.

6 **"peaceable and innocent gun owners"**: Wayne LaPierre, "Standing Guard," *American Rifleman,* June 1997.

6 **"It's only in mediocre books"**: Boris Pasternak, *Doctor Zhivago* (New York: Pantheon Books, 1991), 298.

7 **"Any gun in the hands"**: Charlton Heston, interview on *Meet the Press,* May 18, 1997.

7 **"This is nuts"**: John D. Thomas, "Accidents Don't Happen," *Emory Magazine,* Summer 1995.

8 **"altercation homicides"**: Arthur L. Kellermann and Donald T. Reay, "Protection or Peril?" *New England Journal of Medicine* 314, no. 24 (June 12, 1986): 1558, https://doi.org/10.1056/NEJM198606123142406.

8 **"Citizens did not realize then"**: Arthur Kellermann, "Guns for Safety? Dream On, Scalia," *The Washington Post,* June 29, 2008.

8 **"so different from the rest"**: Thomas Gabor, *Confronting Gun Violence in America* (New York: Palgrave Macmillan, 2016), 255.

8 **"a white male"**: James Fox of Northeastern University, quoted in Gabor, *Confronting Gun Violence,* 73.

9 **The bedroom:** Marvin E. Wolfgang, "Who Kills Whom?" *Psychology Today* 3, no. 5 (October 1969): 72.

9 **"teen gang disputes"**: George D. Newton, Jr., and Franklin E. Zimring, *Firearms & Violence in American Life: A Staff Report Submitted to the National Commission on the Causes & Prevention of Violence* (Washington, D.C.: U.S. Government Printing Office, 1969), 42.

9 **"There was a domestic fight"**: Ibid., 43.

9 **A study of fifty-one murderers:** Stuart Palmer, *A Study of Murder* (New York: Thomas Y. Crowell & Co., 1960).

9 **"Society's greatest concern"**: Manfred S. Guttmacher, *The Mind of the Murderer* (New York: Farrar, Straus and Cudahy, 1960), 11.

10 **"There is no crime"**: Ibid.

10 **"Nobody is more dangerous"**: James Baldwin, "The Black Boy Looks at the White Boy Norman Mailer," *Esquire,* May 1961.

11 **"perceive themselves as arbiters of disputes"**: Hans Toch, *Violent Men: An Inquiry into the Psychology of Violence* (Washington, D.C.: American Psychological Association, 2017), 162–64.

12 **"pseudoinnocence"**: Rollo May, *Power and Innocence: A Search for the Sources of Violence* (New York: W. W. Norton & Company, 1998), 51.

12 **"the element of mercy"**: Ibid., 53.

12 **"good and evil are present in all of us"**: Ibid., 115.

12 **"Opponents of legislation"**: "Law-Abiding Killers," *Los Angeles Times,* May 29, 1972.

12 **"law and order"**: Ralph McGill, "Cowboy Hat Does Things for a Guy," *The Miami News,* June 12, 1968.

12 **"crime on the streets"**: Ralph McGill, "Crime Goes Far beyond the 'Street,'" *The Miami News,* February 5, 1968.

13 **"the Samaritans have a low boiling point"**: David Hemenway, *Private Guns, Public Health* (Ann Arbor: University of Michigan Press, 2004), 76.

13 **more prone to road rage:** David Hemenway, Mary Vriniotis, and Matthew Miller, "Is an Armed Society a Polite Society? Guns and Road Rage," *Accident Analysis & Prevention* 38, no. 4 (July 2006): 687–95, https://doi.org/10.1016/j.aap.2005.12.014.

13 **illegal to drive:** "Road Rage Shootings Surge on America's Highways and Byways," *The Trace,* April 10, 2017, https://www.thetrace.org/2017/04/road-rage-shootings-guns/.

13 **"This is a bill to make Texas"**: "Texas Gov. Bush Signs Law on Concealed Guns," *Los Angeles Times,* May 28, 1995,

https://www.latimes.com/archives/la-xpm-1995-05-28
-mn-7034-story.html.

13 **Within a year, 940 concealed weapon carriers:** Robert J. Spitzer, *The Politics of Gun Control* (London: Chatham House, 1998), 60.

13 **"we should have already reached":** James E. Atwood, *America and Its Guns: A Theological Exposé* (Eugene, Ore.: Wipf & Stock Publishers, 2012), 67.

14 **"his victims will not tamely submit":** "Making Crime Unattractive," *The American Rifleman,* June 15, 1924. Quoted in Patrick J. Charles, *Armed in America: A History of Gun Rights from Colonial Militias to Concealed Carry* (New York: Prometheus Books, 2018), 184–85.

14 **"A good Samaritan":** The Armed Citizen, *American Rifleman,* November 25, 2016, https://www.americanrifleman .org/the-armed-citizen/.

15 **"the cream of the crop of our community":** Angela Stroud, *Good Guys with Guns: The Appeal and Consequences of Concealed Carry* (Chapel Hill: University of North Carolina Press, 2015), 88.

15 **"our behavior patterns":** Ibid., 88.

15 **"punish the righteous":** Ibid., 126.

15 **"bad guys don't read signs":** Ibid., 89.

15 **The sheepdogs are "the heroes":** Ibid.

15 **"are such a predator":** Ibid.

15 **"just innately bad":** Ibid.

16 **"I have no problem with that":** Ibid., 112.

16 **"Don't piss off an old guy":** Ibid., 43.

16 **"No, you're not gonna talk":** *3½ Minutes, Ten Bullets,* directed by Marc Silver (2015, Candescent Films, Motto Pictures, Participant).

16 **Dunn was a member of the NRA:** This was asserted by

John M. Phillips, attorney for Lucy McBath, Jordan Davis's mother, in the 2015 documentary *The Armor of Light,* directed by Abigail Disney and Kathleen Hughes. Mr. Phillips confirmed the claim in a private telephone conversation with the author on June 14, 2023.

17 **"chosen nation":** May, *Power and Innocence,* 51.

17 **"deep-seated exclusionary principles":** Caroline Light, *Stand Your Ground: A History of America's Love Affair with Lethal Self-Defense* (Boston: Beacon Press, 2017), 174.

17 **"reserved only for the select few":** Ibid.

17 **"It is remarkable":** Stroud, *Good Guys,* 102.

17 **"gangster guys":** Ibid., 101.

18 **"In none of my interviews":** Ibid., 102.

18 **"a code word for whites":** Scott Melzer, *Gun Crusaders: The NRA's Culture War* (New York: New York University Press, 2009), 158.

18 **"you don't have any problems":** Ibid.

18 **"If three big ol' Black dudes":** Ibid.

18 **"If you don't like the damn":** Ibid., 153.

19 **"answer to a plague of locusts":** Tom Teepen, "Gun Lobby's Call to Arms Is Way off Target," *San Gabriel Valley Tribune,* February 19, 2008.

19 **"the tyranny beneath the stripes":** Sojourner Truth, *Narrative of Sojourner Truth,* ed. Nell Irvin Painter (New York: Penguin Classics, 1998), 209.

CHAPTER 2

20 **"It does my spirit good":** Ronald Reagan, "Remarks at the Annual Members Banquet of the National Rifle Association in Phoenix, Arizona," May 6, 1983, Ronald Reagan Presidential Library and Museum, https://www.reaganlibrary

.gov/archives/speech/remarks-annual-members-banquet
-national-rifle-association-phoenix-arizona.

20 **"You live by Lincoln's words"**: Ibid.

20 **"Your philosophy puts its trust in people"**: Ibid.

20 **"And, by the way"**: Ibid.

20 **"a violent, shoot-em-up society"**: Ibid.

21 **"just a minute"**: Ibid.

21 **"And locking them up"**: Ibid.

21 **"a nasty truth"**: Ibid.

21 **"legitimate gun owners like yourselves"**: Ibid.

21 **"plinking as young boys"**: Ibid.

23 **the term "individualism"**: Alexis de Tocqueville, *Democracy in America and Two Essays on America,* ed. Isaac Kramnick, trans. Gerald Bevan (1835; repr. London: Penguin Classics, 2003), 588.

23 **"egoism" or self-love**: Ibid., 587.

23 **was the "menace"**: Ibid., 601.

23 **"Remember, all men would be tyrants"**: Abigail Adams to John Adams, March 31, 1776, in *Familiar Letters of John Adams and His Wife Abigail Adams, During the Revolution. With a Memoir of Mrs. Adams,* ed. Charles Francis Adams (New York: Hurd and Houghton, 1876), 149.

24 **"equal and alike in power, dignity"**: D. B. Robertson, *The Religious Foundations of Leveller Democracy* (New York: King's Crown Press, 1951), 72.

25 **"no strict observers of equity and justice"**: John Locke, *Two Treatises of Government* (1689; repr. Cambridge: Cambridge University Press, 1988), 350.

25 **"partial to themselves"**: Ibid., 275.

25 **"the hands of the community"**: Ibid., 324.

25 **"comes to be umpire"**: Ibid.

25 **"a liberty for everyone to do"**: Ibid., 284.

25 **"where there is no law"**: Ibid., 306.

25 **"who could be free"**: Ibid.

25 **"In order to have this liberty"**: Charles de Montesquieu, *Montesquieu: The Spirit of the Laws,* ed. Anne M. Cohler, Basia Carolyn Miller, and Harold Samuel Stone (1748; repr. Cambridge, U.K.: Cambridge University Press, 1989), 157, 189.

26 **"to assist the executive power"**: Locke, *Two Treatises of Government,* 353.

26 **"always thinks it has a great Soul"**: John Adams to Thomas Jefferson, February 2, 1816, National Archives, Founders Online, http://founders.archives.gov/documents/Jefferson/03-09-02-0285.

26 **"Power must never be trusted without a Check"**: Ibid.

26 **"fiery and destructive passions of war"**: Alexander Hamilton, James Madison, and John Jay, *The Federalist Papers* (1788; repr. London: Penguin Classics, 1987), 228–29.

27 **"the will of the majority"**: Thomas Jefferson, *Writings,* vol. 1: *Autobiography, A Summary View of the Rights of British America, Notes on the State of Virginia, Public Papers, Addresses, Messages, and Replies, Miscellany* (1774; repr. Norwalk, Conn.: Easton Press, 1993), 491.

27 **"the greatest instances of virtue"**: *Cato's Letters,* vol. 1 (London: 1724), 245–46.

27 **"makes a man the idolater"**: Ibid., 245.

27 **"to erect a firm building"**: *Cato's Letters,* vol. 2 (London: 1724), 237.

27 **"big with the seeds"**: Ibid., 55.

28 **"the badge of lost innocence"**: Thomas Paine, "Common Sense: Addressed to the Inhabitants of America," 1776, in *The Writings of Thomas Paine,* vol. 1: *1774–1779* ed. Moncure Daniel Conway (New York: G. P. Putnam's Sons, 1894), 69.

28 **"For were the impulses of conscience"**: Ibid.

28 **"that so far as we approve"**: Ibid., 99.

28 **"What is government itself"**: Hamilton, Madison, and Jay, *The Federalist Papers,* 319–20.

29 **"hostile bodies, invading us"**: Thomas Jefferson, *A Summary View of the Rights of British America,* (1774), The Avalon Project, Yale Law School, https://avalon.law.yale.edu/18th _century/jeffsumm.asp.

29 **"the number of armed men"**: Ibid.

30 **"Influence is not government"**: George Washington to Henry Lee, Jr., October 31, 1786, National Archives, Founders Online, http://founders.archives.gov/documents/ Washington/04-04-02-0286.

30 **"organizing, arming, and disciplining, the Militia"**: Constitution of the United States, Constitution Annotated: Analysis and Interpretation of the U.S. Constitution, https:// constitution.congress.gov/constitution/.

30 **"The common talk"**: Quoted in Charles Brand, "The Bane of Liberty: Opposition to Standing Armies as the Basis of Antifederalist Thought" (PhD dissertation, University of Central Florida, 2013), 21.

31 **universally embraced by:** Bernard Bailyn, *The Ideological Origins of the American Revolution,* enlarged edition (Cambridge, Mass: Belknap Press, 1992), 62.

32 **"made Footballs of that Parliament"**: John Trenchard, *A Short History of Standing Armies in England* (London, 1698), 2.

32 **"I am afraid we don't live"**: John Trenchard, *An Argument, Shewing That a Standing Army Is Inconsistent with a Free Government and Absolutely Destructive to the Constitution of the English Monarchy* (London, 1697), 17.

32 **"In those days"**: Ibid., 7.

32 **"were never lodg'd in the hands"**: Ibid.

33 **"Seriously, Gentlemen"**: Member of Neither House of

Parliament, *A Word in Time to Both Houses of Parliament; Recommended to the Perusal of Each Member, Before He Either Speaks, Or Votes, for Or Against a Militia-Bill: . . . By a Member of Neither House* (London: R. Griffiths, 1757), 12–13.

33   **"half-disciplined Men":** Ibid.

33   **"the constitutional security which our laws":** William Blackstone, *Commentaries on the Laws of England,* vol. 1 (Oxford, U.K.: Clarendon, 1765), 400.

33   **"a well-regulated and well-disciplined militia":** Preamble to 1757 Militia Act, quoted in Patrick J. Charles, "The Constitutional Significance of a 'Well-Regulated Militia' Asserted and Proven with Commentary on the Future of Second Amendment Jurisprudence," *Northeastern University Law Journal* 3 (November 15, 2011): 34, https://papers.ssrn.com/abstract=1586459.

34   **"a state of *political Society* and *Government*":** George Clymer, chairman, "Petition and Remonstrance of the Committee of the City of Philadelphia, against the Address of the Quakers," October 31, 1775, Northern Illinois University Digital Library https://digital.lib.niu.edu/islandora/object/niu-amarch%3A86030.

34   **"the safety of the people":** Ibid.

34   **"the duty of every man who enjoys":** New York State Constitution (1777), Historical Society of the New York Courts, https://history.nycourts.gov/about_period/nys-constitution/.

34   **"in lieu of their personal service":** Ibid.

34   **"That a well-regulated militia, composed":** Virginia Declaration of Rights (1776), The Founders' Constitution, https://press-pubs.uchicago.edu/founders/documents/v1ch1s3.html.

35   **"The people have a right to keep":** Bill of Rights: Massachusetts Constitution of 1780, part 1, The Founders' Constitution, https://press-pubs.uchicago.edu/founders/documents/bill_of_rightss6.html.

35 **"Each individual of the society"**: Ibid.

35 **"No subject shall be hurt, molested"**: Ibid.

35 **"Every subject has a right"**: Ibid.

35 **"government is instituted for the"**: Ibid.

36 **"There can be no question"**: Steven J. Heyman, "Natural Rights and the Second Amendment," *Chicago-Kent Law Review* 76, issue 1 (October 2000): 262.

36 **"It may be laid down"**: George Washington, "Sentiments on a Peace Establishment," May 2, 1783, The Founders' Constitution, https://press-pubs.uchicago.edu/founders/documents/a1_8_12s6.html.

36 **"the Total strength of the Country"**: Ibid.

36 **the habits of Soldiers**: Ibid.

37 **"timid, and ready to fly"**: George Washington, letter to John Hancock, September 25, 1776, National Archives, Founders Online, National Archives, Founders Online, http://founders.archives.gov/documents/Washington/03-06-02-0305.

37 **"dragged from the tender Scenes"**: Ibid.

37 **deserted their posts**: George Washington, letter to John Stanwix, July 15, 1757, National Archives, Founders Online, http://founders.archives.gov/documents/Washington/02-04-02-0200.

37 **"standing force"**: Washington, "Sentiments on a Peace Establishment."

37 **"the Mistress of the World"**: Hamilton, Madison, and Jay, *The Federalist Papers,* 72.

37 **"It belongs to us"**: Ibid., 133.

37 **"Let Americans disdain to be"**: Ibid.

37 **"Let the thirteen States, bound together"**: Ibid., 133.

38 **"men of little faith"**: Cecelia M. Kenyon, "Men of Little Faith: The Anti-Federalists on the Nature of Representative

Government," *The William and Mary Quarterly* 12, no. 1 (1955): 3–43, https://doi.org/10.2307/1923094.

38 **"It is impossible for one code":** Agrippa, "Federal v. Consolidated Government: Agrippa, no. 4," December 3, 1787, in Herbert J. Storing, ed., *The Complete Anti-Federalist* (Chicago: University of Chicago Press, 2008), 76.

38 **"you may be dragged from your":** Centinel, "To the People of Pennsylvania," November 5, 1787, in Storing, *The Complete Anti-Federalist,* 159.

38 **"made the unwilling instruments of oppression":** Ibid.

39 **"like a Prussian soldier":** "An Old Whig, no. 5," 1787, in Storing, *The Complete Anti-Federalist,* 36.

39 **guilt of "manstealing":** Jonathan Elliot, *The Debates in the Several State Conventions on the Adoption of the Federal Constitution: As Recommended by the General Convention at Philadelphia in 1787. Together with the Journal of the Federal Convention, Luther Martin's Letter, Yates's Minutes,* 2nd ed. (Washington, 1836), 207–8.

39 **"the detestable custom of enslaving":** Ibid., 207.

39 **"Perhaps we may never be called":** Consider Arms, Malichi Maynard, and Samuel Field, "Reasons for Dissent," 1788, in Storing, *The Complete Anti-Federalist,* 263.

39 **"liberate every one of your slaves":** Quoted in Paul Finkelman, "Complete Anti-Federalist," *Cornell Law Review* 70, no. 1 (November 1984): 189.

40 **nurseries of tyranny:** Storing, *The Complete Anti-Federalist,* 62.

40 **"places the sword in the hands":** Federal Farmer XVIII, January 25, 1788, in Storing, *The Complete Anti-Federalist,* 342.

40 **"was designed to save men's lives":** Brutus VII, January 3, 1788, in Storing, *The Complete Anti-Federalist,* 401.

40　**"to restrain private injuries":** Brutus II, November 1, 1787, in Storing, *The Complete Anti-Federalist,* 373.

41　**"in which the force of the whole community":** Ibid.

41　**"be left to the state governments":** Ibid., 401.

41　**"to provide for the protection and defence":** Ibid.

41　**Starting with Massachusetts:** H. Richard Uviller and William G. Merkel, *The Militia and the Right to Arms, or, How the Second Amendment Fell Silent* (Durham, N.C.: Duke University Press, 2003), 91.

41　**retouch his "canvas":** Thomas Jefferson, letter to James Madison, December 20, 1787, National Archives, Founders Online, http://founders.archives.gov/documents/Jefferson/01-12-02-0454.

41　**"First the omission of a bill":** Ibid.

42　**"the general voice":** Ibid.

42　**"It seems pretty generally understood":** Thomas Jefferson, letter to James Madison, July 31, 1788, National Archives, Founders Online, http://founders.archives.gov/documents/Jefferson/01-13-02-0335.

42　**"What, Sir, is the use of the militia?":** *The Complete Bill of Rights: The Drafts, Debates, Sources, and Origins,* ed. Neil H. Cogan (New York: Oxford University Press, 2015), 280.

42　**"freedom from a permanent military":** Thomas Jefferson to Francis Hopkinson, March 13, 1789, in *The Works of Thomas Jefferson,* vol. 5: *Correspondence 1786–1789,* ed. Paul Leicester Ford (New York: G. P. Putnam's Sons, 1905), Online Library of Liberty, https://oll.libertyfund.org/title/jefferson-the-works-vol-5-correspondence-1786-1789.

42　**"the substitution of militia for a standing army":** Thomas Jefferson, letter to Joseph Priestley, June 19, 1802, National Archives, Founders Online, http://founders.archives.gov/documents/Jefferson/01-37-02-0515.

43 **"The right of the people to keep":** *The Complete Bill of Rights,* 263.

43 **"A well regulated militia, being necessary":** Ibid., 274.

44 **"What is the liberty of the press?":** Hamilton, Madison, and Jay, *The Federalist Papers,* 476.

44 **"In democratic republics":** Cato II, October 11, 1787, in Storing, *The Complete Anti-Federalist,* 107.

44 **The militia was the embodiment of the principle:** John Taylor, *An Inquiry into the Principles and Policy of the Government of the United States* (Fredericksburg, Va.: Green and Cady, 1814), 452.

45 **"natural despotism":** Cesare Beccaria, "Of Honour," chap. 9 in *An Essay on Crimes and Punishments* (Albany, N.Y.: W. C. Little & Co., 1872), Online Library of Liberty, https:// oll.libertyfund.org/titles/beccaria-an-essay-on-crimes-and -punishments.

45 **"idea of Government":** Hamilton, Madison, and Jay, *The Federalist Papers,* 148.

CHAPTER 3

46 **"a thousand newspapers":** Alexis de Tocqueville, *Democracy in America and Two Essays on America,* ed. Isaac Kramnick, trans. Gerald Bevan (1835; repr. London: Penguin Classics, 2003), 353.

46 **"No country administers its criminal law":** Ibid., 653.

46 **"have no neighbors and thus":** Ibid., 419.

47 **"tyrannical" gun-toting ruffian:** Ibid., 461.

47 **"man of violent disposition and mediocre":** Ibid., 324.

47 **"the necessary qualities to govern a free nation":** Ibid.

47 **"very commonplace feat of arms":** Ibid.

48 **"All these bullies were slaveholders?":** Theodore Dwight

Weld, *American Slavery As It Is: Testimony of a Thousand Witnesses* (New York: The American Anti-slavery Society, 1839), 185.

47 **"the most powerful apostle democracy has":** Tocqueville, *Democracy in America*, 305.

48 **"that a man shall come into the world not a man":** Jean-Jacques Rousseau, *The Social Contract & Discourses*, ed. and trans. G. D. H. Cole (1762; repr. London: J. M. Dent & Sons, 1923), 228.

48 **"a tendency to destroy":** Luther Martin, "Mr. Martin's Information to the General Assembly of the State of Maryland," December 28, 1787, in Herbert J. Storing, ed., *The Complete Anti-Federalist* (Chicago: University of Chicago Press, 2008), 62.

48 **"portentous of much evil in America":** Consider Arms, Malichi Maynard, and Samuel Field, "Reasons for Dissent," 1788, in Storing, *The Complete Anti-Federalist*, 263.

49 **"polished skin":** Mason Locke Weems, *The Devil in Petticoats; or God's Revenge against Husband Killing* (Edgefield, S.C.: Advertiser Print—Bacon & Adams, 1878).

49 **it paid to hold your tongue:** Philip E. Tetlock, review of *Culture of Honor: The Psychology of Violence in the South*, by Richard Nisbett and Dov Cohen, *Political Psychology* 20, no. 1 (1999): 211.

49 **"They're mighty free with pistols":** Edward E. Baptist, *The Half Has Never Been Told: Slavery and the Making of American Capitalism* (New York: Basic Books, 2016), 221.

50 **Harry was killed:** Sarah Morgan Dawson, *A Confederate Girl's Diary* (Boston: Houghton Mifflin, 1913), 12–15.

50 **"this regrettable affair":** "Duel Between Harry Morgan and James Sparks," *The Times-Picayune* (New Orleans, La.), May 1, 1861.

50 **fifty times that of the Northeast:** Baptist, *The Half Has Never Been Told*, 221.

50 **"the offense of riding or going about armed"**: See the discussion of the Statute of Northampton, and its application in the United States, in *State v. Huntley (1843)*. *North Carolina Reports: Cases Argued and Determined in the Supreme Court of North Carolina* (North Carolina Supreme Court, 1843), 285, Google Books, https://www.google.com/books/edition/North_Carolina_Reports/DtszAQAAMAAJ?hl=en.

51 **"in a state of uncivilized nature"**: William Blackstone, *Commentaries on the Laws of England,* vol. 4 (Oxford, U.K.: Clarendon, 1769), 181.

51 **"too tender of the public peace"**: Ibid., 182.

51 **"For the law sets so high"**: Ibid., 186.

51 **"a solemn purgation"**: Ibid., 187.

51 **"true man" doctrine**: *Erwin v. State,* 29 Ohio St. 186 (1876).

51 **"the American mind"**: *Runyan v. State,* 57 Ind. 80 (1877).

52 **"the passions of men"**: Peter Oxenbridge Thacher, *Two Charges to the Grand Jury of the County of Suffolk for the Commonwealth of Massachusetts, at the Opening of the Municipal Court of the City of Boston, on Monday, December 5th, A.D. 1836, and on Monday, March 13th, A.D. 1837* (Boston: Dutton and Wentworth, 1837), 11, 28.

52 **"the man who has so completely chained"**: "The Practice of Bearing Arms," *Western Christian Advocate,* March 13, 1835.

52 **"No one knows himself"**: Ibid.

52 **"The very possession of firearms"**: Joseph Gales, "Early Indiana Trials," in *Early Indiana Trials and Sketches: Reminiscences,* vol. 1 (Cincinnati: Moore, Wilsatch, Keys & Co., 1858), 464–67.

52 **"should not be tolerated"**: Ibid.

53 **"violence shows itself in *spite* of law"**: Charles Sumner, "Charles Sumner on the Barbarism of Slavery. The Social

Tendencies of the Institution Argued. Bitter Reply of a South Carolina Senator," *The New York Times,* June 5, 1860, https://www.nytimes.com/1860/06/05/archives/from -washington-charles-sumner-on-the-barbarism-of-slavery -the.html.

53 **"Through these he governs his plantation":** Ibid.

53 **"Slavery must breed Barbarians":** Ibid.

53 **"not derived from the Common Law":** Ibid.

53 **"known as villeinage":** Ibid.

54 **"guarded his person against mayhem":** Ibid.

54 **"species of Common Law":** Ibid.

54 **"a person is withered into a thing":** Ibid.

54 **"There must be an unhappy influence":** Thomas Jefferson, *The Works of Thomas Jefferson,* vol. 4: *Notes on Virginia II, Correspondence 1782–1786,* ed. Paul Leicester Ford (New York: G. P. Putnam's Sons, 1905), 298, Online Library of Liberty, https://oll.libertyfund.org/titles/jefferson-the-works -vol-4-notes-on-virginia-ii-correspondence-1782-1786.

54 **"odious peculiarities":** Ibid., 299.

54 **"the blighting and dehumanizing effects of slavery":** Frederick Douglass, *Narrative of the Life of Frederick Douglass, an American Slave: Written by Himself,* critical edition, ed. John R. McKivigan, Peter P. Hinks, and Heather L. Kaufman (1845; repr. New Haven: Yale University Press, 2016), 32.

55 **"fatal poison of irresponsible power":** Ibid.

55 **"lamblike disposition gave way":** Ibid., 35.

55 **"Slavery," he concluded, "proved as injurious to her":** Ibid.

55 **"Uncle Abram":** Solomon Northup, *Twelve Years a Slave* (1859; repr. Bedford, Mass.: Applewood Books, 2008), 261.

55 **"upon the black man simply":** Ibid.

55 **"a pitiless and unrelenting race":** Ibid., 262.

56 **"rather more respected, as I thought"**: Ibid., 204.

56 **"loudly justifying"**: Ibid.

56 **"or he would brand him as a coward"**: Ibid.

56 **"Such occurrences"**: Ibid.

56 **"The existence of Slavery"**: Ibid.

57 **shot at point-blank range:** John Brown, *Slave Life in Georgia: A Narrative of the Life, Sufferings, and Escape of John Brown, a Fugitive Slave, Now in England* (London: British and Foreign Anti-Slavery Society, 1855), 59.

57 **"a negro man in the road"**: Weld, *American Slavery As It Is,* 172.

57 **slave worth $2,000:** Ibid., 100.

57 **"Slaves shall be considered as real estate"**: A Marylander, "The Law of Slavery in the State of Louisiana—1847: Ii. Code of Practice of Louisiana," *National Era,* September 2, 1847.

58 **"Run Away—My man Fountain"**: Weld, *American Slavery As It Is,* 63.

58 **"Twenty five dollars reward"**: Ibid., 78.

58 **"Two hundred and fifty dollars reward"**: Ibid., 79.

58 **"Ranaway a negro boy named Mose"**: Ibid., 78.

58 **Sarah Grimké, who observed:** Sarah Grimké, *An Epistle to the Clergy of the Southern States* (New York: American Anti-Slavery Society, 1836).

59 **"dead or alive!"**: William Lloyd Garrison, "Letter to Louis Kossuth, Concerning Freedom and Slavery in the United States, 1852, in *Slavery & Anti-Slavery Pamphlets from the Libraries of Salmon P. Chase & John P. Hale* (Ann Arbor: University of Michigan, microfilms, 1974, accessed via ProQuest), 97.

59 **"Is it not a system of murder?"**: William Lloyd Garrison,

"Anti-Slavery: Lecture V. Humanity! Refinement! Republicanism!" *The Liberator,* June 21, 1839.

59 **"that the man who has been born and bred":** Charles Dickens, *American Notes for General Circulation,* ed. Patricia Ingham (1842; repr. London: Penguin Classics, 2001), 264.

59 **"will shoot men down and stab them when he quarrels?":** Ibid., 264.

59 **"to close our eyes":** Ibid.

59 **"These are the weapons of Freedom":** Ibid., 265.

59 **"A Day in the House":** Joanne B. Freeman, *The Field of Blood: Violence in Congress and the Road to Civil War* (New York: Farrar, Straus and Giroux, 2018), 244.

60 **"When I saw this":** Quoted ibid., 246.

60 **"a field of blood":** Reverend John Turner Sargent, letter to Charles Sumner, May 25, 1856, in Freeman, *Field of Blood,* 231.

61 **"entirely useless for distant service":** Quoted in Patrick J. Charles, *Armed in America: A History of Gun Rights from Colonial Militias to Concealed Carry* (New York: Prometheus Books, 2018), 129.

61 **"distributive justice":** *American State Papers: Documents, Legislative and Executive, of the Congress of the United States,* vol. 1, from the first session of the first to the second session of the Fifteenth Congress, inclusive: commencing March 3, 1789, and ending March 3, 1819 (Washington, D.C.: Gales and Seaton, 1832), 189.

61 **"a growing indifference to any system":** Joseph Story, *Commentaries on the Constitution of the United States: With a Preliminary Review of the Constitutional History of the Colonies and States, Before the Adoption of the Constitution,* vol. 2 (Boston: Hilliard, Gray and Company, 1833), 708.

61 **"to be rid of all regulations":** Ibid.

61 **"the protection intended by this clause":** Ibid.

61 **"foreign invasions, domestic insurrections"**: Ibid.

61 **By the 1840s, compulsory drills**: Charles, *Armed in America,* 136.

62 **"no limits short of the moral power"**: *Bliss v. Commonwealth,* 12 Ky. 90 (1822).

62 **"abhorred by our ancestors"**: *Journal of the House of Representatives of the Commonwealth of Kentucky* (Frankfort, Ky.: A. G. Hodges, 1837), 74.

62 **"applied only to the distinctive arms"**: Ibid.

62 **"such detestable instruments"**: Ibid.

62 **"the history of our ancestors"**: *Aymette v. State,* 21 Tenn. 152 (1840).

62 **"to be exercised by the people"**: Ibid.

62 **"No private defence was contemplated"**: Ibid.

63 **"to their military use"**: Ibid.

63 **"A man in the pursuit of deer"**: Ibid.

63 **"Here we know that the phrase"**: Ibid.

63 **"to pervert a great political right"**: Ibid.

63 **Alabama followed Tennessee**: *State v. Reid,* 1 Ala. 612 (1840).

64 **"peace and domestic tranquility"**: *State v. Buzzard,* 4 Ark. 18 (1842).

64 **"many if not all of the rights"**: Ibid.

64 **"the right of any individual"**: Ibid.

64 **"back to its natural state"**: Ibid.

64 **"object for which the government"**: Ibid.

64 **"a principle pregnant with such dangers"**: Ibid.

64 **individual force**: Ibid.

64 **"Certainly not"**: Ibid.

65 **"public liberty"**: Ibid.

65 **"that this, and this alone":** Ibid.

65 **"surrender his negroes":** *State v. Huntley,* 25 N.C. 418 (1843).

66 **"bear arms for the defense of the State":** Ibid.

66 **"If he employs those arms":** Ibid.

66 **"he deserves but the severer condemnation":** Ibid.

66 **"unusual weapon":** Ibid.

66 **"terrify and alarm a peaceful people":** Ibid.

66 **"no man amongst us carries it":** Ibid.

66 **"that public order and sense of security":** Ibid.

66 **"of all regulated societies":** Ibid.

66 **In North Carolina, it was considered disreputable:** Baptist, *The Half Has Never Been Told,* 221.

67 **"perfectly captured":** *District of Columbia v. Heller* 554 U.S. 570 (2008).

67 **" 'The right of the people to bear' ":** *Nunn v. State,* 1 Ga. 243 (1846).

68 **"natural right":** Ibid.

68 **"any free persons of color":** Carol Anderson, *The Second: Race and Guns in a Fatally Unequal America* (New York: Bloomsbury, 2021), 71.

69 **"would undermine the slavery system":** Mason W. Stephenson and D. Grier Stephenson, Jr., "To Protect and Defend: Joseph Henry Lumpkin, the Supreme Court of Georgia, and Slavery," *Emory Law Journal* 25, no. 3 (1976): 596.

69 **"When insults are given personally":** *Johnson v. Lovett,* 31 Ga. 187 (1860).

69 **"We can hardly venture to consider":** Ibid.

69 **"The South has lost, already, upwards":** *Moran v. Davis,* 18 Ga. 722 (1855).

69 **"Instead, therefore, of relaxing the means":** Ibid.

69 **"to redouble our vigilance":** Ibid.

69 **"irresistible, that dogs may":** Ibid.

70 **"the African":** *Bryan v. Walton,* 14 Ga. 185 (1853).

70 **"the social and civil degradation":** Ibid.

70 **"The argument is, that a negro":** Ibid.

70 ***"pro nullis, pro mortuis,* and for some":** Ibid.

70 **"He is not allowed to keep":** Ibid.

71 **Lumpkin's sweeping mandate of 1846:** *Hill v. State,* 53 Ga. 472 (1874).

CHAPTER 4

72 **punish the Gulf states:** Wendell Phillips, speech, April 9, 1861, quoted in William Schouler, *A History of Massachusetts in the Civil War,* vol. 1 (Boston: E. P. Dutton, 1868), 46.

72 **"the death of a hundred thousand":** Ibid., 45.

72 **"we know not where it will end":** Ibid., 46.

72 **"Suppose we were to conquer":** Thomas Nichols, quoted in Harry S. Stout, *Upon the Altar of the Nation: A Moral History of the American Civil War* (New York: Viking, 2006), 31–32.

73 **"sentiment mightier than logic":** Quoted in James Elliot Cabot, *A Memoir of Ralph Waldo Emerson,* vol. 2 (Boston: Houghton, Mifflin and Company, 1893), 600.

73 **"second founding":** Eric Foner, *The Second Founding: How the Civil War and Reconstruction Remade the Constitution* (New York: W. W. Norton, 2019).

73 **a reign of terror:** Cornel West, in dialogue with and edited by Christa Buschendorf, *Black Prophetic Fire* (Boston: Beacon Press, 2014), 140.

73 **"peonage, persecution, and lynching":** Fanny Bixby

Spencer, *The Repudiation of War* (Costa Mesa, Calif.: H. F. Schick, 1922), 6.

73 **"bitterness of revenge":** Ibid.

73 **"The Civil War":** Ibid.

74 **"a vigorous and masterful people":** Theodore Roosevelt, quoted in Richard Slotkin, *Gunfighter Nation: Myth of the Frontier in Twentieth-Century America* (Norman: University of Oklahoma Press, 1998), 37.

74 **"There is no special providence for Americans":** John Adams, *A Defence of the Constitutions of Government of the United States of America: Against the Attack of M. Turgot in His Letter to Dr. Price, Dated the Twenty-Second Day of March, 1778* (Philadelphia: Budd and Bartram, 1797), 121.

74 **"all of the same clay":** John Adams, *The Works of John Adams, Second President of the United States: With a Life of the Author, Notes and Illustrations* (Boston: Little, Brown and Company, 1851), 10.

74 **Adams complained to Benjamin Rush:** John Adams, letter to Benjamin Rush, October 22, 1812, National Archives, Founders Online, http://founders.archives.gov/documents/ Adams/99-02-02-5883.

75 **"We may boast that we are":** John Adams to John Taylor, July 29, 1814, National Archives, Founders Online, http:// founders.archives.gov/documents/Adams/99-02-02-6322.

75 **"empire of liberty":** Thomas Jefferson, letter to Benjamin Chambers, December 28, 1805, National Archives, Founders Online, http://founders.archives.gov/documents/Jefferson/ 99-01-02-2910.

75 **"Liberty robed in law":** D. D. Barnard, "The President's Message: The War," *The American Review: A Whig Journal of Politics, Literature, Art, and Science* 5, no. 1 (January 1845): 1–15.

75 **"the restrictions of the Constitution":** Ibid.

76 **"conquering peace"**: Quoted ibid.

76 **"the last refuge of a scoundrel"**: Quoted ibid.

76 **"Let him answer with *facts*"**: Abraham Lincoln, *Abraham Lincoln: Speeches and Writings,* vol. 1 (New York: Library of America, 1989), 68.

76 **"escape scrutiny"**: Ibid.

76 **"the most oppressive of all Kingly oppressions"**: Ibid., 176.

76 **"where kings have always stood"**: Ibid.

77 **"to rival the native Spanish moss"**: Ibid., 30.

77 **"the increasing disregard for law"**: Ibid., 29.

77 **"reverence for the laws"**: Ibid., 32.

77 **"the political religion of the nation"**: Ibid.

77 **"Passion has helped us"**: Ibid., 36.

77 **"John Brown was no Republican"**: "Speech of Abraham Lincoln, of Illinois, Delivered at the Cooper Institute, Monday, February 27, 1860," in *The Campaign of 1860: Comprising the Speeches of Abraham Lincoln, William H. Seward, Henry Wilson, Benjamin F. Wade, Carl Schurz, Charles Sumner, William M. Evarts, &c* (Albany: Weed, Parsons & Company, 1860), 7.

77 **"An enthusiast broods over the oppression"**: Ibid., 8.

78 **"the Crime against Kansas"**: Charles Sumner, "The Crime Against Kansas. The Apologies for the Crime. The True Remedy," speech delivered in the U.S. Senate, May 19–20, 1856 (Boston: John P. Jewett and Company, 1856), United States Senate: Art and Artifacts, https://www.senate.gov/artandhistory/history/resources/pdf/CrimeAgainstKSSpeech.pdf.

78 **"How does Heaven help us"**: Quoted in Cabot, *A Memoir of Ralph Waldo Emerson,* 600.

78 **"Why, by a whirlwind of patriotism"**: Ibid.

78 **"collective effervescence":** Emile Durkheim, *The Elementary Forms of Religious Life* (New York: Free Press, 1995), 215–16.

78 **"Go into the swarming town-halls":** Quoted in Cabot, *A Memoir of Ralph Waldo Emerson,* 600.

78 **"I will never again speak lightly":** Ibid.

79 **"a sacred spiritual possession":** William James, *The Works of William James,* vol. 17: *Essays, Comments, and Reviews,* ed. Frederick H. Burkhardt, Fredson Bowers, and Ignas K. Skrupskelis (Cambridge, Mass: Harvard University Press, 1987), 162.

79 **"military feelings":** Ibid.

79 **"Ask all our millions":** Ibid.

79 **"bestial side":** Ibid., 165.

79 **"a world of clerks and teachers":** Ibid., 166.

80 **the War Department had decommissioned:** Brian DeLay, "How the US Government Created and Coddled the Gun Industry," *The Conversation,* October 9, 2017, http://theconversation.com/how-the-us-government-created-and-coddled-the-gun-industry-85167.

80 **"cloaked under the name of natural":** *English v. State,* 35 Tex. 473.

80 **"exchanged under the social compact":** Ibid.

80 **"We must not":** Ibid.

81 **"I have always been":** *Hill v. State,* 53 Ga. 472 (1874).

81 **"the claims of the assassin":** *Andrews v. State,* 50 Tenn. 165, 3 (1871).

81 **"make the Constitution defend lawlessness":** Quoted in Patrick J. Charles, *Armed in America: A History of Gun Rights from Colonial Militias to Concealed Carry* (New York: Prometheus Books, 2018), 160.

82 **"There's no bravery in carrying revolvers":** Quoted in

Alexander DeConde, *Gun Violence in America: The Struggle for Control* (Boston: Northeastern University Press, 2001), 82.

82 **"all homicide is presumed to be malicious"**: William Blackstone, *Commentaries on the Laws of England,* vol. 4 (Oxford, U.K.: Clarendon, 1769), 201.

82 **"The greatest of all public calamities"**: *Trial of Thomas O. Selfridge, Attorney at Law, Before the Hon. Isaac Parker, Esquire: For Killing Charles Austin, on the Public Exchange, in Boston, August 4th, 1806* (Boston: Russell and Cutler, 1807), 128.

83 **"we should soon deservedly cease"**: Ibid.

83 **"overset our Constitution"**: Ibid., 151.

83 **"Where will these ideas carry us?"**: Ibid., 140.

83 **"If heroism and honor and chivalry"**: Ibid., 139.

83 **"a true man"**: *Erwin v. State,* 29 Ohio 186 (1876).

83 **"the tendency of the American mind"**: *Runyan v. State,* 57 Ind. 80 (1877).

83 **"even to save human life"**: Ibid.

84 **"one of the penalties"**: Joseph H. Beale, "Retreat from a Murderous Assault," *Harvard Law Review* 16 (June 1, 1903): 582.

84 **"that one man should live"**: Ibid.

84 **"Such thoughts"**: *Springfield v. State,* 96 Ala. 81 (1892).

84 **"unwritten law"**: Thomas J. Kernan, "The Jurisprudence of Lawlessness," *The American Lawyer* 14 (1906), 452.

84 **"liberty dies"**: Ibid., 453.

84 **"Jurisprudence of Lawlessness"**: Ibid.

84 **"all organized government is shaken to its foundation stones"**: Ibid., 453.

84 **"The law of Texas very strongly adopts"**: *Brown v. United States,* 256 U.S. 335 (1921).

84 **"respectable writers agree"**: Ibid.

84   **"a man is not born to run away":** Quoted in Richard Maxwell Brown, *No Duty to Retreat: Violence and Values in American History and Society* (Norman: University of Oklahoma Press, 1994), 34–36.

84   **"must consider human nature":** Ibid.

85   **none of the killings:** Andrew Somerset, *Arms: The Culture and Credo of the Gun* (Windsor, Ont.: Biblioasis, 2015), 39.

85   **"apostle of violence":** Amos Pinchot, "The Courage of the Cripple," *The Masses*, March 1917, 20.

85   **"the most formidable disaster":** Mark Twain, *Autobiography of Mark Twain*, vol. 3, ed. Benjamin Griffin and Harriet Elinor Smith (Berkeley: University of California Press, 2015), 136.

85   **"all that a president ought not to be":** Ibid., 238.

86   **"Unless we keep the barbarian virtues":** Quoted in Sarah Watts, *Rough Rider in the White House: Theodore Roosevelt and the Politics of Desire* (Chicago: University of Chicago Press, 2003), 46.

86   **"the unfit are weeded out":** Theodore Roosevelt, *Hunting Trips of a Ranchman* (Philadelphia: Gebbie and Company, 1885), 16.

86   **"who will not work, perish":** Ibid., 19.

87   **"nothing but a game preserve":** Theodore Roosevelt, *The Winning of the West: An Account of the Exploration and Settlement of Our Country from the Alleghanies to the Pacific*, vol. 1 (1889; repr. New York: G. P. Putnam's Sons, 1917), 71.

87   **"but a few degrees less meaningless":** Theodore Roosevelt, "The Indian Wars, 1784–1787," chap. 2 in *The Winning of the West*, vol. 3 (1889; repr. Project Gutenberg, ebook, 2004), https://www.gutenberg.org/ebooks/11943.

87   **"wolf-hearted":** Roosevelt, *The Winning of the West*, vol. 1 (1917), 93.

87 occasionally "inhuman" methods: Roosevelt, *The Winning of the West* vol. 3 (2004).

87 "the whites, the representatives of civilization": Ibid.

87 "In the long run civilized man": Theodore Roosevelt, "Expansion and Peace," *The Independent,* December 21, 1899.

87 "consent of the governed": Theodore Roosevelt, "The Strenuous Life," in *The Strenuous Life: Essays and Addresses* (New York: Scribner, 1906), 19.

87 "It is only the warlike power": Roosevelt, "Expansion and Peace."

87 "white civilization": Theodore Roosevelt, "The Issues of 1896. A Republican View," *The Century Illustrated Monthly Magazine,* November 1895, 71.

87 "the higher races": Theodore Roosevelt, *American Ideals* (New York: G. P. Putnam's Sons, 1904), 302.

88 "cumberers of the earth": A frequent term of Roosevelt's, and one that carries theological connotations of permanent damnation. Roosevelt, *The Winning of the West* (1917), 106, 451.

88 "go armed": Theodore Roosevelt, *Ranch Life and the Hunting Trail* (New York: Century Company, 1902), 6.

88 "ready to guard their lives": Ibid., 6.

88 "When a quarrel may very probably": Ibid., 55.

88 "will not submit tamely to an insult": Ibid., 55–56.

88 "a certain French-Canadian": Ibid., 96.

88 "It is a noteworthy fact": Ibid., 13.

88 "who infest every frontier town": Ibid.

88 "often by the most summary exercise": Ibid., 14.

89 "known as 'stranglers,' in happy allusion": Ibid., 114.

89 "most of our territory is now": Ibid., 14.

89 **"a party of returning church-goers"**: Roosevelt, *The Winning of the West* (1917), 458.

89 **"hung him to a sycamore tree"**: Ibid.

89 **"by simply passing resolutions of disarmament"**: Theodore Roosevelt, "An International Posse Comitatus," in *America and the World War* (New York: Charles Scribner's Sons, 1915).

89 **"In every case the result was the same"**: Ibid.

89 **"No greater wrong can ever be"**: Theodore Roosevelt, *The Winning of the West,* vol. 1 (New York: The Current Literature Publishing Company, 1889), 130.

90 **"carnivals of emptiness"**: William James, "Governor Roosevelt's Oration," in *The Works of William James,* vol. 17, 163.

90 **"one foe is as good as another"**: Ibid.

90 **"flood of abstract bellicose emotion"**: Ibid.

90 **"a magnificent opportunity"**: Ibid.

90 **"abstract, aesthetic and organic emotionalities"**: Ibid.

90 **"this vast shaggy continent of ours"**: I quote from the book-length version. Frederick Jackson Turner, *The Frontier in American History* (New York: Henry Holt and Company, 1921), 267.

91 **"American democracy"**: Ibid., 293.

91 **"If there were cattle thieves"**: Ibid., 212.

91 **"grim energy"**: Ibid., 253.

91 **"this expert duelist, and ready fighter"**: Ibid.

91 **"had the instincts of the clansman"**: Ibid.

92 **"individualism, democracy, and nationalism"**: Ibid., 35.

92 **She said it only happened once**: Richard Shenkman, *Legends, Lies, and Cherished Myths of American History* (New York: Morrow, 1988), 113.

93 **"flow" beneath his skin:** Owen Wister, *The Virginian* (1902; repr. New York: Penguin, 1988), 3.

94 **"that particular honesty which respects":** Ibid., 57.

94 **"dangling back in the cottonwoods":** Ibid., 256.

94 **"do it again":** Ibid., 364.

94 **"hideous disgrace":** Ibid., 280.

94 **"ordinary citizens":** Ibid., 281.

94 **"take justice back into his own":** Ibid.

94 **"Wyoming is determined to become civilized":** Ibid., 280.

95 **"average rough male blood":** Ibid., 112.

95 **"All men are born equal":** Ibid., 91.

95 **"equality is a great big bluff":** Ibid., 92.

95 **"old trail of inequality":** Ibid.

95 **"All America is divided into two classes":** Ibid., 95.

95 **"Let the best man win!":** Ibid., 95.

95 **"It had come to that point":** Ibid., 364.

96 **"There's something better than shedding blood":** Ibid., 305.

96 **"I have killed Trampas":** Ibid., 310.

96 **"Oh, thank God!":** Ibid.

96 **"Life imitates art far more":** Quoted in Bruce Bashford, *Oscar Wilde: The Critic as Humanist* (Madison, N.J.: Fairleigh Dickinson University Press, 1999), 62.

97 **"When the legend becomes fact":** *The Man Who Shot Liberty Valance,* directed by John Ford (1962, John Ford Productions).

97 **"always seemed to say":** *Collections of the Minnesota Historical Society,* vol. 6 (St. Paul, Minn.: Minnesota Historical Society, 1891), 385.

97 **"the metaphysics of Indian hating":** Herman Melville, *The Confidence-Man: His Masquerade* (New York: Dix, Edwards & Company, 1857), 224.

CHAPTER 5

99 **"I wanted to make it hard":** Frederick Boyd Stevenson, "'Big Tim,' the Man Who Made the Gun Law," *Brooklyn Daily Eagle,* September 17, 1911. Quoted in Charles, Armed in America, 176.

99 **"save more souls":** "Bar Hidden Weapons on Sullivan's Plea," *The New York Times,* May 11, 1911.

99 **The bill sailed through both chambers:** 46 of 51 senators and 148 of 150 representatives in the lower house voted for the measure.

99 **"anti-American":** Quoted in Patrick J. Charles, *Armed in America: A History of Gun Rights from Colonial Militias to Concealed Carry* (New York: Prometheus Books, 2018), 182.

99 **"national suicide":** Ibid., 179.

99 **A cartoon in *Outdoor Life:*** Ibid., 182.

99 **advocate of military preparedness:** Donald George LeFave, "The Will to Arm: The National Rifle Association in American Society, 1871–1970" (PhD dissertation, University of Colorado at Boulder, 1970).

100 **"applied Americanism":** Ibid.

101 **"The Ku Klux Klan," we are told:** *The Birth of a Nation,* directed by D. W. Griffith (1915, David W. Griffith Corp.).

102 **"Not whether a negro shall be":** Thomas Dixon, Jr., *The Clansman: An Historical Romance of the Ku Klux Klan* (New York: Grosset & Dunlap, 1905), 292.

102 **"to demonstrate to the world":** Quoted in Erin Blakemore, "'Birth of a Nation': 100 Years Later," JSTOR

Daily, February 4, 2015, https://daily.jstor.org/the-birth-of-a -nation/.

102 **"It's like writing history with lightning":** Mark E. Benbow, "Birth of a Quotation: Woodrow Wilson and 'Like Writing History with Lightning,'" *The Journal of the Gilded Age and Progressive Era* 9, no. 4 (2010): 509–33.

102 **"Lynch him!":** David L. Lewis, *W.E.B. Du Bois: A Biography* (Macmillan, 2009), 331.

102 **with outfits and burning crosses:** Charles A. Gallagher and Cameron D. Lippard, eds., *Race and Racism in the United States: An Encyclopedia of the American Mosaic,* vol. 1: *A–E* (Westport, Conn.: Greenwood Publishing Group, 2014), 126.

102 **"at most gun shows":** Joan Burbick, *Gun Show Nation: Gun Culture and American Democracy* (New York: The New Press, 2007), 26.

103 **"white terrorism":** Randolph Bourne, "The State," in *Untimely Papers,* ed. James Oppenheim (New York: B. W. Huebsch, 1919), 160.

103 **"almost a sport":** Ibid.

103 **"The net gain":** Fanny Bixby Spencer, *The Repudiation of War* (Costa Mesa, Calif.: H. F. Schick, 1922), 11.

103 **"100 per cent Americanism in every":** Ibid.

103 **"life, liberty and the pursuit of happiness":** Thorstein Veblen, *An Inquiry into the Nature of Peace and the Terms of Its Perpetuation* (New York: Macmillan, 1917), 32.

103 **"any multitude of sins":** Ibid., 40.

103 **"If the Klan is against":** Quoted in David M. Chalmers, *Hooded Americanism: The History of the Ku Klux Klan,* 3rd ed. (Durham, N.C.: Duke University Press, 1987), 1.

104 **"stands ready to protect our country's":** Quoted in Alec Campbell, "Where Do All the Soldiers Go? Veterans and the Politics of Demobilization," in Diane E. Davis and An-

thony W. Pereira, eds, *Irregular Armed Forces and Their Role in Politics and State Formation* (Cambridge, U.K.: Cambridge University Press, 2003), 110.

104 **"to Italy what the American Legion"**: Ibid.

104 **General James A. Drain:** LeFave, "The Will to Arm," 67.

104 **"the patriotic animus"**: Veblen, *An Inquiry into the Nature of Peace,* 31.

104 **"a work of preconception"**: Ibid., 72.

105 **An Ohio congressman:** LeFave, "The Will to Arm," 103–4.

105 **"outstanding fact of our deplorable murder"**: Frederick Ludwig Hoffman, *The Homicide Problem: A Paper* (New York: Prudential Press, 1925), 4.

105 **"the paramount example"**: Quoted in Alexander De-Conde, *Gun Violence in America: The Struggle for Control* (Boston: Northeastern University Press, 2001), 126.

105 **"one good reason"**: Ibid., 121.

106 **"As a civilian's weapon"**: Allyn H. Tedmon, "Truth is Mighty and Shall Prevail: An Editorial for White Americans," *The American Rifleman,* December 15, 1923.

106 **"If nobody had a gun"**: Quoted in DeConde, *Gun Violence in America,* 122.

106 **"It has been proved time"**: George P. LeBrun, "Pistols and Self-Defense," *The New York Times,* May 26, 1922.

106 **"A man is awakened in the middle"**: "Enright on Self-Defense," *The New York Times,* May 19, 1922.

106 **"The pistol is the curse of America"**: William McAdoo, "Causes and Mechanisms of Prevalent Crimes," *The Scientific Monthly* 24, no. 5 (1927): 417.

106 **"to kill or maim human beings"**: Ibid., 418.

106 **"Time and again"**: Ibid., 419.

106 **"utterly and positively useless"**: Ibid.

106 **"I would," he wrote:** Ibid.

107 **"the armed bandit":** Quoted in Charles, *Armed in America,* 192.

107 **"The successful suppression of Aguinaldo's":** "Let Philadelphia Be Disarmed," *The American Rifleman,* May 1, 1924.

107 **"the Apaches of New York City":** Harry Chase, "Letter," *Forest and Stream,* October 7, 1911, 551.

107 **"the universal brotherhood of man":** "Pacifists," *The American Rifleman,* November 1, 1924.

108 **"the melting pot":** Ibid.

108 **"If there is to be but one race":** Ibid.

108 **"I have seen fine dogs":** Ibid.

108 **"a thousand years from now":** Ibid.

108 **"the white American to make":** "The Question of Intent," *The American Rifleman,* March 15, 1925.

108 **"the anti-firearm movement":** Allyn H. Tedmon, "Truth Is Mighty and Shall Prevail: An Editorial for White Americans," *The American Rifleman,* December 15, 1923.

108 **"The growth of murder in America":** "The Foreign Gunman in American Crime," *The American Rifleman,* September 1, 1925.

108 **"we have had drained in upon us":** Ibid.

108 **"We have taken in a stream":** Ibid.

109 **"the foreign killer behind the gun":** Ibid.

109 **"Our old native stock":** Ibid.

109 **the "vipers" arriving:** Ibid.

109 **"Out with them!":** Ibid.

109 **studied thousands of cases:** LeBrun, "Pistols and Self-Defense"; "George P. LeBrun, Centenarian, Dies," *The New York Times,* November 14, 1966.

109 **"The vigilante method"**: "Vigilante Method Is Short and to the Point," *The American Rifleman,* August 1928.

109 **"stamped out by an aroused armed citizenry"**: "The Attorney General Is Inconsistent," *The American Rifleman,* January 1934.

109 **"pioneer forefathers"**: "Shades of the Pioneers," *The American Rifleman,* September 1934.

110 **"emasculate California's free citizenry"**: Ibid.

110 **"when the pioneer vigilantes"**: Ibid.

110 **"Crime is a disease"**: Philip B. Sharpe, "Thug Medicine," *The American Rifleman,* November 15, 1926.

110 **"It is like certain tree diseases"**: Ibid.

110 **"of the firm belief that"**: Ibid.

110 **"the predatory classes"**: Karl T. Frederick, "Pistol Regulation: Its Principles and History, Part III," *Journal of Criminal Law and Criminology (1931–1951)* 23, no. 3 (1932): 540.

110 **"potential murderer"**: Karl T. Frederick, "Pistol Regulation: Its Principles and History, Part I," *The American Journal of Police Science* 2, no. 5 (1931): 442.

110 **"in entirely legitimate and desirable ways"**: Frederick, "Pistol Regulation, Part III," 533.

110 **"the late President Roosevelt"**: Ibid.

111 **"Here, and here alone"**: Karl T. Frederick, "Pistol Regulation: Its Principles and History, Part II," *The American Journal of Police Science* 3, no. 1 (1932): 75–76.

111 **"the rats"**: Frederick, "Pistol Regulation, Part III," 533.

111 **"Two negro burglars"**: Frederick, "Pistol Regulation, Part II," 80.

111 **"the negro who was elected"**: Frederick, "Pistol Regulation, Part III," 531.

112 **"There are very few people"**: Franklin D. Roosevelt, *Public Papers of Franklin D. Roosevelt, Forty-Eighth Governor of the State of New York, Second Term, 1932* (Albany: J. B. Lyon Company, 1939), 136.

112 **"the value of a revolver for this purpose"**: Ibid.

112 **"unselfish" view of the question:** Ibid.

112 **"is out of step with modern thought"**: Franklin D. Roosevelt, *Public Papers of Franklin D. Roosevelt, Forty-Eighth Governor of the State of New York, Second Term, 1931* (Albany: J. B. Lyon Company, 1937), 182.

113 **"to crucify the interests of ten million"**: "Federal Firearms Law," *The American Rifleman*, September 1933.

113 **"leave the criminal the only properly armed"**: Ibid.

113 **"How are we going to know?"**: "Reckord, Copeland Clash on Firearms," *The Sun*, May 29, 1934.

113 **"how are you going to know who they are?"**: Ibid.

113 **"If I can freely ship a gun to you"**: Ibid.

113 **"Under that provision"**: Ibid.

114 **dark and vicious "underworld"**: Ibid.

114 **"protect the men and women"**: *To Regulate Commerce in Firearms: Hearings before a Subcommittee of the Senate Committee on Commerce, United States Senate, Seventy-Third Congress, Second Session* (Washington, D.C.: U.S. Government Printing Office, 1934), 63.

114 **"playing Hamlet with Hamlet left out"**: Quoted in Carl Bakal, *The Right to Bear Arms* (New York: McGraw-Hill, 1966), 177.

114 **"Do you think all owners of pistols"**: Quoted in Patrick J. Charles, *Vote Gun: How Gun Rights Became Politicized in the United States* (New York: Columbia University Press, 2023), 62.

114 **"fondly known to generations of"**: Ibid.

115 **"Show me the man":** Quoted in DeConde, *Gun Violence in America,* 146.

115 **"barrage of letters and telegrams":** Charles, *Vote Gun,* 62.

CHAPTER 6

117 **"climbed toward unanimity":** Richard Harris, "If You Love Your Guns," *The New Yorker,* April 20, 1968.

117 **"What is at stake here":** *Congressional Record: Proceedings and Debates of the United States Congress,* vol. 114 (Washington, D.C.: U.S. Government Printing Office, 1968), 12433.

117 **"It is past time that we":** United States Congress Senate Committee on the Judiciary Subcommittee to Investigate Juvenile Delinquency, *Federal Firearms Act: Hearings, Ninetieth Congress, First Session, Pursuant to S. Res. 35* (Washington, D.C.: U.S. Government Printing Office, 1967), 160.

118 **"For over thirty years":** Mark J. Greenlynn Hinerman, "For Gun Legislation," *The New York Times,* July 4, 1968.

118 **"preparatory armed carriage":** Patrick J. Charles, *Vote Gun: How Gun Rights Became Politicized in the United States* (New York: Columbia University Press, 2023), 44.

118 **"even hunters":** George Gallup, "Favor Tighter Curbs on Purchase of Guns," *The Boston Globe,* August 30, 1959.

119 **Only 16 percent of all American homes:** George Gallup, "Ban on Pistols Favored for All Except Police: Gallup Finds Public Ready for Drastic Measures; Half of Homes Have Guns," *Los Angeles Times,* September 4, 1959.

119 **"Public Would Outlaw All Pistols Except for Police":** "Public Would Outlaw All Pistols Except for Police," *El Paso Times,* September 5, 1959.

119 **"Pistol Ban for All but Cops Backed":** "Pistol Ban for All but Cops Backed," *The Tampa Tribune,* September 4, 1959.

119 **"Public Favors Outlawing Pistols":** "Public Favors Outlawing Pistols," *Orlando Sentinel,* September 4, 1959.

119 **"sterile equality of death":** "Equality of the Grave," *The Washington Post,* August 17, 1968.

119 **"What paralysis of feeling":** "Human Sacrifice," *The Washington Post,* October 22, 1965.

119 **"the daily record of senseless, needless":** "Killers," *The Washington Post,* November 15, 1966.

119 **"the Nation's basic concepts of individual":** "Editorial," *The Philadelphia Inquirer,* April 26, 1968.

119 **"In a civilized society based":** "Guns Should Be Regulated," *The Atlanta Constitution,* June 17, 1968.

120 **The right was limited:** Thomas F. Pettigrew, "Our Society Is Violent Not by Nature but by Structure," *The New York Times Magazine,* April 28, 1968.

120 **only prohibition:** Thomas J. Dodd, "The Use of Firearms: Right or Privilege?" quoted in Charles, *Vote Gun,* 129, 384.

120 **"weaken the security of the state":** Jerome Wilson, "Murder in the Mail: Anyone (Even a Kid, If He Tells Enough Lies) Can Buy a Deer Rifle or an Anti-Tank Gun Right Out of a Catalogue," *The Sun,* April 3, 1966.

120 **the world's lowest crime rates:** Bill Riviere, "The Great: 40 Million Firearms Owners Insist Right to Bear Them Is Sacred," *The Boston Globe,* April 7, 1968.

120 **"In that country":** William C. Selover, "Gunplay Exceeds Warfare Toll: Gains for Criminals Contrasting Rates," *The Christian Science Monitor,* June 7, 1968.

121 **"The question of freedom":** Quoted in Carl Bakal, "The Traffic in Guns: A Forgotten Lesson of the Assassination," *Harper's,* December 1964.

121 **It was a "pseudopatriotism":** Ibid.

122 **"angry shootings by average citizens":** Carl Bakal, *The Right to Bear Arms* (New York: McGraw-Hill, 1966), 3.

122 **"The names are real"**: Ibid., 5.

122 **who were law-abiding citizens**: Ibid., 42.

122 **"murder were left to only"**: Ibid.

122 **"a mere fraction"**: Ibid., 42–43.

122 **"There is a great deal of crime"**: Ralph McGill, "Crime Goes Far beyond the 'Street,'" *The Miami News,* February 5, 1968.

123 **"One of the disturbing oversimplifications"**: "Gun Control Merits," *The Sun,* June 21, 1968.

123 **"bevy of letters"**: "Bonanza," *The Washington Post,* January 4, 1966.

123 **"most estimable citizens"**: Samuel Cornelius Greenbelt, "Sacred Right?," *The Washington Post,* January 4, 1965.

123 **"Few of them have real appreciation"**: Ibid.

124 **"sacred right"**: Ibid.

124 **"Put simply"**: James Ridgeway, "The Kind of Gun Control We Need," *The New Republic,* June 22, 1968.

124 **"Those who cry, 'Law and order'"**: Quoted in Charles, *Vote Gun,* 180.

124 **"Submachine Gun for Father's Day"**: Bakal, *The Right to Bear Arms,* 25.

124 **"We cannot wash our hands"**: "The American Condition," *The Nation,* December 21, 1963.

124 **"a stranger to the American heritage"**: Ibid.

124 **"the typical American boy"**: Albin Krebs, "The Texas Killer: Former Florida Neighbors Recall a Nice Boy Who Liked Toy Guns," *The New York Times,* August 2, 1966.

125 **"a private arsenal so accessible to its citizens"**: Henry Fairlie, "Our Fetish of the Gun: Rest of World Asks, Is U.S. Brave Enough to Take Legislative Aim at Uncurbed Purchase of Firearms?," *The Washington Post,* August 7, 1966.

125 **the gladiator that posed as the Socrates:** "Nimrod as Solon," *The Washington Post,* February 18, 1965.

125 **"there are psychological quirks":** "The Irresponsibles," *The Washington Post,* May 14, 1967.

125 **"There is a savagery behind this twaddle":** Ibid.

125 **"The time is long overdue":** Ibid.

126 **"licensing law aimed at severely curtailing":** Quoted in George D. Newton, Jr., and Franklin E. Zimring, *Firearms & Violence in American Life: A Staff Report Submitted to the National Commission on the Causes & Prevention of Violence* (Washington, D.C.: U.S. Government Printing Office, 1969), 160.

126 **"The revolver":** *Congressional Record,* 114:12487.

126 **"I am one of those persons":** Ibid., 114:12490.

127 **"justifiable" and should not be:** Willard Clopton, Jr., "Book on Guns Under Fire: Rifle Group Brands Work, on 'Death by Shooting' as Full of 'Inaccuracies and Innuendoes' Rifle Association Official Hits Book's 'Inaccuracies,'" *The Washington Post,* August 18, 1966.

127 **bought and paid for:** Charles, *Vote Gun,* 154.

127 **"belt buckles":** "Gallup Poll Hits Gun Owners," *The American Rifleman,* October 1959.

127 **"We, as a people":** Louis Lucas, "Individual Preparedness," *The American Rifleman,* October 1959.

128 **was a "calamity":** "Realistic Firearms Controls. An Editorial," *The American Rifleman,* January 1964.

128 **"highly emotionalized reaction":** Ibid.

128 **"The President's death demands":** Al Bennett, "Outdoor Life," *Bridgeport Post,* December 15, 1963. Quoted in Patrick J. Charles, *Armed in America: A History of Gun Rights from Colonial Militias to Concealed Carry* (New York: Prometheus Books, 2018), 242.

128 **"The unfortunate incident at Dallas"**: Quoted in Bakal, *The Right to Bear Arms*, 222–23.

128 **"just because a few people misuse"**: Quoted in Charles, *Armed in America*, 252.

129 **"Mr. Kennedy was not killed by a gun"**: United States Congress Senate Committee on Commerce, *Hearings, Reports and Prints of the Senate Committee on Commerce* (Washington, D.C.: U.S. Government Printing Office, 1964), 324.

129 **The combined circulation of newspapers advocating**: Bakal, *The Right to Bear Arms*, 97–98.

129 **Great Migration**: For classic accounts see Richard Wright, *Black Boy* (New York: HarperCollins, 2009), and Isabel Wilkerson, *The Warmth of Other Suns: The Epic Story of America's Great Migration* (New York: Knopf Doubleday Publishing Group, 2010).

130 **"In the final analysis"**: Quoted in *Congressional Record*, 114:12498.

130 **"Long Hot Summer Special"**: *Congressional Record* 114:12794.

130 **"Shoot a nigger with it"**: Bakal, *The Right to Bear Arms*, 28.

130 **an appeal for white posses**: Ben A. Franklin, "Gun Problem: The Citizens Arm as Congress Looks the Other Way," *The New York Times*, April 21, 1968.

130 **"code words for race"**: Quoted in Charles, *Vote Gun*, 180.

130 **"Register Communists Not Firearms"**: Quoted in Charles, *Vote Gun*, 140.

130 **"I wish to assure all Americans that Mississippi"**: "Cartoon by Herblock," *The Washington Post*, February 18, 1965.

131 **"the mad dogs against the people"**: Lawrence E. Davies, "Reagan Brands Those in Riots 'Mad Dogs Against the People,'" *The New York Times*, July 26, 1967.

131 **Newspapers reported that white communities**: "Guns in

Everyone's Hands," *The Christian Science Monitor,* April 15, 1968.

131 **One dealer admitted to selling guns:** Bob Jackson, "Easy Gun Purchases Linked to Constitution: And If Law-Abiding Citizen Can Buy Weapons—So Can Law Breaker," *Los Angeles Times,* September 11, 1966.

131 **"I'll be frank":** Quoted in Franklin, "Gun Problem."

131 **"We are," he lamented, "two nations":** Garry Wills, *The Second Civil War: Arming for Armageddon* (New York: The New American Library, 1968), 14.

131 **"*my* country":** Ibid., 15.

131 **"the Negro is clearly not part":** Ibid., 15.

131 **"It is in the realm of behavior":** Mildred A. Schwartz, *Trends in White Attitudes Toward Negroes* (Chicago: National Opinion Research Center, 1967), 10.

132 **"The real issue over gun control":** Quoted in Newton and Zimring, *Firearms & Violence in American Life,* 196.

132 **"The fact that this domestic arms":** Franklin, "Gun Problem."

133 **called "metapolitics":** Peter Viereck, *Metapolitics: From Wagner and the German Romantics to Hitler* (London: Routledge, 2017).

133 **Disinformation and intimidation:** Harris, "If You Love Your Guns."

133 **"I have just received a bulletin":** Bakal, *The Right to Bear Arms,* 226.

133 **"What are you catholics and commies":** Ibid., 223.

134 **"I'd rather be a deer in hunting season":** Quoted in Harris, "If You Love Your Guns."

134 **"Most of us are scared to death":** *Congressional Record,* 114:12489.

134 **"What really concerns me"**: Quoted in Bakal, *The Right to Bear Arms*, 226.

134 **In 1965, Senator Dodd confronted Franklin Orth**: Bakal, *The Right to Bear Arms*, 372.

135 **"All I can say"**: Ibid.

135 **"Some people call it lying"**: Ibid.

135 **"deliberate yelling of 'Fire!' in a theater"**: Quoted in *Congressional Record*, 114:12499.

135 **"The NRA's lies"**: *Congressional Record*, 114:12500.

135 **"New York State has the toughest gun laws"**: Quoted in Bakal, *The Right to Bear Arms*, 269.

135 **"honest, law-abiding citizens"**: United States Congress Senate, *Hearings, Eighty-ninth Congress, 1965–66, V. 12*, 1965, 242.

135 **"much-maligned Sullivan law"**: Ibid., 243.

136 **"keep good people"**: Bakal, *The Right to Bear Arms*, 59.

136 **"Congress might as well try to"**: Elsie Carper, "Rifle Unit Accused of Using 'Hysteria' to Fight Regulation: Brings Rifle," *The Washington Post*, April 13, 1967.

136 **"the rootingest-tootingest sheriff"**: Bakal, *The Right to Bear Arms*, 204.

136 **"Who shall I shoot?"**: Ibid.

136 **The group contained 750 members**: "Lost Leader," *The Washington Post*, November 4, 1966.

136 **"must take a share of the responsibility"**: "RFK Assails Rifle Unit for Opposing Controls," *The Washington Post*, August 25, 1967.

137 **"could have been prevented"**: Ibid.

137 **"vendetta" against the NRA**: Quoted in Charles, *Vote Gun*, 150.

137 **a "smear" campaign**: Ibid.

137 **"great American organization"**: Ibid.

137 **"all the violence and murder"**: John Herber, "Kennedy Heckled in Oregon over Gun Controls: Opposition on Issue Is Called Factor in Primary Today—Senator Cites Violence," *The New York Times,* May 28, 1968.

137 **"Nazi Germany started with the registration"**: Ibid.

138 **"WRITE YOUR SENATOR"**: Charles Nicodemus, "NRA Shoots Back at Ad Opposition: Smacks of McCarthy Vicious at Worst," *The Washington Post,* September 15, 1968.

138 **"a majority of Americans probably"**: Quoted in Charles, *Armed in America,* 266.

138 **the darkest instincts**: Nicodemus, "NRA Shoots Back at Ad Opposition."

138 **"Can three assassins kill"**: "Can Three Assassins Kill a Civil Right?," *The American Rifleman,* July 1968.

138 **"The rights of 200 million law-abiding"**: Ibid.

138 **"had struck a staggering blow"**: Ibid.

139 **twelve days after King was murdered**: "Do Americans Really Want New Gun Laws?" *The American Rifleman,* April 1968.

139 **a bullish apologia**: Warren W. Herlihy, "Happiness Is a Warm Gun," *The American Rifleman,* May 1968.

139 **"inconvenience"**: *Congressional Record,* 114:12503.

140 **"Idaho does not ask to write"**: Ibid.

140 **"We ask only to be left the master of our own house"**: Ibid.

140 **"art of the possible"**: Quoted in Charles, *Vote Gun,* 168.

140 **"Today the nation cries out"**: Lyndon Johnson, "Message to Congress: Johnson on Firearms Control," in *CQ Almanac 1968,* vol. 24, online edition (Washington, D.C.: United States Congressional Quarterly, 1969).

140 **"Criminal violence from the muzzle of a gun"**: Ibid.

140 **"the terrible toll inflicted"**: Ibid.

140 **"but we can expect the Congress"**: Ibid.

140 **"So today, I call upon the Congress"**: Ibid.

141 **"a crimp in the mail order gun business"**: "Wanted: An Anti-Gun Lobby," *The Washington Post,* December 15, 1968.

141 **"falls short"**: Lyndon B. Johnson, "Remarks Upon Signing the Gun Control Act of 1968," October 22, 1968, The American Presidency Project, https://www.presidency.ucsb .edu/documents/remarks-upon-signing-the-gun-control -act-1968.

141 **"The voices that blocked these safeguards"**: Ibid.

141 **"They were the voices of a powerful lobby"**: Ibid.

141 **"strict firearms control laws"**: Lyndon B. Johnson, "Special Message to the Congress on Crime in America," February 6, 1967, The American Presidency Project, https:// www.presidency.ucsb.edu/documents/special-message-the -congress-crime-america.

141 **"a measure of a civilized society"**: Ibid.

141 **"Government of law"**: Quoted in DeConde, *Gun Violence in America,* 183.

142 **"A nation that could not devise"**: Richard Hofstadter, "America as a Gun Culture," *American Heritage,* October 1970.

CHAPTER 7

143 **"I don't know why any individual"**: Quoted in Meenal Vamburkar, " 'People Should Not Have Handguns': Records Show Nixon Wanted Gun Ban, Considered Taking On Gun Lobby," *Mediaite,* March 11, 2013.

143 **"people should not have handguns"**: Ibid.

143 **"Goddamn it!"**: Quoted in Frederic J. Frommer, "Nixon

Backed Gun Control, Eyed Ban on All Handguns," *Worcester Telegram & Gazette,* March 9, 2013.

144 **"Guns are an abomination":** Quoted in William Safire, "Essay; An Appeal for Repeal," *The New York Times,* June 10, 1999.

144 **"diametrically opposed":** Quoted in Patrick J. Charles, *Vote Gun: How Gun Rights Became Politicized in the United States* (New York: Columbia University Press, 2023), 253.

144 **"the Amendment applies only":** Ibid., 269.

145 **"glorified lynch law":** Peter Viereck, "But—I'm a Conservative!" *The Atlantic,* April 1, 1940.

145 **"give us only the negative liberty":** Ibid.

145 **"will everywhere answer illegal force":** Ibid.

145 **"weaken the magic of all good":** Ibid.

146 **"We are the barbarians within":** Bradley J. Birzer, *Russell Kirk: American Conservative* (Lexington: University Press of Kentucky, 2015), 85–86.

146 **"We have dealt more death and destruction":** Ibid., 86.

146 **"terrible simplifiers":** Russell Kirk, "The Promises and Perils of Christian Politics," *The Intercollegiate Review,* 1982, https://theimaginativeconservative.org/2016/05/russell-kirk-promises-and-perils-of-christian-politics.html.

146 **"liberty under law":** Russell Kirk, *The Conservative Mind: From Burke to Eliot* (Washington, D.C.: Regnery Publishing, 2001), 94.

146 **Men like Buckley and Goldwater:** Peter Viereck, "Conservatism Under the Elms," *The New York Times,* November 4, 1951, and "The New Conservatism," *The New Republic,* September 24, 1962.

147 **"a sane Conservatism in American life":** Quoted in Birzer, *Russell Kirk,* 164.

147 **"the good guys"**: William F. Buckley, Jr., "Wait until the Apocalypse?," *National Review,* February 25, 1968.

147 **"the great oppressor"**: Russell Kirk, "A Dispassionate Assessment of Libertarians," May 28, 1988, posted at *The Imaginative Conservative,* February 21, 2015, https://theimaginativeconservative.org/2015/02/russell-kirk-a-dispassionate-assessment-of-libertarians.html.

147 **"that the state is natural and necessary"**: Ibid.

147 **"primary function of government is restraint"**: Ibid.

148 **"a conflict between absolute good"**: Richard Hofstadter, "The Paranoid Style in American Politics," *Harper's,* November 1964.

148 **"the battle shifted"**: Phil Gailey, "Gun-Control Advocates Are Feeling Surrounded," *The New York Times,* December 27, 1981.

148 **For Carter, the problem always seemed to be "us"**: Philip Jenkins, *Decade of Nightmares: The End of the Sixties and the Making of Eighties America* (New York: Oxford University Press, 2006), 175, 210.

148 **"We know that living in this world means"**: Ronald Reagan, "Address to the National Association of Evangelicals at Sheraton Twin Towers Hotel, Orlando, Florida," March 8, 1983, Voices of Democracy: The U.S. Oratory Project, https://voicesofdemocracy.umd.edu/reagan-evil-empire-speech-text/.

149 **"kept alight the torch of freedom"**: Ibid.

149 **"the aggressive impulses of an evil empire"**: Ibid.

149 **"if America ever ceases to be good"**: Ibid.

149 **"the corruption of all other nations"**: Alexis de Tocqueville, *Democracy in America and Two Essays on America,* ed. Isaac Kramnick, trans. Gerald Bevan (London: Penguin Classics, 2003), 710.

149 **"it wearies even those who are disposed"**: Ibid.

149 **"moral equal of our Founding Fathers"**: Quoted in Gerald M. Boyd, "Reagan Terms Nicaraguan Rebels 'Moral Equal of Founding Fathers,'" *The New York Times,* March 2, 1985.

149 **"I saw that picture"**: Tip O'Neill, "The Speaker Speaks Out," *Chicago Tribune,* September 13, 1987.

149 **Such was the thinking:** Charles Nusser, "'Contras' Not Like the Lincoln Brigade," *The New York Times,* November 10, 1984.

150 **"We're a free people"**: Ronald Reagan, "Remarks at the Annual Members Banquet of the National Rifle Association in Phoenix, Arizona," May 6, 1983, Ronald Reagan: Presidential Library & Museum, https://www.reaganlibrary.gov/archives/speech/remarks-annual-members-banquet-national-rifle-association-phoenix-arizona.

150 **"the best means of preserving"**: Ibid.

150 **"the guerrillas"**: Ibid.

150 **"a group which has had great success"**: Ibid.

150 **"we crack down on criminals"**: Ibid.

150 **"truly protects the rights"**: Ibid.

150 **Carter changed the spelling of his name:** "Leader of Rifle Group Affirms That He Shot Boy to Death in 1931," *The New York Times,* May 6, 1981.

151 **"bill of rights for America's gun owners"**: Osha Gray Davidson, *Under Fire: The NRA and the Battle for Gun Control,* rev. ed. (Iowa City: University of Iowa Press, 1998), 58.

151 **against the recommendation:** Gailey, "Gun-Control Advocates Are Feeling Surrounded."

151 **"Only a madman"**: Quoted in Davidson, *Under Fire,* 59.

151 **In 1980, 14,287 Americans were murdered:** Davidson, *Under Fire,* 59.

151 **A Gallup poll in 1981:** "The Gun Message Is Getting Through," *The Washington Post,* April 4, 1981.

151 **"You recall when Moses came down":** *Hearings before the Committee on the Judiciary, House of Representatives, Ninety-Ninth Congress, First and Second Sessions, on Legislation to Modify the 1986 Gun Control Act, October 28, 30, November 9, 1985; February 19 and 27, 1986* (Washington, D.C.: U.S. Government Printing Office, 1987), 208, 209.

151 **"to control the rocks":** Ibid.

151 **"for the purposes of disarming the people":** Frank Smyth, "Gunning for His Enemies," *The Washington Post,* July 9, 1995.

152 **"What are they going to do":** Jim Stewart and Andrew Alexander, "Anti-Gun Activists Threatened," *Austin American-Statesman,* June 18, 1989.

152 **"There's always going to be":** Quoted in Nicholas M. Horrock and Tom Hundley, "NRA's Romantic View Fading into Sunset," *Chicago Tribune,* March 22, 1989.

154 **Congress voted to defund research:** Arthur L. Kellermann and Frederick P. Rivara, "Silencing the Science on Gun Research," *JAMA* 309, no. 6 (February 13, 2013): 549–50, https://doi.org/10.1001/jama.2012.208207.

154 **"Tragedy," he said:** Charlton Heston, "A Reminder from Charlton Heston," *The Daily Iberian,* August 23, 2010; "National Rifle Association Convention," May 1, 1999, C-SPAN, https://www.c-span.org/video/?122961-1/national-rifle -association-convention.

155 **"America must stop this predictable pattern":** Ibid.

155 **"When an isolated terrible event occurs":** Ibid.

155 **"the Big Guns of the ACLU":** William F. Buckley, Jr., "Who Did It?," *National Review,* May 31, 1999.

155 **"Guns are valuable hobgoblins":** Ibid.

155 **"Guns were used, after all":** Ibid.

155 **"If only we could just blame"**: Ibid.

155 **"The little monsters of Littleton"**: Ibid.

156 **"Yeah, it must have been the guns"**: "Consequences for Juvenile Offenders Act of 1999," in *Congressional Record*, vol. 145, 1999, H4366.

156 **"It couldn't have been because half our children"**: Ibid.

156 **"Nah, it must have been the guns"**: Ibid.

156 **"Guns are a two-edged sword"**: Molly Ivins, "Gun Debate One of Congress' Dumbest," *The Buffalo News,* June 23, 1999.

157 **"that guns had nothing to do"**: Ibid.

157 **"What is the Cold War now about?"**: E. P. Thompson, *Beyond the Cold War* (London: Merlin Press, 1982), 17.

CHAPTER 8

158 **"the death of liberty"**: Molly Ivins, "Silence Says a Lot about Gun Views," *The Charleston Gazette,* June 15, 1999.

158 **"I've been writing in favor of"**: Ibid.

158 **"Let me say that I am indeed"**: Molly Ivins, "Assault-Gun Ban Should Have Been a No-Brainer," *The Seattle Times,* May 9, 1994.

158 **"I firmly believe we need"**: Ibid.

159 **"Fourteen-year-old boys"**: Ibid.

159 **"It says quite clearly"**: Ibid.

159 **"The reasons for keeping them"**: Ibid.

159 **"No sane society would allow this to continue"**: Ibid.

159 **The NRA's position was a perfect inversion:** Tom Teepen, "NRA Puts the Constitution on Hold, Again," *The Palm Beach Post,* December 1, 1993.

159 **"magical body count"**: Tom Teepen, "American Public

That Favors Gun Control Held Hostage by NRA," *The Atlanta Journal-Constitution*, March 12, 2000.

159 **"On average"**: Ibid.

160 **"the regular organized militia of the state"**: *Presser v. Illinois*, 116 U.S. 252 (1886).

160 **"Military Code"**: Ibid.

161 **"to the public peace, safety, and good order"**: Ibid.

161 **"especially under the control"**: Ibid.

161 **"The Constitution and laws"**: Ibid.

161 **"obvious purpose"**: *United States v. Miller*, 307 U.S. 174 (1939).

161 **"must be interpreted and applied"**: Ibid.

161 **"civilians primarily, soldiers on occasion"**: Ibid.

161 **"the common defense"**: Ibid.

161 **"as a guarantee of an individual's right"**: *The Challenge of Crime in a Free Society: A Report by the President's Commission on Law Enforcement and Administration of Justice* (Washington, D.C., 1967), 242.

162 **"The argument that the Second Amendment"**: Ibid., 242.

162 **"for the regulation or abolition"**: Karl T. Frederick, "Pistol Regulation: Its Principles and History. Part III," *Journal of Criminal Law and Criminology* 23, no. 3 (1932): 540.

162 **"recognize the fact that constitutional provisions"**: Ibid., 541.

162 **"It is not to be found in the Constitution"**: Ibid.

162 **"From all the direct and indirect"**: Quoted in Patrick J. Charles, *Armed in America: A History of Gun Rights from Colonial Militias to Concealed Carry* (New York: Prometheus Books, 2018), 227.

163 **"We prefer to believe that the simple"**: Ibid.

163 **"the keeping and bearing of arms":** Ibid.

163 **"the history of the construction":** Jack J. Basil, "The Right to Bear Arms" (master's dissertation, Georgetown University, 1959).

163 **A quantitative analysis:** Matthew J. Lacombe, "Gunning for the Masses: How the NRA Has Shaped Its Supporters' Behavior, Advanced Its Political Agenda, and Thwarted the Will of the Majority" (PhD dissertation, Northwestern University, 2019), 81.

164 **"to bear arms in a coat":** Stephen P. Halbrook, *A Right to Bear Arms: State and Federal Bills of Rights and Constitutional Guarantees* (Westport, Conn.: Greenwood Publishing Group, 1989), 101.

164 **"carrying weapons on the person":** Ibid.

164 **To bear arms in a coat was:** Garry Wills, "To Keep and Bear Arms," *The New York Review of Books,* September 21, 1995.

165 **"detailed exploration of":** Don B. Kates, "Handgun Prohibition and the Original Meaning of the Second Amendment," *Michigan Law Review,* April 15, 1983, 228.

165 **" 'One loves to possess arms,' Thomas Jefferson":** Ibid.

165 **"While on the subject of papers":** Thomas Jefferson, letter to George Washington, June 19, 1796, National Archives, Founders Online, http://founders.archives.gov/documents/Jefferson/01-29-02-0091.

165 **"when guns are outlawed, only outlaws will have guns":** Don B. Kates, "A Modern Historiography of the Second Amendment," *UCLA Law Review* 56, no. 5 (June 2009): 234.

166 **"where bearing firearms is punished":** Charles de Montesquieu, *Montesquieu: The Spirit of the Laws,* eds. Anne M. Cohler, Basia Carolyn Miller, and Harold Samuel Stone

(Cambridge, U.K.: Cambridge University Press, 1989), 517–18.

166 **"Locke, Trenchard, [and] Rousseau"**: Kates, "Handgun Prohibition and the Original Meaning of the Second Amendment," 233.

166 **"Arms were never lodg'd"**: John Trenchard, *An Argument, Shewing That a Standing Army Is Inconsistent with a Free Government and Absolutely Destructive to the Constitution of the English Monarchy* (London, 1697), 7.

167 **"growing body of scholarly commentary"**: Quoted in Peter Finn, "NRA Money Helped Reshape Gun Law," *The Washington Post*, March 13, 2013.

167 **"Plainly it was not meant as such"**: Richard Hofstadter, "America as a Gun Culture," *American Heritage*, October 1970.

167 **"The right to bear arms"**: Ibid.

167 **"largely confined to the obstinate lobbyists"**: Ibid.

167 **"has been the subject of one"**: Interview with Warren Burger, *PBS NewsHour*, December 16, 1991.

167 **"Now, just look at those words!"**: Ibid.

167 **"a well–regulated militia"**: Warren Burger, "The Right to Bear Arms," *Parade*, January 14, 1990. See also Warren Burger, "Second Amendment Does Not Guarantee the Right to Own a Gun," in *Gun Control*, ed. Charles P. Cozic (New York: Greenhaven Publishing, 1992), 99–102, U.S. Department of Justice: Office of Justice Programs, https://www.ojp.gov/ncjrs/virtual-library/abstracts/second-amendment-does-not-guarantee-right-own-gun-gun-control-p-99.

167 **"The Second Amendment doesn't guarantee"**: Quoted in Adam Liptak, "A Liberal Case for Gun Rights Sways Judiciary," *The New York Times*, May 6, 2007.

167 **"to ensure that the 'state armies'"**: Warren E. Burger, "2nd Amendment Has Been Distorted," Associated Press, December 11, 1991.

168 **an "unfettered" one:** Ibid.

168 **"If we win":** Quoted in John Mintz, "In Bush, NRA Sees White House Access," *The Washington Post,* May 4, 2000.

168 **"the right of law-abiding, responsible citizens":** Opinion (Antonin Scalia), *District of Columbia v. Heller* 554 U.S. 570 (2008).

169 **"a dramatic upheaval in the law":** Dissent (John Paul Stevens), *District of Columbia v. Heller* 554 U.S. 570.

169 **Others called it "hubris":** William G. Merkel, "Heller as Hubris, and How McDonald v. City of Chicago May Well Change the Constitutional World as We Know It," *Santa Clara Law Review* 50, no. 4 (January 2010): 43.

169 **"unloaded, disassembled":** Hearing and Disposition before the Committee on the District of Columbia, House of Representatives, Ninety-Fourth Congress, Second Session on H. Con. Res. 694 to Disapprove the Firearms Control Regulations Act of 1975, August 25, 1976 (Washington, D.C.: U.S. Government Printing Office, 1976), Internet Archive, http://archive.org/details/firearmscontrol00colugoog.

169 **"the Militia of the States":** *Parker v. District of Columbia,* 478 F.3d 370 (2007).

170 **the Second Amendment could not:** I'm grateful to William Merkel for identifying this point. William G. Merkel, "The District of Columbia v. Heller and Antonin Scalia's Perverse Sense of Originalism," *Lewis & Clark Law Review* 13, no. 2 (2009): 362.

170 **"It had nothing to do with":** "Oral Arguments in the Supreme Court of the United States, District of Columbia v. Dick Anthony Heller," March 18, 2008, 8, Supreme Court of the United States, https://www.supremecourt.gov/oral _arguments/argument_transcripts/2007/07-290.pdf.

170 **"not the discourse"**: Ibid.

170 **"the only use of the phrase"**: Ibid.

170 **"the use of weapons"**: Ibid., 6.

170 **"of people living in the wilderness"**: Ibid., 30.

171 **"The militia that resisted the British"**: Ibid., 69.

171 **"Doesn't 'well regulated' mean 'well trained'?"**: Ibid., 26.

171 **"It doesn't mean—it doesn't mean 'massively regulated'"**: Ibid.

171 **authorizes personal "confrontation"**: *District of Columbia v. Heller* 554 U.S. 570.

172 **"virtually all"**: Ibid.

172 **"prefatory" and "operative"**: Ibid.

172 **"Before addressing the verbs 'keep' and 'bear'"**: Ibid.

172 **"The 18th-century meaning"**: Ibid.

172 **"Timothy Cunningham's important"**: Ibid.

172 **"then as now"**: Ibid.

172 **"to weapons that were not specifically designed for military"**: Ibid.

173 **"instruments of offence"**: Ibid.

173 **"technical meaning"**: Ibid.

173 **"At the time of the founding"**: Ibid.

173 **"From our review of founding-era sources"**: Ibid.

173 **"we conclude that this natural meaning"**: Ibid.

173 **"to retain; not to lose"**: Ibid.

173 **"to retain in one's power or possession"**: Ibid.

173 **"the most natural reading of 'keep Arms'"**: Ibid.

174 **"to keep and bear Arms"**: Ibid.

174 **"unambiguously military and collective"**: William G. Merkel, "Heller as Hubris, and How McDonald v. City of

Chicago May Well Change the Constitutional World as We Know It," *Santa Clara Law Review* 50, no. 4 (January 2010): 1221–61. The author is quoting the work of Nathan Kozuskanich in the *Journal of the Early Republic.*

174 **"clearly related to rendering":** Ibid., 1227.

174 **"idiomatic," and one that:** *District of Columbia v. Heller* 554 U.S. 570.

174 **"Giving 'bear Arms' its idiomatic meaning":** Ibid.

175 **"fits poorly":** Ibid.

175 **"*person* religiously scrupulous of bearing arms":** Neil H. Cogan, ed., *The Complete Bill of Rights: The Drafts, Debates, Sources, and Origins* (New York: Oxford University Press, 2015), 263.

175 **"compelled to render military service in person":** Ibid.

175 **"Putting all of these textual elements together":** *District of Columbia v. Heller* 554 U.S. 570 (2008).

176 **"We must determine":** Ibid.

176 **"the organized militia":** Ibid.

176 **"congressionally-regulated military forces":** Ibid.

176 **"fully consistent with the ordinary definition":** Ibid.

177 **defined "regulate" as:** Ibid.

177 **"security of a free state":** Ibid.

177 **"preserving the militia":** Ibid.

177 **"the people have a right to bear arms":** Ibid.

177 **"an individual's right to defend his home":** Carl T. Bogus, "Brief of Amici Curai Jack N. Rakove, Saul Cornell, David T. Konig, William J. Novak, Lois G. Schwoerer, et al. in Support of Petitioners," Supreme Court of the United States, 2008, 23, SCOTUSblog, https://www.scotusblog.com/wp-content/uploads/2008/01/07-290_amicus_historians.pdf.

177 **"the defense of themselves and their own state"**: Ibid.

178 **"the colonial government's failure to organize"**: Ibid.

178 **"the United States"**: Ibid.

178 **"standing armies"**: Ibid.

178 **"peculiar" that anyone**: *District of Columbia v. Heller,* 554 U.S. 570.

178 **tyranny and oppression**: William Blackstone, *Commentaries on the Laws of England,* vol. 1 (London: S. Sweet, 1844), 251. I am grateful to Heyman for clarity on this point. See Steven J. Heyman, "Natural Rights and the Second Amendment," *Chicago-Kent Law Review* 76, issue 1 (October 2000), 258.

178 **his "auxiliary" rights**: Blackstone, *Commentaries on the Laws of England,* vol. 1 (Oxford, U.K.: Clarendon, 1765), 139.

178 **"when the being of the state"**: Ibid., 244. Far from advocating an individual right of resistance, or a personal right of self-defense, Blackstone emphasizes that this right of resistance is collective and determined by consensus. To grant "to every individual the right of determining this expedience, and of employing private force to resist even private oppression," he explains, would be a "doctrine productive of anarchy, and (in consequence) equally fatal to civil liberty as tyranny itself. For civil liberty, rightly understood, consists in protecting the rights of individuals by the united force of society: society cannot be maintained, and of course can exert no protection, without obedience to some sovereign power: and obedience is an empty name, if every individual has a right to decide how far he himself shall obey."

179 **"wild and savage"**: Ibid., 121. This condition of "Political" or "civil, liberty," explains Blackstone, "is infinitely more desirable, than that wild and savage liberty which is sacrificed to obtain it. For no man, that considers a moment, would wish to retain the absolute and uncontrolled power of doing whatever he pleases; the consequence of which is, that every other man would also have the same power."

179   **"virtually all interpreters"**: *District of Columbia v. Heller,* 554 U.S. 570.

179   **"perfectly captured"**: Ibid.

180   **"in continuity with the English right"**: Ibid.

180   **"Those who believe that the Second Amendment"**: Ibid.

180   **"a military sense, and no other"**: *Aymette v. State,* 21 Tenn. 152.

180   **"exercised by the people in a body"**: Ibid.

181   **"the connotation" of the right**: *District of Columbia v. Heller,* 554 U.S. 570.

181   **"the defense of the State"**: *State v. Huntley,* 25 N.C. 418 (1843).

181   **"A gun is an 'unusual weapon'"**: Ibid.

181   **"No man amongst us carries it"**: Ibid.

181   **"in our peace-loving and law-abiding State"**: Ibid.

181   **submitted by "GeorgiaCarry.org"**: "At about the same time, various state supreme courts were declaring expansive rights to keep and bear arms," alleges the brief, followed by the reference to "*State v. Huntly*" [*sic*]. "Brief for Georgia Carry.org, Inc. as Amicus Curiae Supporting Respondent," February 2008, 10.

182   **"patrons of anarchy"**: John Locke, *Locke: Two Treatises of Government* (Cambridge, U.K.: Cambridge University Press, 1988), 330.

182   **blamed gun regulations on "communists"**: "He Won the Biggest Gun Rights Case in U.S. History. But Dick Heller Is a Hard Man to Please," *The Trace,* March 20, 2016.

POSTSCRIPT

183 **"The South is armed for revolt"**: Quoted in Russell Warren Howe, "A Talk with William Faulkner," *The Reporter,* March 22, 1956.

183 **"Go slow"**: Ibid.

183 **"the Southern whites are back in the spirit of 1860"**: Ibid.

183 **"If that girl goes back to Tuscaloosa"**: Ibid.

184 **"I'd fight for Mississippi"**: Ibid.

184 **"The central question"**: William F. Buckley, Jr., "Why the South Must Prevail," *National Review,* August 24, 1957.

184 **"What has once become ridiculous"**: Voltaire, *The Works of Voltaire. A Contemporary Version,* trans. William F. Fleming, vol. 11 (New York: E. R. Du Mont, 1901), 177.

185 **"three quarters of its strength"**: Simone Weil, *The Iliad, or the Poem of Force,* trans. James P. Holoka (New York: Peter Lang Inc., International Academic Publishers, 2006), 18.

185 **"possibilities of salvation"**: *McDonald v. Chicago,* 561 U.S. 742 (2010).

186 **"during the time of their being under arms"**: United States Congress, "Public Acts of the Second Congress, 1st session, chapter 33," in *United States Statutes at Large,* vol. 1 (New York: Little, Brown, 1845).

186 **"these bastard laws of violence"**: Thomas J. Kernan, "The Jurisprudence of Lawlessness," *American Lawyer* 14 (1906): 453.

188 **"While they prate of economic laws"**: Franklin D. Roosevelt, "Address Accepting the Presidential Nomination at the Democratic National Convention in Chicago," July 2, 1932, The American Presidency Project, https://www.presidency.ucsb.edu/documents/address-accepting-the

-presidential-nomination-the-democratic-national
-convention-chicago-1.

188 **"no society can remain free":** *To Establish Justice, to Insure Domestic Tranquility: Final Report of the National Commission on the Causes and Prevention of Violence* (Washington, D.C.: U.S. Government Printing Office, 1969), xvi.

189 **"our democratic society":** Ibid.

189 **"dangerous investment":** Ibid., 175.

189 **"humanitarian war":** Joanna Bourke, *Deep Violence: Military Violence, War Play, and the Social Life of Weapons* (New York: Counterpoint, 2015), 99.

190 **"Here's my commentary":** Karen Valby, "Jodie Foster: Candid Q&A with 'Brave One' Star," *EW.Com*, August 31, 2007.

190 **"They talked loud of liberty":** James Sullivan, *An Impartial Review of the Causes and Principles of the French Revolution. By an American* (Boston: Benjamin Edes, 1798), 44.

190 **"one trusts neither oneself":** Friedrich Nietzsche, *The Portable Nietzsche* (New York: Penguin, 1977), 284.

191 **"Rendering oneself unarmed":** Ibid., 72.

191 **"From that point on":** Martin Luther King, Jr., *The Autobiography of Martin Luther King, Jr.,* ed. Clayborne Carson (London: Little, Brown and Company, 1999), 82.

191 **"I was much more afraid":** Ibid., 82.

Index

About the Author

DOMINIC ERDOZAIN is a writer and historian with a passion for bringing the past into dialogue with the present. Erdozain has written widely on the intellectual origins of democracy and has published opinion pieces for CNN, placing America's gun problem in a broader philosophical context. A graduate of Oxford and Cambridge, he is currently a visiting professor at Emory University.